IT WAS AN AWFUL SUNDAY

IT WAS AN AWFUL SUNDAY

The 2nd Battalion Royal Inniskilling Fusiliers at the
Battle of Festubert 15-17 May 1915

MICHAEL JAMES NUGENT

Reveille
PRESS

Reveille Press is an imprint of
Tommies Guides Military Booksellers & Publishers

Gemini House
136–140 Old Shoreham Road
Brighton
BN3 7BD

www.tommiesguides.co.uk

First published in Great Britain by
Reveille Press 2015

For more information please visit
www.reveillepress.com

© 2015 Michael James Nugent

A catalogue record for this book is available
from the British Library

ISBN 978-1-908336-36-1

Cover design by Reveille Press
Typeset by Vivian@Bookscribe

Printed and bound in Great Britain

CONTENTS

DEDICATION

---ᨸᨸᨸ---

For my great uncle James and his fallen comrades.

*Also for my father James Nugent 1926-2005, who would have
been proud to have seen this in print.*

ACKNOWLEDGEMENTS

The completion of this work would not have been possible without the assistance of a number of individuals and institutions.

Special thanks are due to Richard Doherty for his advice and guidance throughout this project and for reviewing the manuscript. His encyclopaedic knowledge of Irish military history and points of contact proved invaluable and gave me the confidence to complete this project. Invaluable assistance was also provided by Natasha Martin at the Inniskillings Museum in Enniskillen. Her knowledge and practical assistance kept me on the right track whilst carrying out research. Thanks also Natasha for replying to my emails in an informative manner, no matter how obscure the subject!

To Catherine Coffey, thanks for your excellent translation of the official history of the German 55th Infantry Regiment. This translation gave the perspective of the battles of Aubers Ridge and Festubert from a German viewpoint, and showed that the Germans retained great respect for the fighting qualities of the Allied soldiers. Also in relation to the German accounts, thanks are due to Jack Sheldon for his advice on locating records.

Thank you to Sir David Stewart who showed great interest in my research into his late uncle, Lt John Houghton Stewart and provided me with family details and photographs. Also to Nigel Henderson for advice and access to his database of 'Ulster & the War' columns from the *Belfast News Letter* and his prodigious database of servicemen's photographs – www.greatwarbelfastclippings.com. I am also grateful to Walter Millar for uncovering previously unknown memorial information relating to my great uncle James.

Thanks are also due to Noel Irwin, branch chairman of the Dungannon and Moy branch of the Royal British Legion and Martin Brennan from the Friends of the Somme, Mid-Ulster branch for their support for my research. To Harry Donaghy and the other members of the 6th Connaught Rangers Research Group, thanks for your continued shared interest and support.

To the staff at the Public Records Office Northern Ireland, National Archives, Imperial War Museum and the many museums and libraries of Ireland that I have plagued for information, thanks for all your help and assistance. I think I finally know how to load a microfiche now!

Thanks must also go to the editors and staff of the *Belfast Telegraph, Belfast News Letter, Irish News, Derry Journal, Londonderry Sentinel, Tyrone Constitution, Mid Ulster Mail, Tyrone Courier* and *Fermanagh Herald*, for their encouragement and support. In this regard, a special word of thanks to Marie-Louise McConville at the *Irish News* for the excellent article she produced on my research, which generated a lot of further leads. Thanks also to Sarah Gilbert and Rowan Hand of the Destination Newry online TV station for their interest and interview.

For answering all my research queries swiftly, a special word of thanks has to go to the members of the Great War Forum. No matter how obscure the question, an answer was received, usually within hours at the latest. An amazing resource!

To my colleagues when I was working in foreign climes (you know who you are!), thanks for your patience in listening to my accounts of progress, fast or slow and for listening to peculiar facts which I had unearthed.

Finally, this work could not have been completed without the help and support of my family. To Sebastianne and Gabrielle, thanks for listening and for your advice (particularly on IT issues!) To Alison, I couldn't have done this without your limitless patience, encouragement and support. Dragging you around muddy fields in northern France, where there is not a shop for miles could not have been your idea of a great trip, but you smiled throughout.

To Ryan Gearing, Reveille Press and the Western Front Association, thanks for making this publication possible.

STRUCTURE OF BRITISH EXPEDITIONARY FORCE

The following table shows the structure of the BEF for much of the war.

Approx. Number of Men	Name of Unit	Commander	Composition
12	Section	Corporal or Lance Corporal	Not Applicable first unit of the structure
48	Platoon	Lieutenant or Second Lieutenant	Four sections
200	Company	Major or Captain	Four platoons and company headquarters
1,000	Battalion	Lieutenant Colonel	Four Companies, Battalion Headquarters and Specialists
5,000*	Infantry Brigade	Brigadier General	Five Infantry Battalions, Engineers, Machine Gun Company and Trench Mortar Battery
20,000	Division	Major General	Three Infantry Brigades, a pioneer battalion and artillery
60,000	Corps	Lieutenant General	Two or more Divisions
200,000	Army	General	Two or more Corps

*At this stage of the war an infantry brigade comprised five battalions. As the war progressed, this was reduced to four.

LIST OF MAPS

FOREWORD

THE CENTENARY OF the outbreak of the First World War brought a wide range of publications, TV programmes and other media features on the war and what it meant. Since then several anniversaries within the history of the war have been marked in various ways, including wreath laying services, parades and publications.

One factor becomes clear on examining the renewed interest in the Great War, as it was known until a second and even more cataclysmic war broke out: there is a general lack of informed knowledge about events on the Western Front and elsewhere. Sadly, the 'Blackadder school of history' has succeeded in planting a mythologised view of the war in too many minds. One of the main effects of that has been to create a focus on events along the Somme in 1916 and around Ypres in the summer and autumn of the following year. There is little awareness of the early battles, other than Mons and le Cateau and the first Battle of Ypres, or of the battles of 1915, while the Allied advances of 1918 are also obscured, if not all but forgotten.

It is, therefore, good to see a study such as this by Michael Nugent of a battalion of British regular infantry at the Battle of Festubert in May 1915. As Michael comments in his own preface, Festubert has been largely ignored by historians over the years. His personal interest in it arose because one of his great-uncles, James Nugent, aged 17, was killed in the battle, serving with 2nd Royal Inniskilling Fusiliers. He was one of the 650 Inniskillings who became casualties on that day, over two-thirds of the battalion's strength.

That lack of information and a desire to know more about the circumstances in which James Nugent died led Michael to carry out a forensic analysis of the Battle of Festubert. Although the focus of attention is on the Inniskillings, he examines the broader battle and the circumstances surrounding it, including the logistical aspects with particular attention to munitions. One part of the story that he deals with is the allegation contained in the history of another regiment, the Worcesters, that the Inniskillings compromised the element of surprise at Festubert, an allegation that he shows to be false. He also emphasises the part played by Indian soldiers on the Western Front, another all but forgotten part of the story of the Great War.

As well as attention to detail, this book also shows an empathy with the soldier on the ground, including as it does many accounts written by such men. Thus the author succeeds in providing a view of the battle that reaches from the higher command levels to that of the ordinary fusilier in the trenches. It is a rare skill that can weave such aspects of an action together so well and one that makes this book a pleasure to read as well as being a deserving tribute to Private James Nugent and all his comrades who died at Festubert.

Richard Doherty

PREFACE

ALTHOUGH THE IDEA to write a book is a fairly recent development, I have always had an interest in military history in general and the First World War in particular. The idea that you could be standing in the trenches, and someone of your own age would blow a whistle and you would unquestioningly climb over the parapet into a hail of shells and bullets and almost certain death, has long fascinated me.

My family has no great military tradition with no close relatives having recently served, however, I was always aware that in times of war the family responded to the nation's call. Through general family conversation over the years, I became aware that two brothers of my paternal grandfather were killed in the First World War. That was it. There were no descriptions of their pre-war lives or detailed mention of them, just that they were killed. A potential source of primary evidence, my grandfather Thomas Nugent, died in 1972 when I was thirteen. I wasn't sufficiently aware of the circumstances of my great uncle's death at that time and so a valuable opportunity to develop my interest was lost. One thing he did which perpetuated my interest, was to name my father James, after one of his brothers who died in the war. This tradition continued with the name James being given to me by my father as a middle name.

Growing up just outside Belfast in the 1970s provided many other distractions and it was not until close to forty years had passed and I had married and had grown-up children of my own that I found the time to consider some more in-depth research. I have always been an avid reader, mostly of books on military history, but the biggest motivator by far had to be the advent of the internet. Tentative steps initially through the internet identified the family background and the fact that five of my grandfather's brothers served in the First World War and that my great uncle Robert, attached to the 1st Battalion Royal Inniskilling Fusiliers, having survived Gallipoli, died of wounds received at Carnoy, France, on 15 February 1917 aged 23 and is buried at Rouen, France. His younger brother James, attached to the 2nd Battalion Royal Inniskilling Fusiliers, was killed in action at Festubert on the 15/16 May 1915. He was 17 years of age, and has no known grave, but is commemorated on Le Touret Memorial to the Missing.

The fact that there was a dearth of oral family history on the brothers sparked my interest and perhaps because of his youth and the fact that he has no known grave, I made a conscious decision to concentrate on finding as much detail as possible of the circumstances of James' death. To say that this has become a fixation may be not too far from the truth! Unfortunately, James' service record, like the vast majority of others serving in the First World War has not survived, so I have had to piece together what I could from family sources. One anecdote I came across was that James had already made one attempt to enlist against his mother's wishes and that his elder sister Charlotte was despatched to the recruiting office to bring him home. Any existing family memorabilia was in all likelihood destroyed on Easter Tuesday 15 April 1941, when the family home at 31 Percy Street, Belfast, received a direct hit from a German bomb in the Belfast blitz.

As I obtained books, read and researched on the internet focusing on 2nd Inniskillings, I discovered that Festubert is largely a forgotten battle. There are no books solely dedicated to it and although a chapter in the *Official History of Military Operations in France and Belgium 1915,* by Brigadier General Sir James Edmonds is devoted to it, it receives scant attention in many excellent and well regarded works of the time. *The Royal Inniskilling Fusiliers in the World War*, by Sir Frank Fox, widely recognised as the official history of the regiment's participation in the war devotes four paragraphs to it out of over three hundred pages. This is astonishing considering the casualties sustained, of which more later. The excellent *1915: The Death of Innocence*, by Lyn Macdonald which runs to some six hundred pages does not even mention Festubert in its own right, but merely as a follow on to the battle of Aubers Ridge. Martin Gilbert's authoritative *First World War*, has no mention of the battle at all. Perhaps this is not altogether surprising, as the battle (which took place six days after the disastrous Battle of Aubers Ridge) was fought over nearly identical ground and against the same resolute and deeply entrenched German defenders. Some British press accounts refer to the Battle of Richebourg, after the nearby village of Richebourg L'Avoue and combine Aubers Ridge and Festubert, which is erroneous as Aubers Ridge was a one day battle, and was an unmitigated disaster resulting in 11,619 British casualties,[1] whereas the Battle of Festubert lasted from 15 to 27 May, resulting in 16,648 British casualties.[2] The Germans meanwhile, refer to the battles of Aubers Ridge and Festubert as the battle of La Bassee, after the town of the same name which was behind their lines.

There are few in Ireland and particularly Northern Ireland who have no knowledge of the Battle of the Somme on 1 July 1916 and the heroic exploits of the 36th Ulster Division which have rightly been eulogised in many books and articles to the extent that they have become part of Ulster folklore and culture. The Inniskillings were represented on that day by five battalions, two regular (including 2nd Inniskillings) and three service battalions. The total number of Inniskilling's casualties, dead, wounded and missing on that day was 2,208[3] or 44.16 per cent of total strength. By comparison, at the Battle of Festubert, 2nd Inniskillings sustained around 650 casualties[4] or 67 per cent of the battalion's battle strength in a little under 48 hours.

As I researched in greater depth and came across biographical material and accounts from individual officers and men, I became more convinced that there was a need to document and examine the experiences of the Inniskillings on the period leading up to, and their involvement at Festubert. My aim in compiling this account is to shine a light on long forgotten, hidden, but connected events and to provide some explanation of circumstances which culminated in such a catastrophic loss of life. In doing so, I decided to incorporate as far as possible the personal accounts of those men that I could find through research, to give a flavour of what life was really like at the front.

There were a number of issues that impacted on those experiences which I believed required further examination: the reorganisation of the battalion following its participation in the battles of autumn 1914, the subservience of the British Expeditionary Force (BEF) to the demands of the French generals, the lack of vision and in some cases competence of some British generals, the overall lack of British preparedness to fight a large scale war, including the munitions scandal, the fact that the battle was the first night attack undertaken by the BEF in the First World War and, an ever present issue in First World War literature, the conditions on the battlefield.

The Inniskillings have a proud history and at the time of the First World War, 2nd Inniskillings were a battalion with strong family links recruiting predominantly but not exclusively from a tightly knit community in the northern provinces of Ireland and particularly from Tyrone, Belfast and Londonderry. It was a culturally and religiously mixed battalion, with devout Catholics serving alongside their Protestant countrymen, many of whom were Orangemen and members of the nascent Ulster Volunteer Force (UVF). Not only did the battalion have a religious mix, but there was also the class division, with men very much working class like my great uncle James, before the war a message boy from the Shankill area of Belfast, being led by officers not much older but the sons of the aristocracy and the products of England's leading public schools.

They lived together, fought together and died together, with a strong sense of duty, and of doing the right thing, but also with loyalty to their colleagues, the battalion and their country.

Their experiences need to be given greater exposure than has been the case to date. Hopefully what follows will go some way to honour their sacrifice.

1   Edmonds, *Military Operations in France and Belgium, 1915*, p76

2   Ibid,p.39

3   Fox, *The Royal Inniskilling Fusiliers in the World War*, p.72

4   Edmonds in the Official History enumerates Inniskilling casualties at 19 officers and 630 other ranks. Fox meanwhile cites 19 officers and 652 other ranks.

··· CHAPTER 1 ···
THE INNISKILLINGS GO TO WAR

A SHORT PARAGRAPH tucked away on page 5 of the *Dover Express and East Kent Times*, between details of the finals of the club competition of the Institute Bowling Club and the latest Breakwater Swim results announced the arrival of the 2nd Battalion Royal Inniskilling Fusiliers at Dover, at 6.00 am on Monday 29 September 1913. The underwhelming nature of the announcement was compounded by the statement that the battalion, which was replacing the 1st Battalion Royal Berkshire Regiment as garrison of Dover Castle and Fort Burgoyne, was not very strong, numbering under 500.[1]

Despite their lack of personnel and the less than enthusiastic welcome, the Inniskillings settled in well with the Dover community and were soon actively participating in many local sporting leagues fielding teams at football, hockey, cricket and cross-country running. The battalion also gave a good account of itself in inter service and public boxing tournaments held in the town. Inevitably, and as was the case in all garrison towns there were those who fell foul of the law. On 29 December 1913 Privates Dennis McGuigan and Robert Nixon of B company, and Samuel Boyd and Bernard McMullan of D company were found guilty at Dover Police Court of assaulting Constable Cadman, whilst the worse for wear through drink. The chief constable giving evidence stated that 'soldiers had behaved very well over Christmas.'[2] Fining each ten shillings, the chairman stated, 'Your conduct is anything but what we would expect of young men wearing the King's uniform.'[3] Of the four, Dennis McGuigan, 20, from Convoy in County Donegal would be dead within the year, killed at Ploegsteert Wood, Belgium on 20 October 1914.

As time progressed the town warmed to the Inniskillings and in May of 1914 they were offered and accepted 'Mastership of the Hunt' by the West Street Harriers, the intention being to give young officers the experience of riding to hounds. There was, however, the backdrop of an inexorable drift towards war. Articles in one local paper gave details of a potential spy recruited by the German Navy intending to come to Dover to spy on the port, using the cover of a nursery governess.[4] Throughout the spring and early summer of 1914, the Inniskillings were engaged in preparations for active service including manoeuvres in many of the small villages surrounding the town as well as quality time honing rifle skills spent at the ranges in nearby Lydd and Hythe where the Army School of Musketry was based.

As July turned into August the battalion found itself engaged in guard duties at the coastal batteries, guarding piers and erecting barbed wire defences. At 4.00 pm on 3 August, as had been expected, the word 'mobilise' was received.[5] In essence, this was the instruction for the battalion to prepare for war and set in train a myriad of actions to prepare for the orders to move which would surely come sooner rather than later. Chief among these was building the complement of officers and men. As in most home-based infantry battalions in a peacetime role, the numbers attached to the battalion were nowhere near what was required for offensive operations.

It may be of value at this point to describe the composition of the British fighting forces. A British battalion was commanded by a lieutenant colonel and at active service strength consisted of 36 officers and 1,000 men.[6] In reality the numbers actually deployed in battle were closer to 800, comprised of four rifle companies each consisting of four platoons of around 50 men each. Specialist troops such as machine-gunners and bombers were added to this complement and commanded by a lieutenant. Each company was commanded by a captain and each platoon by a lieutenant or 2nd lieutenant, assisted by a serjeant.[7] At this stage of the war five infantry battalions constituted a brigade, which was commanded by a brigadier general. Three brigades accompanied by Royal Artillery and Royal Engineers personnel constituted a division which numbered around 20,000 and was commanded by a major general.

When the call to mobilise for war was made this was accompanied by a Royal Proclamation ordering the calling up of the Army Reserve, the first replacements to bring the battalion up to fighting strength. This ensured that the Inniskillings reservists on hearing of the call up reported to the regimental depot at Omagh, where they were issued equipment and prepared for travel. The first batch of reservists – 342 in number, left Omagh on 6 August by train and arrived at Dover the following evening at 8.30 pm and were posted to companies. Medical inspection rejected very few as unfit for service overseas. All ranks were also inoculated against enteric fever, nowadays known as typhoid. This was to prove a great success as the casualties to sickness in the Great War were much less than that in the South African War 12 years earlier when typhoid fever decimated the Army. The numbers required to bring the battalion to war strength were six officers and 680 other ranks.[8] This figure gives some indication of the general unpreparedness of the British Army for war, as the Inniskillings were by no means unique in operating at half their active service strength. Without demeaning the skills of the reservists, they had not all recently been regular soldiers and not used to the current skills and the rigours and discipline of army life. Some though had had previous experience with the battalion in the South African War of 1899-1902 and their experience of battle was to prove invaluable. With this depletion of the reserve, efforts had to be made to find suitable replacements. In essence, reservists were those who had previously served in the armed forces. By the regulations which pertained at that time, soldiers signed up for seven years with a further five years being spent on the reserve, liable to be recalled for war service. The Special Reserve by contrast came about as one of the reforms recommended by Sir Richard Haldane, the Secretary of State for War in 1908, the purpose being to create a pool of trained reservists. Members of the Special Reserve (which was the militia renamed), received six months full-time training and three to four weeks a year thereafter. The difference between them and the Territorial's was that Special Reservists could be sent overseas in time of war.[9]

One way of attracting replacements was reported in the *Derry Journal*, where it was described how the 2nd Inniskillings band attended the half yearly hiring fair in Letterkenny, County Donegal. This was a regular occurrence at hiring fairs throughout Ireland. The recruiting serjeant who accompanied the band, always had plenty of tales of adventure and exotic locations to appeal to those whose outlook consisted of relentless hard physical work on the farm or in the mill. The lure of steady employment and the regular daily wage of one shilling a day proved attractive to many young men.[10]

The battalion left Dover on 8 August, handing responsibility over to an English reserve battalion and moved to join the rest of 12 Infantry Brigade who were stationed at Drayton.[11] Here, intensive training took place to get the battalion and particularly the new arrivals up to speed before joining the rest of the 4th Division at Neasden, near Harrow. On 21 August the battalion travelled by trains to Southampton, where at 1.40 pm on 22 August they sailed on the SS *Corsican* for Le Havre.[12] If some of the conditions they had experienced in their hastily prepared training seemed spartan, the crossing in the SS *Corsican* was a step up in class. Built in Glasgow in 1907, the SS *Corsican* was one of a number of steamships operated by Allan Brothers and Company on transatlantic routes between United Kingdom ports and those on Canada's east coast. The 11,500 ton and 500ft in length ship was modern and quite luxurious as befitted a transatlantic passenger vessel, with 'No effort spared to obtain construction of the finest quality – the vessel conformed to the highest class of the British Corporation.' It was very attractive to the War Ministry for use as a troopship as it had capacity for over 2,000 passengers – in peacetime, 300 first class, 400 second class and 1,500 third class passengers. Indeed, shortly after the Inniskillings cross channel passage it was diverted in September 1914 to a route which more suited its ocean going capabilities, transporting troops from Bombay to Alexandria.[13]

SS Corsican

In essence then, the majority of the battalion had gone from being a civilian army reservist to being in a war zone in just over two weeks. As with most battalions of the British Expeditionary Force arriving in France, they were accorded an enthusiastic reception by the locals who showered them with gifts of fruit and cigarettes as they marched through Le Havre. If the troops thought that they were on some hospitable trip around France however, they were in for a nasty surprise.

On the morning of 26 August, a mere three days after arriving in France, the 2nd Inniskillings found themselves on the extreme left of the British Expeditionary Force's 4th Division and therefore on the extreme left of the entire British line at Le Cateau. The general situation which existed was that the BEF had to stop the rapid German advance which threatened to outflank the British lines which were protecting the left flank of the French Army. The order was to check the German advance before retiring with the rest of the division. B and C companies 2nd Inniskillings under the command of Major Charles Wilding (soon to assume command of the battalion on 9 September), had the honour of the first engagement of the war, a brief but vicious skirmish with German troops of the 7th and 8th Jagers.[14] Joined by the other two companies of the battalion, the Inniskillings held the Germans at bay all that day inflicting heavy losses before taking part in the planned 4th Divison withdrawal. This initial contact with the enemy was a bloody taste of the realities of modern warfare for the Inniskillings who lost 36 killed and many more wounded in that engagement.[15]

Among the Inniskillings casualties that day was 19-year-old Second Lieutenant Oliver George Norman Stacke, attached to A company. He was the youngest son of Henry Aloysius Stacke, a barrister born in Listowel, County Kerry.[16] Second Lieutenant Stacke had been born in London and had attended Sherborne public school in Dorset before entering Sandhurst in 1913 as a gentleman cadet. In a true *Boys Own* scenario, he was initially reported killed in the engagement, but was in fact wounded and captured by the Germans. Remarkably however, he escaped and made his way to England dressed as a French peasant.[17] He rejoined the battalion before Christmas and was promoted to lieutenant in April of 1915, commanding one of the platoons in the battalion's A company.

Over the following two months the 2nd Inniskillings were continually on the move as efforts continued to thwart the German advance. In October the battalion crossed the frontier into Belgium and were involved in the defence of Ypres, the historic Belgian town which despite continuous attempts throughout the war never fell into German hands. Throughout October and into November, the battalion was involved in numerous actions against the Germans at places such as Ploegsteert Wood, (known as Plug Street Wood to the soldiers), the name of which is synonymous with some of the most bitter fighting of the early years of the war.

From their arrival at Le Havre on 23 August and being thrust into battle on 26 August, the battalion was continually on front line duty until 6 December when it was ordered to the rear to reorganise. This involved several days marching back through north-western France as transport was precious and priority was given to moving supplies to the front. Finally, the battalion arrived at their new temporary home, a large convent at Wisques near the picturesque and historic town of St Omer, which coincidentally housed the Headquarters of the British

Expeditionary Force. Here the battalion was given the opportunity to rest and recuperate. The previous four months had taken a heavy toll with many officers, NCOs and men having been killed or wounded. This period of rest enabled some of those who had been wounded in the early battles to return to the battalion and for a large number of replacements to fill the ranks of the fallen. A large draft of around 200 replacements arrived in France on 24 November[18] and further drafts arrived on 19 and 27 December. By this time however, the pool of army reservists that had joined with enthusiasm in August was all but exhausted and the replacements consisted of Special Reservists and new recruits with no experience of army life at all. Not all those who travelled as replacements to the front went with excitement and enthusiasm for the task ahead. There were plenty who, having realised the reality of warfare had second thoughts, or were looking forward with trepidation. One who expressed concern was 20-year-old Private Joseph Nelson, from Beechfield Street in East Belfast. At a training camp in November 1914 in County Donegal, he expressed his fears and reservations in a letter to his mother:

> *Dear Mother,*
> *This would not work, but if you would send up a telegram I would get away easy,*
> *but I think I would need my fare and if you can't afford it you need not mind, but*
> *I am for the front all wright. I have sined my will over to mother and we are to*
> *go anytime, but God send me back to come back safe try and get me down for a*
> *few days as it would ease my mind. Let on to be bad, send a telegram on return*
> *of post and if you can send my fare send it in the telegram.*
> *God Bless You, will write soon*
> *From Joe*[19]

It is not recorded whether this plan worked or not, but Private Joseph Nelson arrived with the Inniskillings in France on 27 December 1914 and was posted to D company.

By the year's end with the addition of Special Reservists and new recruits, the strength of the battalion had been brought up to 28 officers and 995 other ranks.[20]

On Christmas Day 1914, the battalion had church parade and was then visited and addressed by the Colonel of the Regiment, Lieutenant General Sir Archibald Murray, Chief of the Imperial Staff, who had commanded the 2nd Inniskillings in the South African War. In a rousing and complimentary speech he congratulated the battalion on their exploits to date, but prophetically as it turns out, warned of greater hardships ahead:

> *In attacking or defending positions, he told them that their native spirit made it a matter of consequence that they would acquit themselves well. That was not the part of this war which they might find trying or difficult. It was the bearing of hardships that he wanted them to excel in, and he repeatedly emphasised the Regimental motto – 'Hardships have no terror for us'. If they had to stand up to their knees in mud and water, he wanted them to do it and all hard things cheerfully, for the honour of their King, their Country and their Regiment.*[21]

On a more practical note and probably more welcome and of greater significance to the men was the distribution of a supply of plum puddings and other comforts, the organisation of which had been undertaken by Major Pierce who was at home recovering from wounds.[22]This action exemplified the close-knit ties and sense of family which existed in the battalion.

In common with many other regular battalions of the BEF, the end of 1914 found them in a completely different state to that which had existed five-and-a-half months earlier. In essence, the pre-war regular army had been greatly depleted, and senior officers in battalions throughout the BEF were faced with the prospect of trying to reconstruct their fighting force with raw recruits. They knew from experience that this took patience and time, the very essentials which were not available to them.

---

1   *Dover Express and East Kent Times*, 3 Oct 1913 p.5 at www.britishnewspaperarchive.co.uk
2   Ibid, 2 Jan 1914, p.6
3   Ibid
4   Ibid 18 Mar 1914 p.5
5   Alexander, *With the 2nd Battalion Royal Inniskilling Fusiliers in France 1914-16*, p.1
6   Bristow, *A Serious Disappointment:The Battle of Aubers Ridge 1915 and the Munitions scandal* p.27
7   Ibid.
8   Alexander, op. cit., p.2
9   www.1914-1918.net/recruitment
10   *Derry Journal* 17 May 1915, p.2
11   At this stage an Infantry Brigade consisted of five infantry battalions. A Division consisted of three Infantry brigades
12   Alexander, op. cit., p.3

13 www.norwayheritage.com. Used as a troopship until 1917, it was then bought by the Canadian Pacific Company and renamed the *SS Marvale*, resuming the transatlantic passenger route until it struck a reef off the Newfoundland coast and foundered, with no loss of life in May 1923.

14 *Sprig of Shillelagh*, the regimental journal of the Inniskillings, November 1914, p..11

15 www.cwgc.org The majority of those killed have no known grave and are commemorated on the La Ferte Sous Jarre Memorial to the Missing, in the town of the same name some forty miles east of Paris.

16 Ancestry.co.uk, 1911 Census

17 Alexander, op. cit., p.47

18 Fox, *The Royal Inniskilling Fusiliers in the World War*, p50

19 www.soldierswills.ie Pte 3108 Joseph Nelson was killed in the advance of 16 May 1915. He has no known grave and is commemorated on the Le Touret Memorial to the Missing.

20 Alexander, op. cit., p.35

21 Ibid, p.34

22 Ibid

··· CHAPTER 2 ···
FAILING TO PREPARE

The story of 1915 is but a commentary on the straits to which the British Empire was reduced by lack of preparedness for war, and the consequent heavy cost in life and material without result. (Brigadier General Sir James E Edmonds, *Military Operations France and Belgium, 1915*)[1]

It is beyond argument that the British Expeditionary Force performed splendidly and above expectation in the autumn battles of 1914. However, the result was the destruction of the regular army. Part of the reason that the BEF performed so well was that the highly trained soldiers operated exceptionally well in the kind of warfare conducted in open country which had characterised the battles of 1914. By the end of the year, however, this open warfare had ground to a halt and would not resume again for the duration of the war. When the German advance was halted each side dug in, literally, with trenches eventually stretching from Dixmude near the Belgian coast to the French/Swiss border, a distance of nearly 500 miles, preparing for a long struggle. Ominously, over the horizon was the spectre of large scale battles, which the Germans were prepared for, but the BEF in particular was not.

The pre-war British Army was a small but highly trained organisation designed to protect the outposts of the Empire and suitable for participation in colonial conflicts where the enemy was generally not as well organised and was preferably armed with spears. It was not designed or equipped to fight a large-scale conflict in continental Europe. The Royal Navy, ruler of the seas, was there to deter any threat of invasion of the British Isles, so it did not appear necessary to have a large army. Unlike the French and German armies, the British Army consisted of volunteers and was backed as has already been stated, by a system of recall of reserves and of the recently created Special Reserve. Beyond that was the Territorial Force who were intended for home defence. The French and Germans had large standing conscript armies with the facility to recall soldiers to duty once their period of conscription was completed. This foresight had the impact of being able to replace casualties quickly and effectively with soldiers who had recent military experience, required little training and were aware of current operational tactics.

The Haldane reforms which emanated from a review of the performance of the British Army in the South African War had established the concept of an 'expeditionary force' and to a point this worked well, but it was never foreseen as a force to fight a large-scale war for a protracted length of time.

When the decision was made by the British government to send the British Expeditionary Force to France, it could have been assumed that its commander, Field Marshal Sir John French had been issued with clear and concise instructions over its purpose, objectives, its sphere and limitation of operations and precise details of command and control at a strategic level. However, this appears not to have been the case. The instruction from the Secretary of State for War – the recently appointed Lord Kitchener, to the Field Marshal Commander in Chief, British Armies in France August 1914, is a vague document full of generalities.

Paragraph two, for example states 'the special motive of the Force under your control is to support and cooperate with the French Army against our common enemies. The peculiar task laid upon you is to assist the French Government in preventing or repelling the invasion by Germany of French and Belgian territory.[2]'

Paragraph four states, 'The place of assembly, according to present arrangements is Amiens and during the assembly of your troops you will have every opportunity for discussing with the Commander in Chief of the French Army the military position in general and the special part which your force is able and adapted to play. It must be recognised from the outset that the numerical strength of the British Force and its contingent reinforcement is strictly limited, and with consideration kept steadily in view, it will be obvious that the greatest care must be exercised towards limited loss and wastage.[3]'

Paragraph five states, 'Therefore, while every effort must be made to coincide most sympathetically with the plans and wishes of our Ally, the gravest consideration will devolve upon you as to the participation in forward movements where large bodies of French troops are not engaged and where your force may be unduly exposed to attack. Should a contingency of this sort be contemplated, I look to you to inform me fully and give me time to communicate to you any decision to which His Majesty's Government may come to in the matter. In this connection I wish you to understand that your command is an entirely independent one and that in no case will you come in any sense under the orders of any Allied general.[4]'

This document placed Field Marshal Sir John French in a very awkward if not untenable position. Paragraph two authorises him to 'support and cooperate' with the French Army. This immediately infers that the BEF is the junior partner in the enterprise, but falls short of implicitly stating that fact. This ambiguity is reinforced in paragraph five where it states, 'In this connection I wish you to understand that your command is an entirely independent one and that in no case will you come in any sense under the orders of any Allied general. The inference here being that the BEF was an autonomous body in full control of its decision making process, which, as it transpired was never the case. The reticence with which the British Government perceived the entire exercise is exemplified in paragraph four which emphasises to Field Marshal French the limits on manpower and the inherent dangers of incurring losses, an occupational hazard in warfare it could be suggested. Perhaps the most galling part of the document from French's point of view is contained in paragraph five, where he is ordered to report back to the Secretary of State for War before taking any offensive action outside of joint operations with the French Army.

This document basically emasculated Field Marshal French and more importantly failed to provide clarity to him over the prosecution of the war. The view could be taken that the tone of the document hints at a lack of confidence in the Commander in Chief by those in higher authority. There may be some truth in this supposition. As with most people of ambition, Field Marshal French had enemies, those jealous of his position and the opportunity afforded him. He had serious personality clashes with Lord Kitchener whom he had served under in the Boer War. Whilst Kitchener was introverted and austere, French was gregarious, especially in his dealings with women. Both were also stubborn, and whilst each praised the other in public, privately each had little enthusiasm for the other's military prowess. In addition, relations with one of his Corps Commanders, Sir Douglas Haig were far from straightforward. French and Haig had served together in the South African War where Haig had been French's Chief of Staff. At one time they were close friends. This is evidenced by the loan to French by Haig of the princely sum of £2,000 in 1898, to cover losses French had accumulated speculating in South African gold shares. This sum is worth around £190,000 in today's money,[5] and its loan in all probability saved French's military career. Haig was also French's brigade major, whilst French was commanding the cavalry brigade at Aldershot in the years following the Boer War.[6] Deeply ambitious himself, Haig whilst appearing as a loyal subordinate, privately had little confidence in French's abilities as a military commander and, as an ascetic Scot, he deeply disapproved of French's serial womanising – French at the time was carrying on a long-term, passionate and indiscreet affair with Mrs Winifred Bennett, a diplomat's wife.

A unique opportunity at self-promotion fell into Haig's lap when in 1905 he married Dorothy Maud Vivian, maid of honour to Queen Victoria and Queen Alexandra, the marriage taking place in the Buckingham Palace chapel. This gave Haig access to royal patronage, an opportunity he grasped with both hands, soon becoming an unofficial military advisor to King George V. Haig used this patronage to advance his own career, by continually damning French with faint praise to the king in an attempt which ultimately proved successful, in replacing French by the end of 1915 as commander in chief. Those in charge of the British war effort then were familiar with each other through their military careers, but this familiarity bred privately held contempt and the relationships were riven by petty jealousies and overpowering ambition. Sir John French was always in an awkward position with Sir Douglas Haig with the knowledge that he was indebted to Haig, for having saved his military career. That those at the upper echelons of British military command were not a cohesive unit would have implications as the war progressed.

So in essence, relations with the French high command suffered from a lack of clarity from the start. The French regarded the BEF very much as the junior partner in the enterprise. Whilst grateful for British assistance in thwarting the successful completion of the German Schlieffen plan objectives of encircling and destroying the French Army, General Joffre, the commander in chief of the French Army was generally dismissive of the British effort at that time. He had some justification in holding this view as the French had 100 divisions in the field whilst the British had seven.[7]

French national pride had been severely dented by the ease in which the German troops had swept through Belgium and had occupied French soil. The sole objective of the French was to drive the Germans out of French territory and back across the Rhine. To do this they envisaged a series of massive Franco-British offensives, with themselves in command of course. This made perfect sense to the French as their sacred soil had been invaded and they were expending the greatest of efforts and sacrificing their youth to restore their honour. The fact that the British were unable to commit vast resources and equipment to the enterprise was a source of constant friction between Joffre and Field Marshal French and led to constant pressure being placed on the British to do more. The Belgians having also been invaded had the same objectives as the French, to force the Germans out of their territory. As Britain had entered the war due to the fact that Belgian neutrality had been violated, the Belgians, not unreasonably, expected the British to assist them in their quest.

Field Marshal French then was being pulled in different directions by Allies who had different objectives and at the same time was constrained in his actions by the directions of the Secretary of State for War. Remarkably, there was no Allied strategic command, so in effect France, Belgium and Britain were fighting three separate wars against the same enemy.

Whilst he may have wanted to contribute more, French was not in a position to do so. It is a matter of public record that at the outbreak of war, the majority of the British population expected it to be over by Christmas and this led to the rush to the recruiting offices by thousands of young men eager to see some action before the war was over. One realist who held a different view was Sir Douglas Haig. At a war council meeting in Downing Street on 5 August 1914, Haig advanced his personal view that: '1. As Britain and Germany were fighting for their existence, it was bound to be a long war, 2. GB must take in hand immediately the creation of an Army of at least a million, 3. Only a small number of trained officers and NCO's were available. These must be economised as efficient instructors would be required. 4. As strong a BEF as possible to assist the French should be sent ASAP and increased.'[8]

This realisation that it may be a long war had further serious implications for Sir John French. It meant a lack of resources of both replacement men and equipment for his already depleted army. In this context the idea that he would send experienced officers and NCOs back to Britain to train raw recruits when they were needed to hold the army together at the front was an anathema to him, and he repeatedly refused in 1914 to part with a single officer or man to assist in training troops at home.[9] This placed French in an invidious position. He could hold on to his experienced men to maintain the standard of his depleted army, but as a consequence it would delay the arrival of much needed reinforcements which in turn would alleviate pressure from the General Joffre to do more. Faced with this dilemma, French retained his experienced men, hoping for reinforcements by early 1915. In hindsight, this was perhaps the wrong decision, for as the new divisions arrived they were certainly enthusiastic, but inexperienced and poorly trained. By contrast, the Germans by using a cadre of 25 per cent old soldiers, managed in three months to put 12 new 'reserve divisions' into the field.[10]

Nor was the lack of manpower Field Marshal French's only problem. The means to prosecute offensive action was also a pressing issue. The British munitions industry was wholly unprepared for the demands placed upon it. Traditionally its output was adequate for a small professional army engaged in colonial wars and limited campaigns, but was completely overwhelmed when the initial battles of the First World War took place. To give some scale of the expenditure of shells, during these 1914 battles the BEF artillery expended more ammunition than it had fired in the entire South African War.[11]

Producing more shells was not the panacea to this problem. The entire industry was unproductive, unprepared for war and in desperate need of modernisation. To meet the need of realities on the battlefield required the acquisition of land or properties and the construction of factories. Workers had to be recruited and trained to work in the factories and this all took time. This was exacerbated by the fact that suitably skilled and trained workers had been allowed to leave in the rush to 'join up'. The recruitment of women and unskilled workers to fill these places was vehemently opposed by the unions, who saw a dilution of their power. In addition to this, as the war looked like lasting longer than Christmas, new artillery pieces had to be manufactured for the artillery who were using obsolete weapons which had seen action in the South African War and in colonial conflicts before that. As the open warfare ground to a halt around Christmas 1914, it was evident that a massive increase in high explosive shells suitable for the destruction of fortified emplacements would be required. Shrapnel shells, which constituted the majority of available stock were suitable for attacking troops in the open, but wholly ineffectual against strongly constructed positions.

British unpreparedness for war and a lack of appreciation of prosecuting modern warfare manifested itself in another vital area of munitions supply, that of machine guns. The machine gun was first introduced as a weapon in the American Civil War of the 1860s, the first prototype having been invented by Dr Richard Gatling in 1861. The Gatling gun was a primitive weapon which consisted of six barrels that required to be hand cranked to continue firing. Other models appeared in the following years, but it was not until 1884 that what we would recognise as the modern machine gun was invented. The Maxim gun was invented in London by an American born inventor, Hiram Stevens Maxim[12] and proved a massive step forward in design as the gun used a recoil mechanism to feed the next round into the chamber. This massively increased the rate of fire from the original hand cranked version with early prototypes having a rate of fire of 600 rounds a minute.[13]

Machine guns were issued to the British Army as early as 1885 and they were used on colonial expeditions in Africa, where their mere presence was often enough to cowe the indigenous peoples into submission. But as an innovation in warfare, they were not highly regarded by the British. This was perhaps due to a combination of factors. Early versions came on two-wheeled carriages and were cumbersome to manoeuvre, they were also prone to jamming, and most importantly they did not fit in with British military tactics at that time, a situation which was to remain with disastrous consequences for many years to come.

Unfortunately and with great irony, it was the Germans who recognised the potential of this British invention. The then Prince Wilhelm of Prussia, soon to become Kaiser Wilhelm, received a demonstration in the operation of the machine gun whilst visiting his grandmother, Queen Victoria in the summer of 1887.[14] Wilhelm had a passionate interest in all things military and was very taken by the demonstration by the Prince of Wales' own regiment, the 10th Royal Hussars. He was even more impressed when the Regiment, on a reciprocal visit to Berlin presented him with a machine gun of his own.[15]

The German Army under the watchful eye of the new kaiser immediately realised the potential of this new weapon and adopting the Maxim model began producing their own in the 1890s. By the turn of the century, the German Army possessed more machine guns than any other army in Europe. Although still a cumbersome weapon, being part of a Maxim gun team in the German Army was a prestige appointment and regular training and competitions honed skills. With constant development and refinement, in 1908 the Germans produced the Maxim heavy machine gun, the *Maschinegewehr 08*, or MG 08, which was to wreak such havoc amongst Allied soldiers throughout the war. It was called the heavy machine gun and with some justification, it weighed 152 lbs, was mounted on a sled and had a crew of four. When operational it could fire over 400 rounds a minute to an effective range of over 2,000 yards.[16] By the outbreak of war the Germans had over 2,000 such weapons issued to the army and their machine gun teams were a well-trained, practised and integral part of each infantry unit.

The pre-war British Army by contrast had not grasped the significance of this weapon or had the foresight to see its potential. One possible reason for this is that the majority of members of the General Staff were cavalrymen who did not see the need for the infantry to have such a weapon. Sir John French and Sir Douglas Haig were both cavalrymen, as was Sir William Robertson, Chief of the Imperial General Staff. As far as they were concerned, the infantry existed to charge with the bayonet and clear a gap for the cavalry to exploit. Unfortunately, this view persisted long into the First World War when it had become obvious that due to the trench emplacements and fortifications, that the days of great cavalry charges were consigned to history.

The emphasis placed on the use of machine guns in the British Army can be judged from the coverage they merit in the *British Army Field Service Regulations 1909*. This publication deals with the 'General principles which govern the leading in war of the Army'[17] and is in effect the British Army's bible. In Part 1- Operations, which runs to some 300 pages, one paragraph of 18 lines are devoted to the principles of deploying machine guns, whereas the various styles of marching by contrast merits 11 pages. It is no coincidence that one of the main contributors in compiling the Field Service Regulations was none other than the cavalryman, Sir Douglas Haig. Even as the stalemate of trench warfare continued, Haig did not change his stance. Following the battle of Neuve Chapelle in March 1915, Haig in a minute to the Army Council stated that the machine gun was 'a much overrated weapon', and that two machine guns per battalion 'were more than sufficient.'[18] In making this comment, Haig may have been referring to its value when attacking fortified defences. The Germans however, valued it highly for defending such constructions.

Certainly the Inniskillings were already aware of the offensive capabilities of the machine gun under the right circumstances. Under the command of their machine gun officer Lieutenant Ralph William Gore Hinds, they had seen action early on in the war:

> *On Sept 1 came a heavy trial; after marching all the previous day through the forest of Compeigne, the 2nd Inniskillings formed an outpost line for the 12th Bde along the south edge of the forest. At dawn a Company of German cyclists in close formation appeared out of the mist only 200 yards in front of Lt Hinds' two machine guns which were covering the road. He ordered them to open fire on this excellent machine gun target and caused great slaughter.*[19]

So while the British Army were making good offensive use of their two machine guns per 1,000 men, it is thought-provoking as to what results could have been achieved with a more substantial complement. The short sightedness of the British high command concerning machine guns continued into 1915 and it took those from outside military circles to correct the imbalance. Lloyd George as Minister for Munitions in 1915 was contemptuous of the Generals in the field. Aware that Haig had deemed two machine guns were sufficient per battalion: 'Kitchener thought that 4 per battalion would be useful and more than that a luxury.' Lloyd George told his assistants, 'Take Kitchener's maximum, square it, multiply the result by two and when you are in sight of that double it again for good luck.' This feat of arithmetic would have given 64 machine guns per battalion.[20]

The lack of initiative in relation to the supply and deployment of machine guns was to have a devastating impact on the British Army in 1915. With trench lines established at the limit of the German advance, the Germans were not averse to making minor corrections here and there involving the giving up of a worthless piece of ground to settle on a better defensive site. The German Army was fighting a war on two fronts, with the Allies on the western front and against the Russians on the eastern front. The initial German plan had been to deal with the Allies quickly and then concentrate on the Russians, but the gallant rear-guard of the BEF in 1914 stymied that plan, so they were forced into setting up defensive lines in France and Belgium whilst they concentrated on defeating the Russians in the east. This strategy caused friction within the German high command with the easterners, Lieutenant General Erich von Ludendorff and Field Marshal Paul von Hindenburg believing that the war would be won by devoting resources to the east, whilst the Chief of the General Staff of the German Army, General Erich von Falkenhayn believing that the greatest threat was in the west. The easterners view held sway and so the Germans dug in for a long struggle along defensive lines in the west.

The French meanwhile, were committed to driving the Germans out of French territory with the assistance of their ill-prepared British Allies. In mounting offensives in 1915 the French hoped to strike a heavy blow against the Germans which would have the effect of tying down German forces and alleviating pressure on the other member of the entente cordiale, Russia.

The Germans in setting up their defensive lines throughout northern France had ample opportunity to fortify their defensive positions and to site their overwhelmingly superior numbers of machine guns with precision to cause maximum damage. A prophetic and ironic warning of what could be expected when the time came to try and dislodge the Germans is contained within the *British Field Service Regulations*, which stated, 'Machine guns are best adapted for use at effective infantry ranges, but when good cover from view and fire exists they may be usefully employed at close infantry ranges.'[21] The German intention was to ensure that they were certainly usefully employed.

By Christmas 1914, Field Marshal French realised that his army was not ready to fight, and needed time to rest, recuperate and resupply. They were short of men, short of all types of munitions and were hopeful of improvements on both counts in the spring. Field Marshal French was keen to avoid any large-scale battles until the deficiencies were rectified, but unfortunately time, and the designs of the French high command were working against him.

1   Edmonds, *Military Operations France and Belgium 1915*, Preface v

2   Neillands, *The Death of Glory:The Western Front, 1915*, Appendix. (Kindle ebook)

3   Ibid

4   Ibid

5   www.measuringworth.com £189,000 against the retail price index, an even more staggering £752,000 when compared with relative wages.

6   Bristow, *A Serious Disappointment, the battle of Aubers Ridge 1915 and the Munitions Scandal*, p.5

7   Ibid p.3

8   Sheffield, G & Bourne, J, *Douglas Haig, War Diaries and Letters 1914-1918*, p55

9   Edmonds, Preface viii

10 Ibid

11 Neillands. op.cit., (Kindle ebook) Loc 573

12 www.Wikepedia.org/wiki/Maximgun. Accessed 20 September 2013

13 Ibid

14 MacDonald, *1915: The Death of Innocence*, p.11

15 Ibid p.13

16 www.Wikepedia.org/wiki/MG08. Accessed 20 September 2013

17 War Office, *Field Service Regulations(FSR) 1909 Part 1 Operations*, Frontpiece

18 Bristow, op. cit., p.37

19 Fox, *The Royal Inniskilling Fusiliers in the World War* p.42

20 Taylor, *The First World War,* p.86

21 *British Army Field Service Regulations.* op.cit., p.20

··· CHAPTER 3 ···
LIFE AT THE FRONT

The town is very full now, Monday is market day and it's just like Dungannon, fowl, stalls of boots and clothes and a large sale of vegetables, eggs are plentiful too. (Lieutenant Charles Alexander, Transport Officer, 2nd Battalion Royal Inniskilling Fusiliers describing the French town of Bethune in a letter to his mother at home in County Tyrone on 3 May 1915)[1]

Whilst at rest at Wisques, the Inniskillings received large drafts of reinforcements from the Regiment's Reserve and Special Reserve, and also equipment and uniforms to replace those which had been damaged and destroyed. To the ordinary soldier at the front, the means by which the army sustained him, with food, supplies of every kind and replacements was a complete mystery. All the soldier at the front was aware of was that these items automatically appeared from what was known as 'the rear'.

In the case of the replacements which the Inniskillings received in November and December 1914, even though the war had been raging for less than six months, a complex system already existed to ensure that units at the front were kept up to strength so as not to diminish their fighting ability. This system was run by the Adjutant General's department and a lot of organisation and manpower was expended to ensure the smooth delivery of reinforcements to the front.

As the ship docked at one of the main French ports such as Boulogne or Le Havre (ports which also contained large supply depots), the first contact new troops would have of the BEF would be the military landing officer, who came on board with a nominal roll and checked that all those who were expected were present. Troops were then given instructions as to where to form up and disembarked the ship. On forming up, packs were removed and along with other equipment were collected by soldiers detailed for baggage duty. These soldiers also looked after vehicles and horses.

If the replacements were going directly to the front they would be given the time of departure and marched, led by a guide, to the awaiting train which would be at the railhead beside the port. Prior to boarding or if there was a delay, soldiers had the opportunity to avail of facilities established for their comfort at base railway stations. These consisted of covered waiting facilities, a place to draw rations for the journey, an office issuing maps and in some cases a barber's. There was also a coffee shop run by British ladies who had volunteered for the task and a shop selling last minute items such as bootlaces, cigarettes and tobacco, sweets and of great importance, writing paper and postcards.

When the allotted time to board the train came, it was done speedily and with the minimum of fuss as the units had been briefed beforehand. Here, class came into its own. Officers were allocated seats in passenger compartments, whereas the men boarded covered vans, common throughout Europe which had stencilled on the side 'Cheveaux 8, Hommes 40' (horses 8, men 40), indicating the capacity of the cargo. In these there were no seats, but perhaps some straw scattered on the floor, and a bucket in one corner as a toilet. Here, the men made themselves as comfortable as possible. At the disembarkation point, the replacements were met by a detachment from their unit and marched to the battalion headquarters where they were allocated to a company and met their new colleagues for the first time.

An alternative existed for the situation where troops were held at a base depot. Perhaps the most infamous of which was at Etaples, near Le Touquet on the French coast, where a vicious mutiny by the troops held there against what was perceived as a repressive regime took place in 1917.

Troops were held at base depots so that they could undergo final or refresher training before being sent to the front as needs required. It was utilised by replacements coming from Britain and those returning to their units after having been wounded. The stay was for an indefinite period, but in reality was never that long. The arriving troops were marched there under the care of a guide and billeted with others from the same unit. There were always some personnel from an individual's unit at the depot as they rotated through on their way to the front. Each battalion retained the same rows of tents in the same area, which over time were adorned with crests and signs signifying the identity of its residents. This gave a semblance of permanency and must have helped implant a sense of familiarity in the new arrivals.

Facilities were generally good at the base depots with canteens, cinemas, reading and games rooms and facilities provided by the Church Army and YMCA. However, they were far from holiday or rest camps and daily drilling, bayonet practice and forced marches over the nearby sand dunes were the order of the day. It is small wonder then that most troops were glad to make it to their battalion at the front. The journey from the base depot to the front line was made in the same fashion as those who had gone straight after disembarkation.

The management of all supplies for the army was also run from bases at the sea port or close to them. Whereas the management of men was run by the adjutant general's department, the management of the supply of materials and horses was run by the quartermaster general's department. A sub-division of this, the Army Service Corps (ASC) managed all food for men and animals which was transported by road, whilst movements by rail and canal were managed by the Railway Transport Department. The Army Ordnance Department (AOD), meanwhile looked after everything except food and medical stores.

When ships arrived carrying food, they were unloaded into massive hangars on the quayside and non-perishable goods were kept there until they were loaded onto trains for despatch to the front. Perishables such as meat were kept frozen on refrigerated ships until they were required and were loaded directly onto the trains. Bread was baked daily at the bases and loaded directly onto trains. High value items such as wine, spirits and medical supplies were kept under armed guard in locked warehouses to prevent pilfering.

The AOD warehouses were situated beside those of the Army Service Corps. Whilst the ASC had predictable requirements to meet, the AOD also had to deal with the unpredictable, which must have proved a procurement and logistical nightmare. For example during the cold and wet winter of 1914-1915, they had to source and despatch vast quantities of whale oil with which to prevent the occurrence of trench foot. Also, cold weather clothing, braziers and water pumps, all to alleviate the conditions encountered by the men in the trenches had to be found at short notice. Items urgently required at the front, for example a replacement part for a machine gun were ordered by telegram and despatched by the next available transport. Outside of the predictable items, the urgent requests were averaging 250 a day in early 1915.[2]

The AOD fulfilled another very important function, that of returned to store items. These were items that were no longer required by the unit, or more often, recovered from the battlefield. These items, be they rifles, machine guns, saddles, greatcoats, etc were examined to assess the possibility of repair and then delivered to expert tradesmen in situ who would repair or refurbish the item for reissue.

As can be imagined the bases were a hive of industry and employed many thousands of expert tradesmen from dockers to armourers all seconded as reservists for the duration of the war. They were supplemented by soldiers who were unfit for active service, but still willing and able to play a vital role in supporting those at the front.

Perhaps besides food, what lay most dear to the soldier's heart when at the front, was news from home. At the bases, and under the command of the Inspector General of Communications (reporting to the Adjutant General), was the Army Postal Service (APS). Their remit was the carriage, distribution and delivery to units of all letters and small parcels. When you imagine the confusion and disruption caused by warfare and the state of communications existing in 1915, it seems that the APS had a difficult, if not at times impossible job. However, the remarkable thing is that the service due to its extremely competent organisation worked remarkably well.

The system worked well because of its simplicity. The staff were mainly postal service workers from Britain seconded to the Royal Engineers Special Reserve for the duration of the war. Initial sorting of mail was done in Britain and post was placed in sacks according to unit. On arrival in France the ships were unloaded by soldiers not fit for front line duty and loaded onto trains with the other supplies, care being taken to check if the unit had moved. In early 1915 7,000 sacks of mail containing 500,000 letters, 60,000 parcels and 2,000 registered letters were being handled daily.[3] The system worked so well that a soldier of the Inniskillings serving in the front line in northern France regularly received letters from home in County Tyrone in three days.[4] It is arguable whether such prompt service exists today. The parcel allowance was a generous 11lbs, enabling those at the front to receive forgotten or requested items of clothing, or other comforts.

Postal rates were advertised in local newspapers, so that family members were able to budget to send home comforts be it items of clothing, cakes, cigarettes or confectionary to the front. One such advert in the *Belfast News Letter* in 1915 indicated that letters to the British Expeditionary Force in France or Belgium cost one penny per ounce. Parcel charges were on a sliding scale, with a three pound weight parcel costing one shilling, whilst a parcel of the maximum eleven pound weight cost one shilling and seven pence.[5]

In addition, the postal service arranged for the distribution of daily papers which were provided free of charge to the BEF by patriotic newspaper proprietors. Close to 100,000 papers daily were sorted at base depots so that a variety of papers were sent to each unit, enabling those at the front to have a connection with events back home, soon after they had happened. When all material, foodstuffs, clothing, weapons, ammunition, post and newspapers were assigned, they were loaded onto a train in the care of an officer and uniformed guard to prevent theft and made their journey to a railhead close to the front. Here, they were handed over by issuers to supply columns from the various battalions based in that area.

In the case of the 2nd Inniskillings the supply column came under the command of the transport officer, Lieutenant Charles Adam Murray Alexander. Lieutenant Alexander was born in 1889 into a prominent County Tyrone family who resided at Athenree, Termon, Carrickmore. His father Lieutenant Colonel Charles Murray Alexander was a land agent and the officer commanding the 4th (Extra Reserve) Battalion Royal Inniskilling Fusiliers. The young Lieutenant Alexander attended Wellington College and was commissioned into the 2nd Battalion Royal Inniskilling Fusiliers in 1910. He embarked for France with the rest of the battalion in August 1914 and initially was attached to A company. Having been through the battles of 1914, he was appointed transport officer in January 1915, a job which he realised was a necessity, but apparently endured rather than enjoyed. He was a prolific letter writer (courtesy of the Army Postal Service!), particularly to his mother Mary and his letters to her in the early part of 1915 provide an authentic and invaluable personal record of life at the front. As he took up the post of transport officer, he appeared unsure as to what his responsibilities actually were. Luckily, a handwritten document in the form of an aide memoire survives and details the duties as follows:

TRANSPORT

Duties of a Transport Officer – is responsible for the efficiency of the Transport.

Responsible that horses selected are fit and good steady workers, that harness is in good repair also vehicles – these should be carefully inspected, especially shafts and wheels.

After mobilisation he will tell off the drivers and carts for their respective duties.

Each Coy provides – 4 drivers, 3 carts, 4 horses.

So Batt, will have, drivers, carts, horses.

These will be divided into 2 Lots.

1st line Transport – all carts carrying ammunition and tools and rations (1 cart per Coy, these form part of the fighting efficiency of the unit – ie carrying ammo etc) and will always march as close behind fighting troops as possible.

2nd Line Transport – ie the supply and baggage train – All other carts ie for Supplies, (meal, flour), (1 per 2 Coy's) and the carts with Baggage.

This train will march under the Bn Transport Officer and will follow at a safe distance behind. An armed escort under an officer should be detailed to accompany the train for its protection.[6]

This was a vitally important role, as the transport officer was the final link in the chain in getting everything needed to sustain the battalion from the railhead to the front. But it was not a particularly glamorous appointment and Lieutenant Alexander tried over the succeeding months to get another posting. He may have been chosen for this role due to his familiarity with horses, the care of which features in many of his letters.

Whilst the Inniskillings remained at Wisques a training area was set aside to continue platoon, company, and battalion exercises and for the first three weeks of January 1915, considerable effort was expended in getting the replacement troops 'up to speed'. This rest and recuperation period was finite though and on 25 January 1915 in a divisional reorganisation, the 2nd Inniskillings were posted to 5 Infantry Brigade of the 2nd Division, under the command of Brigadier General Arlington Augustus Chichester.[7] On 30 January, the battalion marched to the suburbs of Bethune where they met up with the other infantry battalions in 5 Infantry Brigade: 2nd Battalion Oxfordshire and Buckinghamshire Light Infantry, 2nd Battalion Worcestershire Regiment, 2nd Battalion Highland Light Infantry and the 1/9th Highland Light Infantry, also known as the Glasgow Highlanders, who were a territorial battalion.[8]

As the war had now reached a stalemate, both the Germans and the Allies assessed their positions and began to dig in for the long haul. The Germans were keen to make defensive positions which could be held whilst their army dealt with the Russians in the east, whereas the British were engaged in constructing trenches, which while affording protection could be used as jumping off points when the planned offensives of the spring took place. As they were now again part of an operational division, the Inniskillings had to take their turn in the front line. At this time the 2nd Division held the line from the La Bassee canal in the south to just north of the village of Festubert,[9] an area the Inniskillings would become well acquainted with over the next few months with fateful consequences. At this time, the Inniskillings spent four days in the front line and then were relieved by the 2nd Ox and Bucks LI, with the reverse taking place the following week.

The Allied Offensives, May 1915[10]

The major problem which existed at this time was the state of the ground, where the term 'trenches' as we would understand in the context of the First World War was a misnomer. Lieutenant Alexander described the state of the ground where the Inniskillings found themselves:

> It cannot be said that trenches as we understood them to be, existed. The line in most places consisted of a series of 'Grouse Butts' built of sods, hurdles and mud, supplemented by any old material found lying about. The ground was so wet and marshy, trenches were out of the question, and all available men were concentrated in building breastworks which were a bad substitute when a bombardment took place.[11]

At the end of the battles of 1914, the British Army in this part of the country had ended up in the worst place geographically possible. The 2nd Division sector consisted of low lying marshy country criss-crossed by canals and broad, deep drainage ditches which was prone to flooding, even before shellfire disrupted the existing watercourses. The water table in this area was very high, barely half a metre below the surface in many places which made the digging of meaningful trenches impossible and even attempts to dig shallow scrapes were unsuccessful, as they filled with water as quickly as they were dug. The *Manual of Field Engineering*, published by the War Office in 1911, was the British Army's bible for any types of construction on the battlefield and gave detailed instructions in how to construct trenches to include firing steps, shelters, ammunition recesses and loopholes for firing through. But the conditions existing in this part of the line rendered these instructions redundant. The front line troops were forced as is highlighted above to build from the ground up, but the recognised means of doing this – with sandbags, was hampered due to them being in short supply. Where they were available, the instruction in the manual was that each filled sandbag (with sand) should measure 20 x 10 x 5 inches and weigh around 60lbs.[12] Bearing in mind that the Inniskillings were using glutinous mud instead of sand, the work must have been backbreaking. According to the battalion war diary, on the night of 13 February 1915, the Inniskillings managed to fill 1,600 of them. Duckboards to raise the level of the footway above the water would have been useless and at this early stage in 1915 were unheard of in this stretch of the line. The flimsy structures constructed by the troops afforded little protection and even the slightest bombardment caused them to collapse, often burying the unfortunate inhabitants. This is another indicator of the general British unpreparedness for war. It is arguable that a state of perpetual trench warfare could not have been foreseen in 1914, but it could be contended that as an army, failing to prepare is preparing to fail. As it was, the Inniskillings had to rely on their own initiative and ingenuity to scrounge materials to make life in the trenches more bearable. This included wooden fittings, doorposts and the like taken from abandoned or destroyed French houses. In a letter to his mother on 13 February 1915, Lieutenant Alexander stressed the urgency of the situation stating that; 'The country is still very wet. A very busy day getting hurdles and paling posts for the trenches and carting them up, part of them by day and the rest by night'.[13] The battalion war diary indicates that whilst in the trenches during February, the Inniskillings were engaged in this type of work every night in order to improve the trench or breastwork conditions. This work was also carried out under the ever present threat of snipers and shelling which the Germans carried out intermittently. On 11 February (according to the diary, but other records indicate 10 or 12 February), one Inniskilling fell prey to a German sniper whilst engaged in breastwork construction. He was 29-year-old Private Francis McKernan who had been with the 2nd Battalion at the front for three months. He was a member of the Inniskilling's 4th (Extra Reserve) Battalion, known colloquially as the Fermanagh Light Infantry and prior to being mobilised was an agricultural labourer. He lived with his parents Patrick and Mary Ann, an elder brother and two sisters at 8 Strand Street, Enniskillen. In his will, which was written shortly after he arrived in France in early November 1914, he left '*the whole of his property and effects*'[14] to his mother Mary Ann. Private Francis McKernan is buried close to where he fell, at Brown's Road Military Cemetery, Festubert.

To compound issues with the topography, the Inniskillings also had to contend with the weather. It rained, and rained incessantly adding to the water levels in what passed for the trenches and turned common use areas leading to the trenches into a glutinous mire. Between 25 October 1914 and 10 March 1915 there were only 18 dry days and on 11 of these the temperature was below freezing.[15] Weather records at the time indicated just how wet the winter of 1914-1915 was in the north European battlefields. Unusually heavy falls of rain had been experienced from the middle of August 1914. These continued and November brought gales, heavy rain and then frost. In December, rainfall at Boulogne a short distance away on the French coast was over six inches and rainfall in January at Dunkirk, again not far away was recorded at 5.8 inches – 300 per cent of the average. In fact in the period August 1914 to April 1915, rainfall recorded at Dunkirk was nearly three and a half inches greater than average figures taken over a 30 year period.[16]

Breastworks and mud, Rue de Bois, February 1915
(Image courtesy of Imperial War Museum, Q56217)

The wet winter was so out of the ordinary that serious consideration was given by members of the Royal Meteorological Society to the supposition that the use of artillery in the area may have contributed towards the heavy rainfall. A paper considered in 1915 by the society put forward the following hypothesis:

> *If by concussion an upward tendency is given to saturated air it must of necessity produce rain. Can the concussion from the guns firing over the battlegrounds produce this upward tendency of the surface air? It is not suggested that in the recent wet weather the rainy conditions have been generated by gun firing, but it seems quite possible that at times when the conditions are favourable to rain, the rains have been augmented or accelerated by the concussion initiated over the battleground.*[17]

Bearing in mind that this study was completed in 1915, long before the advent of cloud seeding technology, the honourable members were sceptical of the supposition, but did not exclude it in the absence of further and more comprehensive data.

All this meant little to the Inniskillings in the front line. They just knew that a stretch in what passed for the trenches equated to a week of abject misery, as you wore the same clothes from when you went into the trenches until you came out four or five days later. The conditions coupled with the winter cold led to a number of Inniskillings being hospitalised with frostbite. One soldier, Private Michael Deery from Howard Place in Derry was so badly affected with frostbite that he was medically discharged. His health did not improve however and he subsequently died in his home city on 24 April 1915. Preventative measures were employed including the issue of whale oil and lard to rub on the feet to alleviate trench foot – caused by the feet being immersed for long periods in water. Waders and wellington boots were a luxury and not on general issue, however other supplies were. In a letter to his mother on 13 February 1915, Lieutenant Alexander stated that, 'although it had been wet all week the men were sticking the winter wonderfully well. All got issued a waterproof coat yesterday, and now they wonder how they will carry all their kit.' (The fact that they were only receiving waterproof coats in mid-February makes you wonder how they had coped up until then!) He went on to say that 'fuel was in plentiful supply and that the battalion was receiving a wagon of coke a day for fuel and for braziers in the trenches.'[18] The fact that the Inniskillings were at the time based in a coal mining area would have ensured that at least the men in the trenches had some means of keeping warm.

Thankfully there was always a bit of light at the end of the tunnel – providing you emerged unscathed of course. Coming out of the line meant there was an opportunity to have a bath. Divisional bath houses were set up in large facilities such as breweries, brick works and factories. Here the men had an opportunity to get themselves cleaned and avail of the opportunity of clean underwear. In keeping with the times, facilities were separate and of differing quality for officers and men. Officers usually bathed on their own in whatever was available, an issue foldaway canvas bath, sometimes a proper tin bath, sometimes a wooden tub or something constructed especially for the occasion. For the men though it was a communal bath, a vivid description of the experience at the time exists in Richard Van Emden's exceptional *The Soldiers War, The Great War Through Veterans Eyes* from Lance Corporal Cook of the Somerset Light Infantry:

Had a lovely hot bath and change of clothing this morning. On arrival at this brewery where we were going to have our bath, we undressed in a room, taking off everything except our shirts and boots. Our Khaki coats, trousers and caps, less the chinstraps, were tied in a bundle and placed in the fumigator, and our vests, pants and socks were carted off (lice and all) for boiling. We then had to go out in the open and proceed along the canal towpath for about 50 yards. In full view of the ladies on the canal bank. Remember, we only had shirts on and it was bitterly cold, so we did not loiter for the benefit of the Mademoiselles much, but high winds did not help conceal our modesty! We were glad to get inside the bathroom which was nice and warm. Our bathtub consisted of large beer vats. Ten men were allotted to each vat, so on discarding shirts and boots we clambered up into the vats like a lot of excited kids. Every now and again we peeped over the side to see if our boots were ok, for we had been told to keep our eye on them as they were likely to be pinched. By this time we were a very lousy crowd, the lack of facilities had bred louse by the thousand, and the surface of our bath water had a thick scum of these vermin. But we didn't care, we helped scratch each other's backs (which already looked like a lot of cats had been scratching them) to ease the itching. We were of course given a piece of soap and a towel, and after ten minutes we were ordered out and dried ourselves and were given a clean shirt. We then had to retrace our steps along the towpath to the dressing room where the girls were still waiting. It must have been cold for them but I suppose they thought it worth their while! We were then issued with clean vests, pants and socks, then out came our clothes, all steaming hot, which we put on. My! What a sight we looked with everything creased and our hats all shapes. Anyway, we felt nice and clean for a while, but it would not be long before our warm bodies became alive again with nits that had not been destroyed in the washing process, making themselves active in our vests and pants.[19]

Where possible it was arranged that a bath was available each time the troops rotated from the trenches to billets.

With the realisation that the war was likely to be a long one, the issue of home leave had to be addressed, especially so in the case of the Inniskillings and other battalions, who had been at the front since arriving in France in August 1914. Initially, leave was meant to be seven days and in early 1915 was granted to one officer and seven other ranks per battalion. Seven days was fine if you lived in Kent or Sussex on the south coast of England, where a short train and boat journey brought you to your door. For the vast majority of the Inniskillings though, both the outward and return journey took up over half of the leave period and as the war progressed, the entitlement was increased to ten days to take account of those living in the farthest outreaches of Britain and Ireland. In early March 1915 though, Lieutenant Alexander commented that the Inniskillings commanding officer, 'Lt Col Wilding arrived back from leave, he only got two and half days at home.'[20]

Leave was managed by the battalion on a rota basis with officers tending to get leave every six to eight months and other ranks every 14 months. Leave, however, was subject to the 'exigencies of duty' and could be cancelled, postponed, restricted or stopped altogether as the progress of the war dictated. Managing such a system usually fell to the adjutant and must have been an administrative nightmare. Those due leave too became apprehensive as the departure date approached, becoming especially wary of any potential danger which they could foresee and waiting with trepidation in case there was some action on the part of the British or Germans that would inevitably lead to crushing disappointment. The ad hoc nature of leave is mentioned again in another of Lieutenant Alexander's letters of 6 March 1915, 'John Stewart (a 2nd Lt and member of another prominent Co Tyrone family) only got four days leave, that's all officer's get now. I hear now that there will be no more leave.'[21] The dissemination of an order to the effect that; 'there will be no more leave' was usually a fair indication to the astute observer that the battalion was soon to be involved in some form of proactive action.

The ratio of those entitled to leave, one officer and seven other ranks per battalion per week, seems at first sight somewhat unfair on the soldiers, given as we have seen that the strength of the battalion at the end of 1914 was twenty-eight officers and 995 men. Assuming there were no delays and cancellations, at that rate it would have taken 142 weeks to grant leave to all the other ranks. Reinforcing this was the fact that officers were entitled to leave twice as often as those in the ranks. Whilst it could be said that this is an example of class bias, there may be another reason-the opportunity to alleviate stress.

The role of the officer, particularly junior officers of Second Lieutenant and Lieutenant rank, were the most dangerous jobs in the army. In his excellent book, 'Six weeks: the short and gallant life of the British Officer in the First World War', John Lewis-Stempel indicates that if anyone was likely to die in an attack it was the officer. Using available figures to highlight his point he quotes from 'The General Annual Report of the British Army 1913-1919 which makes the general point of officer losses: in the period 1 October 1914 – 30 September 1915 the percentage of officers killed was 14.2, whereas for other ranks it was 5.8.'[22] Allied to this was the fact that the junior officers in the Inniskillings, in common with other infantry battalions, were for the most part teenagers. This fact as we shall see later is borne out by the ages of those Inniskillings officers who made the ultimate sacrifice at Festubert. It may seem unbelievable to us now in the second decade of the twenty-first century, but in 1914 a second Lieutenant could serve in a war situation at 17 years of age. As the war progressed, this age was raised due to the fact that so many officers of such a young age were being killed.

The vast majority of the officers were, as we have already seen in the cases of Lieutenant's Oliver Stacke, Charles Alexander and John Stewart, from prominent and wealthy families, what would be termed upper middle or upper class. These families all had servants at home, (both the families of John Stewart and Oliver Stacke had three).[23] Whilst growing up therefore, these boys were used to seeing their parents giving orders to those of a perceived lower class. This was reinforced when they attended public schools which were ingrained with the leadership ethos and where the boys were reminded constantly that they were born to be leaders.

When they joined the battalion therefore, they knew that their place was to lead their men. But with leadership came responsibility. They were ultimately responsible for the lives of their men. At 17 years of age it could be contended that that was a massive burden to carry, especially as in some cases the soldiers were old enough to be their father. Learning to lead in a civilian situation is one thing but to be in charge of the lives of 50 men in a war situation is quite another. When the order came to advance, it was the officer who led. No matter how scared personally he felt – and he would have been acutely aware of his own chances of survival – he could show no fear as it would unsettle the men. The fear of failure was uppermost in his mind. He did not want to let down his men, he did not want to let his family down and he did not want to bring disgrace on his school. These were powerful motivating factors, but ones which heaped pressure on the young officers. Perhaps the granting of more frequent leave was a way of alleviating that pressure and ensuring that those officers who survived the 'six weeks' went on to play a meaningful role with the battalion.

Some of the Inniskillings officers, as we have seen in the cases of Charles Alexander and John Stewart had connections to Ireland and particularly the Inniskillings recruiting area, so pre-war would have been well used to daily contact with the type of working class men from Counties Tyrone, Derry and Antrim who made up the battalion. For those with no connection to Ireland and from a privileged upper class background such as Second Lieutenant Alfred Douglas Wingate, who was born and brought up in India, attended Dulwich College and whose father was at a high level in the Indian Civil Service,[24] and the wonderfully named Second Lieutenant Lionel St George Mordaunt-Smith, who attended Charterhouse public school and whose father was a banker,[25] it must have been a severe culture shock to meet their soldiers for the first time.

Understanding what each other was saying would have been a trial, so it was fortuitous that in each case they had experienced and reliable serjeants to look after and guide the young officers. These men were all experienced soldiers, mostly in their early 30s and chosen for their knowledge and ability to guide teenaged officers. They included men like Serjeant Thomas McFarland from Tattynure outside Omagh. Having completed nine years with the battalion, he left and emigrated to Canada, but on the outbreak of war he immediately returned and was reappointed to the 2nd Inniskilling's D company, as experienced NCOs were a precious commodity. The system worked. The soldiers looked to their officer for leadership which he was programmed to provide, and the officers relied on the serjeants to guide them in dealing with the men. Getting to know the men, their strengths and weaknesses was a vital part of a young officer's job. One area which aided the officers in getting to know the men was that of censorship.

Censorship was introduced in order that no military advantage could be gleaned from letters or postcards if they fell into the wrong hands. Soldiers of all ranks were not allowed to state the location where they were, or geographical details of any planned action or recent action they had been involved in. Some soldiers got round the censor by use of ingenious codes agreed with those back home, whilst others took the chance that what they had written was innocuous or the censor may miss or overlook the sentence. In a letter to his mother dated 25 February 1915, Lieutenant Alexander stated; 'Today we are moving into that large town 'B' for four days'.[26] This is a reference to the town of Bethune, in the vicinity of which the Inniskillings were to remain for the first months of 1915. It was a duty of the young officers to check the outgoing mail of the men for any such indiscretions. This had additional value however, as through reading the letters they got to know the family circumstances of the men, which helped them to strike up a conversation or to assess their strengths and weaknesses. It also served as an early warning system should some situation at home have a destabilising influence on the soldier and enabled the officer and serjeant to implement measures in regard to the soldier's welfare.

For the Inniskillings, January and February of 1915 were spent alternating with the 2nd Ox and Bucks LI in the sodden trenches around Festubert, with periods of trench duty, sometimes four days, sometimes eight, broken by periods of comparative rest in the villages behind the front line. Although time spent in the front line was always dangerous, at this time there were no major actions and apart from occasional shelling, a culture of 'live and let live' appeared to exist between the British and Germans in this part of the line. At the beginning of March, however, this state of affairs was about to change.

1   PRONI, D/4121/F/4/B/2/6/2A 3 May 1915 CAM Alexander papers

2   Swinton, ED & Percy AIP, *A Year Ago; Eye-Witness's Narrative of the War from March 20th to July 18th, 1915* p.181

3   Ibid p184

4   PRONI D/4121/F/4/B/2/5/10a 6 March 1915 CAM Alexander papers

5   Ulster and the War, *Belfast News Letter*, 23 Jun 1915.

6   PRONI D/4121/F/4/D/1/17 Undated CAM Alexander papers

7   Brigadier General Chichester came from a distinguished military family from Devon. He was mentioned in despatches eleven times during the course of the war and finished the war with the same rank that his father attained – Major General.

8   Alexander, *With the 2nd Battalion Royal Inniskilling Fusiliers in France, 1914-16*, p36

9   Ibid p37

10 Edmonds, Sketch 2, page 2

11 Alexander Op. Cit, p37

12 War Office, *Manual of Field Engineering, 1911*, p13

13 PRONI D/4121/F/4/B/2/5/7 13 Feb 1915, CAM Alexander papers. Hurdles were basically wicker effect fences which were secured to the ground by stakes or paling posts and used to support entrenchments or earth was piled against them to create a defensive barrier.

14 Francis McKernan Will available online @soldierswills@nationalarchives.ie

15 Clark, *The Donkeys*, p39

16 Harding, *Battle Weather in Western Europe, 9 months from August 1914-April 1915. Quarterly Journal of the Royal Meteorological Society* Volume 41, Issue 176, pp338 and 341. Available online@ onlinelibrary.wiley.com

17 Ibid p343

18 PRONI D/4121/F/4/B/2/5/7 13 Feb 1915, CAM Alexander papers

19 Van Emden R, *The Soldiers' War. The Great War through veteran's eyes*,(E book) Loc 987

20 PRONI D/4121/F/4/B/2/5/11a 9 March 1915 CAM Alexander papers

21 PRONI D/4121/F/4/B/2/5/10a 6 March 1915 CAM Alexander papers

22 Lewis-Stempel, *Six Weeks: The short but gallant life of the British Officer in the First World War*, p183

23 Ancestry.co.uk, UK 1911 Census, Stacke, Channel Islands 1911 Census, Stewart.

24 Ancestry.co.uk, De Ruvigny's Roll of Honour, AD Wingate

25 www.laugharnememorial.co.uk p33

26 PRONI D/4121/F/4/B/2/5/8a 25 Feb 1915 CAM Alexander papers

··· CHAPTER 4 ···
NEUVE CHAPELLE AND AUBERS RIDGE

Our bombardment seems to have been accurate, but the enemy had placed machine guns under his parapet to fire just above the level of ground... The muzzles could not be seen or hit by shell fire.[1] (Diary entry for Sunday 9 May 1915 by then General Sir Douglas Haig, Commander, 1st Army, describing his perception of the failed attack on Aubers Ridge.)

As the crow flies, it is just under three and a half miles between the villages of Neuve Chapelle and Festubert which lie on the plain of French Flanders. Overlooking them is Aubers Ridge, which in geographical terms would be insignificant as it reaches 70 feet at its highest, but in the circumstances prevailing in 1915 it was of immense strategic importance, as it overlooked the low lying ground where the British had been forced to dig in following the autumn battles of 1914 and was in the hands of the Germans. In the 78 days between March 10 and May 27 1915, three major battles were fought over this ground, Neuve Chapelle 10-12 March, Aubers Ridge 9 May, and Festubert 15-27 May, resulting in close to 40,000 British and Empire casualties – dead, wounded and missing. The 2nd Inniskillings were involved in a peripheral role in both Neuve Chapelle and Aubers Ridge and sustained casualties in both engagements, including six dead at Neuve Chapelle.

In understanding the experiences of the Inniskillings at Festubert it is important (without dissecting the entire course of each battle), to examine why and how the battles of Neuve Chapelle and Aubers Ridge were fought and what lessons if any were learned from these battles of early spring 1915 which could, or should have affected the outcome of Festubert.

Whilst the Inniskillings had been spending January and February alternating in and out of the sodden trenches at Festubert and Givenchy, opposite them the German Army was undergoing a reorganisation. As the easterner's in the German high command, Major General Erich Ludendorff and Field Marshal Paul von Hindenburg had prevailed in their view that Russia required to be dealt with before focusing on the Western Front, it became obvious that they required extra troops for the task. General Erich von Falkenhayn the German Army chief of staff in assessing the situation, believed that he could supply the troops and that the French Army could be held by strong defensive lines until the Russian theatre was satisfactorily dealt with. He was dismissive of the situation regarding the British Army which he regarded as neither having the will nor the material to mount a meaningful offensive. As it turned out, in relation to material, he was correct. In relation to will he was not.

In the early months of 1915, Field Marshal Sir John French was in something of a dilemma. He was desperately concerned about the low levels of artillery ammunition and equipment in general. He was also concerned that the promised new divisions to enable him to prosecute an offensive had not yet arrived. He was also not happy that the troops had been static in atrocious conditions for over two months and were at risk as he saw it, of losing their 'offensive spirit'. But most of all he was under severe pressure from the French high command to assist them as had been promised – as the French were at pains to point out, to drive the Germans back.

A joint offensive was initially planned to take place in the La Bassée area in March, but this depended on the British being able to relieve French troops to the north of Ypres to free them up for the battle, something Field Marshal French was unable to do even if he had wanted to, due to troops scheduled for the western front being diverted to the planned Allied offensive in the Dardanelles. This situation reinforced the French view that the British were not pulling their weight and were really of little value to the French war effort. The situation was not helped by Sir John French's personal relationship with General Joffre. Neither completely trusted the other and these communication difficulties were compounded by Sir John being barely able to speak a word of French.

Sir John French was frustrated by the constant French demands to do something – anything – that would help the war effort, so he elected to have a British only offensive in the area of Neuve Chapelle. The planning for this effort was delegated to the commander of the British First Army General Sir Douglas Haig. Haig's primary concern before beginning his planning was the weather. In a discussion regarding the timing of the forthcoming battle with the Chief of the Imperial General Staff, General Robertson, as early as 19 February Haig stated, 'in reply to questions as to possible date, I said that it all depends on the weather. The rain of last Sunday flooded the country again, and threw operations back a week.'[2] This statement is very important in the context of the planning of the battle as it emphasises the fact that the ground was completely sodden to the extent that operations could not reasonably take place.

By 5 March however, Haig had produced an audacious plan:

We are embarking on a serious offensive with the object of breaking the German line. There is no idea of merely taking a trench here or a trench there. My object is to surprise the Germans and push forward to Aubers Ridge with as little delay as possible.[3]

It could be contended that the objectives of this plan were not only overly optimistic, but foolhardy. It has to be remembered that this was to be the first attack of a new type of warfare and there was a lot of the unknown involved. The battles of 1914 were, albeit on a larger scale, more like the open fast moving warfare that had been the norm in the South African campaign at the turn of the century. This battle was to be the first attack of the war on a static and entrenched defensive line. Aubers Ridge is situated two miles from Neuve Chapelle village and Haig's plan was to capture the village, capture the ridge and open the way for an attack on the strategically important town of Lille which lay beyond. There is also evidence that in his planning, Haig returned to his cavalry roots. General Rawlinson, commander of the 4th Division which was to spearhead the battle – and an infantryman, wrote to Lord Kitchener on 6 March and stated:

Things look hopeful I think for an attack on Neuve Chapelle which is tentatively fixed for the 10th, but if the wet continues it will be absolutely necessary to postpone this date. We shall have a very considerable predominance of artillery and infantry assets which we have never before possessed and we certainly ought to be able to force a big hole in the enemy's line. Whether we shall be able to follow it up and get the Cavalry through behind him is another matter, but I think there is a reasonable prospect of our being able to do so. Anyway conditions are more favourable than they ever have been before and if we cannot obtain a distinct success now, we shall never be able to in this theatre of trenches, wire and mud.[4]

It is not the intention in this book to demonise General Sir Douglas Haig's plan with the benefit of hindsight, but, the last four words in Rawlinson's letter are indicative of the fact that Haig's plan was hopelessly optimistic and did not appear to take into consideration the factors pertaining at the time. The objectives of his plan set up a situation where failure was a real possibility and this had implications for how the battle unfolded.

The British High Command was not immune however, to innovation. In this regard the Royal Flying Corps No 2 and 3 Squadrons had been engaged for the first time in the war in aerial reconnaissance. This innovation incidentally was embraced wholeheartedly by Haig, who immediately grasped the possibilities that the RFC provided. Despite the adverse weather they were able, using rudimentary cameras, to provide an accurate record of the German trench lines, the details of which were clearly of benefit to those planning the initial attack.[5] What the photographs were unable to show were the strongly fortified machine gun posts which were built into the parapet and covered. It should be remembered that the Royal Flying Corps as an entity itself was in its infancy and many of its tactics were based on trial and error. The first attempts of using wireless to communicate between planes and artillery had only been trialled in December 1914. The first camera experiments were made in January 1915 and the first time that they were used to photograph defences from the air was on 2 March 1915 – eight days before the battle.[6] Even in this there was an element of innovation bordering on the farcical. Cameras were initially held over the side of the plane by the observer – no mean feat in a moving platform when your fingers were numb with cold, until it was realised that far superior pictures could be obtained when the camera was fixed to the aircraft. In No 2 Squadron, an observer was appointed Photographic Officer simply because he had owned a camera as a boy.[7] However, the fledgling aircrew persevered and grew in experience with each flight. Photographs taken in the week prior to the battle were subsequently transcribed into maps and used to brief attacking troops.

Preliminary preparation in support of the attack was also carried out by the Royal Artillery. As this was the first large scale offensive of the war, the level of Artillery support required was an unknown quantity. Both field guns of various calibres and howitzers were employed. To explain the difference, field guns fired a shell in a low trajectory and the majority were firing shrapnel shells to cut the enemy wire. These shells were fitted with a powder burning fuze which was set by hand.[8] The fall of shells and consequent adjustment of fuzes was carried out by observation of the fall of shot, with the intention that the shells should burst in the air over the target and scatter steel balls over a radius of about 200 yards, hopefully decimating anything in their path. Howitzers fired a high explosive shell on a high trajectory, with the intention that they should hit the earth at speed before exploding, causing destruction over a radius of 25 yards. They were primarily for use to destroy trench fortifications. In the days before the battle, the artillery were brought into position and their firing was registered along with the routine firing that was taking place. This meant that Forward Observation Officers (FOOs), had to be in a position to gauge the fall of shot and report back to the artillery batteries in order that adjustments could be made. The problem with this was that the ground on the British side was so flat and featureless that this could not be done effectively. The result was that whilst the trench line could be identified, particular concealed features within it, particularly machine gun positions could not.

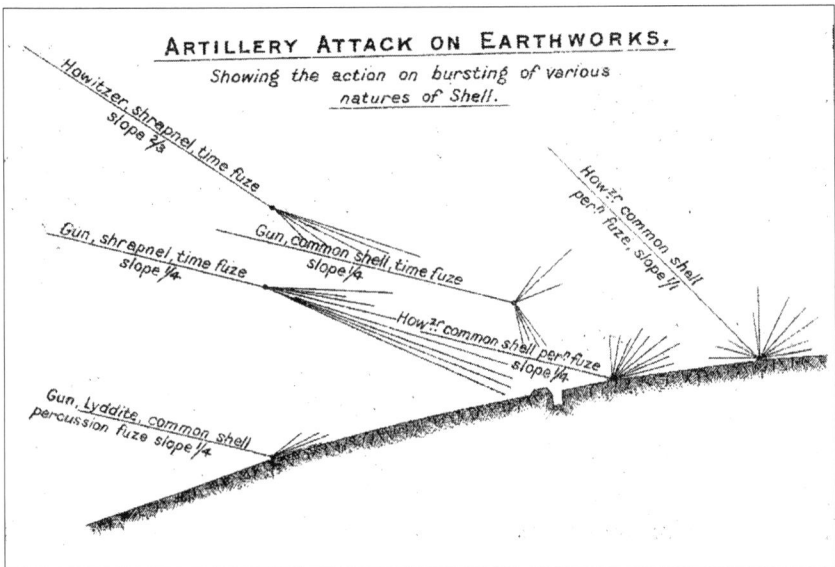

Illustration of the Effect of Shells
(Plate 1, Manual of Field Engineering 1911)

A Special Order for the day was issued to the First Army by its commander, General Sir Douglas Haig, emphasising the overwhelming superiority enjoyed by the British forces. In light of subsequent events, it displays hopeless optimism.

The battle commenced on Wednesday 10 March 1915 at 7.30 am with an artillery bombardment of 35 minutes duration. In this initial bombardment, 240 guns were involved in wire cutting on a 2,000 yard frontage and 99 guns and howitzers concentrated on the trenches.[10] To the troops of the IV and Indian Corps waiting to attack in the trenches, the bombardment which was the greatest in the war to date, was very impressive. The perception was that nothing could survive in the inferno. One officer waiting in the reserve trenches south of Neuve Chapelle stated, 'the din was terrific, the whole air and the solid earth itself became one quivering jelly.'[11]

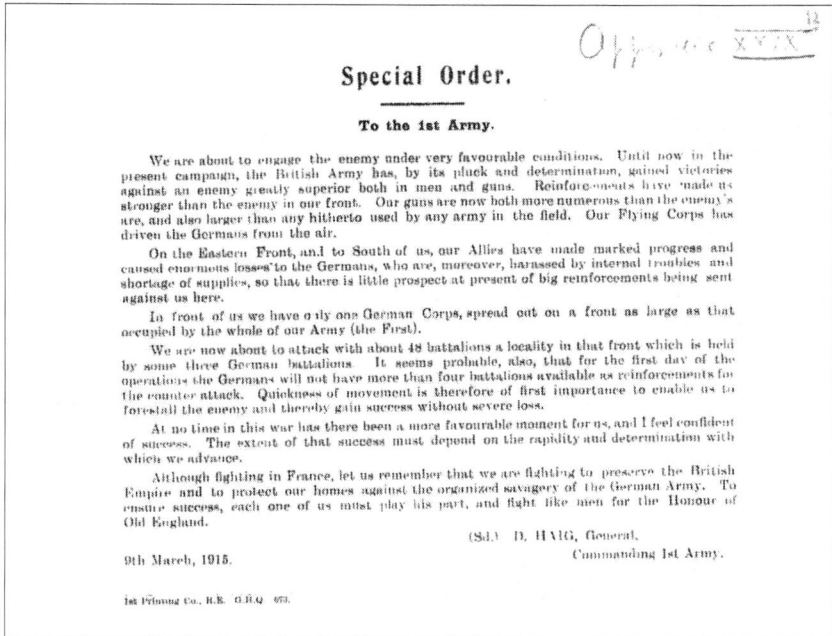

Special Order.

To the 1st Army.

We are about to engage the enemy under very favourable conditions. Until now in the present campaign, the British Army has, by its pluck and determination, gained victories against an enemy greatly superior both in men and guns. Reinforcements have made us stronger than the enemy in our front. Our guns are now both more numerous than the enemy's are, and also larger than any hitherto used by any army in the field. Our Flying Corps has driven the Germans from the air.

On the Eastern Front, and to South of us, our Allies have made marked progress and caused enormous losses to the Germans, who are, moreover, harassed by internal troubles and shortage of supplies, so that there is little prospect at present of big reinforcements being sent against us here.

In front of us we have only one German Corps, spread out on a front as large as that occupied by the whole of our Army (the First).

We are now about to attack with about 48 battalions a locality in that front which is held by some three German battalions. It seems probable, also, that for the first day of the operations the Germans will not have more than four battalions available as reinforcements for the counter attack. Quickness of movement is therefore of first importance to enable us to forestall the enemy and thereby gain success without severe loss.

At no time in this war has there been a more favourable moment for us, and I feel confident of success. The extent of that success must depend on the rapidity and determination with which we advance.

Although fighting in France, let us remember that we are fighting to preserve the British Empire and to protect our homes against the organized savagery of the German Army. To ensure success, each one of us must play his part, and fight like men for the Honour of Old England.

(Sd.) D. HAIG, General,
Commanding 1st Army.

9th March, 1915.

1st Printing Co., H.E. G.H.Q. 473.

Special Order to the Army on the Eve of the Battle of Neuve Chapelle[9]

To the Germans on the receiving end of the bombardment, it must have seemed like the end of the world. At 8.05 am the bombardment lifted to register on targets behind the German lines and the infantry advanced with the village of Neuve Chapelle their primary objective. Fifteen British battalions, roughly 15,000 troops attacked the village which was held by around 1,500 German troops. The reason that the village was so lightly defended was that it was believed that the British had neither the will nor the materiel to mount an attack and resources had been diverted elsewhere. Not surprisingly, progress in the centre of the advance was swift and the village was rapidly taken. Progress on the flanks was slower as the troops there discovered that the wire had not been as completely cut as it had been in the centre and German machine guns in positions to the rear which had been untouched by the bombardment restricted forward momentum.

The problem which now arose was that the attack stalled. Once the attacking troops left the front line trenches, communication with them was a very hit and miss affair. In an ideal world communications were maintained by field telephones, the lines being either dug in during pre-attack night operations, or run out by Royal Engineers personnel who advanced with the attack. The telephone wires were flimsy and prone to breakage. When this happened an attempt could be made at repair. However, first find the breakage whilst under fire! If this failed, commanders at the head of the advance had to rely on runners. A distinctly unenviable task and one for which volunteers were sought, the runner had to go back over the ground which had just been taken, find the headquarters, deliver the message and return with the reply – all this whilst under fire. Not surprisingly the mortality rate was exceptionally high and unless the runner returned to the front line, the commander was never sure if his message had reached its destination. In reality then, once the advancing troops left the trenches, generals and staff officers to the rear had no control over the direction of the battle and had to hope that all went to plan. However as senior officers, the vast majority of whom would have attended staff college, they must have been aware of the maxim of the eminent nineteenth-century German military strategist, Helmuth von Moltke – 'No plan of operations goes with any degree of certainty beyond the first contact with the hostile main force.'

At Neuve Chapelle this communication issue stifled initiative and led to the attack grinding to a halt as the whole picture of the extent of the advance could not be accurately assessed. Lieutenant Colonel Laurie of the 1st Battalion Royal Irish Rifles saw that the brigade to his left was being held up and asked permission to manoeuvre left to help them, but permission was refused.[12] To the right of the village, Lieutenant Colonel Stephens commanding officer 2 Rifle Brigade, saw a disorganised mob of Germans retreating in front of him and asked permission to advance in pursuit, but his request was refused as it deviated from the original plan.[13] Instances such as this literally proved fatal to the British cause. Once the attack stalled and the Germans got over their initial surprise it was inevitable that they would rush to strengthen their line and once this was done, organise a counter-attack. As the morning developed, to all intents and purposes at around 11.00 am on 10 March, the advance for the British was over. Further attempts at advancing on the afternoon of 10 March resulted in minimal gains, as the Germans rushed reinforcements to plug any gaps in their line.

The Inniskillings, for their part were to the south west of Neuve Chapelle in reserve trenches near the village of Le Hamel. They were to support an advance by 6 Infantry Brigade, their sister brigade in the 2nd Division, in an attack on the German lines designed to prevent reinforcements being sent to aid those at Neuve Chapelle. As most of the artillery was concentrated at Neuve Chapelle and probably due to conserving ammunition for the main thrust, an ineffectual bombardment took place between 7.30 am and 7.40 am and was then resumed at 7.50 am until 8.10 am when the assault commenced. The German trenches were 170 yards away and the attack is captured graphically in the war diary of 6 Brigades' 1st Battalion King's Royal Rifle Corps:

> At 8.10 am both assaulting parties having assembled on the White House road endeavoured to rush the enemy's trenches about 170 yards away. The right party advanced at the double over the intervening ground and soon came under a heavy fire (rifle and machine gun) losing many casualties, those remaining continued their advance but within about 30 yards of the wire entanglement were almost annihilated by cross machine gun fire. Some men threw themselves on the ground as they could not get through the entanglement which had nowhere been breeched and which consisted of trestles and high wire entanglement. Only a small number of men succeeded in reaching the wire and none got into the enemy's trench.
>
> The left party advanced at the double and some of them succeeded in getting into the enemy's trench notwithstanding many casualties and I believe some of them penetrated as far as the enemy's support trench, but it is impossible to say with certainty as only from one party has anyone returned.' The KRRC casualties in this attack numbered 255 Officers and men.[14]

As this abortive attack was taking place, the Inniskillings provided covering fire for their colleagues, receiving the attentions of the German artillery in return. In this action the Inniskillings suffered 26 casualties, including six killed.

Two of the six are quite fittingly buried beside each other in Bethune town cemetery.[15] This cemetery was used extensively by the 33rd Casualty Clearing Station located in the town, indicating that both had died of wounds after being conveyed from the battlefield. They were Lance Corporal William Logan, a 20-year-old from Raphoe in County Donegal who was survived by his father, mother, five brothers and three sisters, and Private Samuel Casey, a 28-year-old married man and father of a four-year-old son, from Saint Columb's Wells,

Londonderry. Before joining up he had been employed as a baker in the city. Inscribed on his headstone is a personal touch allowed by the Commonwealth War Graves Commission – and paid for by the family – with the words, 'Jesus have mercy on his soul – inserted by his wife and little children.'[16] Two of their comrades are also buried alongside each other in the Post Office Rifles Cemetery at Festubert, so named because of the large number of soldiers – originally post office workers from this regiment (officially the 1/8th City of London Regiment) buried there.[17] They are Private Daniel Brogan, 24 years, from Ballymoney and Private John Hoynes, originally from Drumquin, County Tyrone. The final two have no known grave and are commemorated on Le Touret Memorial to the Missing, a short distance from Festubert. This memorial commemorates 13,400 Allied soldiers who fell in the area between October 1914 and September 1915 and have no known grave.[18] They are 19-year-old Private John Muldoon, son of John and Annie Muldoon of 57 Main Street, Dungiven,[19] and 27-year-old Private William Cotton who was survived by his wife Louisa of 667 Scholefield Street, Birmingham.[20] Private Muldoon's family were fortunate in that they received some information as to how he met his death. A colleague, Private McConnell, wrote to them as follows:

> We were bombarding the enemy's trenches when a shell struck the parapet, killing him instantly. I was with him to the last, and he was buried with some Irish Guardsmen not far from the firing line. The Roman Catholic chaplain conducted the service at his burial. He was very popular with the men in his company, and you have our deepest sympathy.[21]

The family also received a letter from the chaplain, stating that their son was an excellent soldier, liked by all his officers and comrades. 'He met his death like a brave man, and I buried him in a little cemetery close to a church.' In all likelihood, all traces of Private Muldoon's grave were lost in the continual fighting which took place in this area over the duration of the war. Two officers were amongst the 26 wounded. Captain Charles Caulfield Hewitt and Second Lieutenant John Houghton Stewart were slightly wounded and were able to remain with the battalion after treatment. Both are of particular interest due to their involvement in the Battle of Festubert, some two months away.

Charles Caulfield Hewitt was a native of Weybridge, Surrey. Born in 1883, he attended Charterhouse public school before entering the Royal Military Academy,

Sandhurst. He was commissioned into the Royal Inniskilling Fusiliers in October 1902 and attained rapid promotion to become captain by 1908. By 1913 he was an experienced officer, having served in South Africa, Egypt, Crete and Malta, and in that year became an instructor at the Army School of Musketry at Hythe on the Kent coast. He re-joined the battalion in France as a replacement in December 1914, and took command of D company, a position he continued to hold until Festubert.

Born in 1895, John Houghton Stewart was the eldest son of Lieutenant Colonel George Powell Stewart and Florence Maria Georgina Stewart (nee Godfrey), of Grainville Manor, St Saviour, Jersey. Lieutenant Colonel Stewart was appointed officer commanding the Royal Inniskilling Fusiliers depot at Omagh in December 1914. He was to become the 5th Baronet of Athenree, County Tyrone. The Stewart baronets were major landowners in the county owning nearly 30,000 acres and homes at Ballygawley House and at Loughmacrory Lodge between Mountfield and Carrickmore. John Stewart attended Victoria College Jersey and Bradfield College in Berkshire before entering the Royal Military Academy, Sandhurst. Whilst at Bradfield, he was a member of the school shooting team.

Not surprisingly, on being commissioned he joined his father's regiment, again emphasising the close family ties and local connections of the Inniskillings.

John Stewart with his younger brother Hugh in Army cadet uniform at Bradfield College. (Picture courtesy of Sir David Stewart)

For those wounded, a complex well-organised system was in place to get them away from the battlefield and to receive the best medical attention available in the shortest space of time. This system had been developed following severe criticism of army medical services during the South African War. In these 1915 battles the wounded soldier, if he was unable to walk, was picked up from the battlefield by stretcher bearers, most likely from his own battalion. In the case of the Inniskillings these were the bandsmen, identified by a Red Cross armband. The wounded were initially taken to a regimental aid post, (which was usually in a dugout or some other hardened structure close to the front line), where they received first aid from Royal Army Medical Corps (RAMC) personnel. Each battalion had an RAMC medical officer and a small number of other ranks attached to it. At this stage, wounds were dressed but no real diagnosis carried out. The soldier was then carried by stretcher or horse drawn ambulance to the Divisional Field Ambulance. Field ambulances were run by the RAMC, having a staff of ten medical officers and a total complement of over 200. There were three attached to each division. Once the wounded soldier reached the field ambulance, he had passed out of regimental care and into the divisional medical system. It was at the field ambulance where what we would regard as 'triage' was carried out. The injured were sorted according to the nature of their wound, given anti tetanus injections and if appropriate something to eat and drink. They were then prepared for transport to a Casualty Clearing Station, (CCS)

Once the soldier left the field ambulance en route to the CCS, he passed out of the hands of the division and came under the control of the army medical services. Casualty Clearing Stations were situated at railheads, and could handle around 200 cases. They were a 'holding centre' until an ambulance train became available. The CCS was the first place that the wounded soldier would be in a bed. The most serious cases, ie those unlikely to survive and those whose wounds made movement a risk remained at the CCS. The stay at the CCS was usually only a few hours until a train became available. Each train had a staff of around fifty RAMC personnel and once aboard the train, the soldier passed out of the collection zone and into the evacuation zone.

The ambulance trains took the wounded to base hospitals. In the area of northern France the Inniskillings were operating in, these were at Boulogne, St Omer and Wimereux. The fact that these were all near ports made the situation of the base hospitals there ideal for swift embarkation of the wounded. There were two types of base hospitals, general and stationary. General hospitals were larger and better equipped – sometimes proper hospitals. Stationary hospitals despite their name could be mobile and operated out of hotels or other large buildings. The duration of stay varied due to the nature of the wound. Very severe cases – those unlikely to recover and very slight cases – those who would soon be returning to their unit, stayed. Those who were going to take more than three weeks to recover and were unlikely to be further harmed by the journey, were sent to England by hospital ship. The entire medical system was based on two principals – relieving the troops at the front of the burden of caring for the wounded and, providing the best care in as speedy a manner as possible.[22]

The attack on Neuve Chapelle was ordered to be resumed on the morning of 11 March, preceded by a 15 minute bombardment. This bombardment was largely ineffective as it was not clear where exactly the German defensive lines were due to faulty communications and lack of up-to-the-minute intelligence. In addition, after their efforts on the morning of 10 March, the Artillery were running very short of ammunition, with eighteen-pounder field guns only permitted to fire 15 shells each.[23] This attack was met with stiff resistance by the now reinforced German lines, and no appreciable advance was made, but great loss of life was incurred.

Almost inevitably, the German counter-attack came. Having managed to bring up reserves almost undetected, the first many British troops knew about it was when the grey clad figures emerged from the early morning mist of 12 March. The British were quick to realise the danger, however, and the German counter-attack was halted in its tracks by rapid rifle and machine gun fire resulting in massive casualties for the Germans. The mist stopped any attempt at aerial observation of the extent of the German attack and again lack of clarity of the situation on the battlefield added to the confusion as a further British attack was ordered for 10.30 am, but then postponed to 12.30 pm. In a further indication of the communications problems which existed, this message did not reach all the units and 2nd Battalion Scots Guards and 2nd Border Regiment attacked on their own sustaining heavy casualties. The confusion continued into the afternoon with General Haig believing the Germans were again on the retreat. He ordered an advance to take place at 4.00 pm and issued a directive to his corps commanders which, although based on faulty intelligence seems unduly heartless considering what had preceded:

> *Information indicates that enemy on our front are much demoralised. Indian Corps will push through the barrage of fire regardless of loss, using reserves if required.*[24]

As the true situation became known, however, including the conditions of the troops – some of whom had been fighting for two days and the fact that reserves were not readily available, this attack was initially postponed and then finally cancelled altogether.

So ended the battle of Neuve Chapelle. In its 60 hours duration, total casualties for the British and Indian troops numbered nearly 12,000 dead, wounded and missing. It is believed the German casualty total was similar.

The battle was seen by the relieved British high command as a success, possibly because they needed a success and any advance into territory held by the Germans was deemed a success. Importantly, they were able to prove to the French that they were not just there to make up the numbers and that given the right tools, the fighting spirit of the British Tommy would prevail. News of the attack was well received at home as a timely morale booster. An editorial in *The Times* dated 18 March 1915 stated:

> *Now that there is a lull in the heavy fighting around Neuve Chapelle, we can discern a little more clearly what happened. The British attack on the morning of 10th March evidently came as an almost complete surprise to the enemy. It was admirably planned, was well prepared by terrific Artillery fire, and succeeded in its immediate object. The result of the attack was to give a great fillip to the high spirits of the British Army, and it aroused the warmest admiration in France and Russia. The original statement of SIR JOHN FRENCH that, 'the losses incurred were not great in proportion to the results achieved' was entirely justified. The British casualties were even at first considerable, but the punishment inflicted on the foe reached a far higher point.[25]*

Somewhat predictably, *The Times* article paints a positive and jingoistic picture, but it has to be remembered that good news about the war was in very short supply up until this point and like the British high command, *The Times* was keen to stress the positives for home consumption. The casualty total of 12,000 seems horrendous to us 100 years later, but in the context of what had already happened on the western front the numbers, whilst never acceptable are perhaps understandable. In the autumn battles of 1914 for example, the French Army had lost over 40,000 men killed, in just three days. If we look deeper into the facts surrounding the battle, there are several issues which are worthy of note with regard to the conduct of the subsequent battles in the following months at Aubers Ridge and Festubert.

If we recall, Haig stated that his objective was 'not to take a trench here or there, but to push forward to Aubers Ridge with as little delay as possible.' This objective was clearly not obtained and as was discussed earlier was optimistic in the extreme. In view of the modest British gains this was perhaps conveniently overlooked. Although the element of surprise caught the Germans unawares, the failure of battlefield communications was perhaps the biggest inhibitor of a more comprehensive advance. This manifested itself in a failure to push on utilising the initiative of those in the best position to read the situation – individual battalion commanders.

Aerial reconnaissance as a means of communication was utilised to good effect initially, but this was negated by poor weather conditions and the inherent dangers, with at least one plane being shot down by British artillery whilst providing aerial observation.[26] In addition, whilst the use of aeroplanes was of benefit in spotting large artillery pieces it was – as subsequently noted by General Haig – of limited value in spotting machine gun positions which were dug into the parapets and invisible to aerial observation.

The positioning of machine guns, (much derided as a weapon by the British command) was crucial to the successful German defence once they recovered from the initial attack, a fact which can be attested to by the devastating experience of the Kings Royal Rifle Corps, yet few of these positions appear to have been neutralised in the artillery bombardment. Where this initial bombardment was successful was in cutting the wire in front of Neuve Chapelle, but difficulties with observation and again, lack of communication with advancing troops caused serious difficulties. Perhaps the greatest problem with the artillery was the condition of some of the artillery pieces and the lack of ammunition. The damning fact is that this was known to the British high command prior to the commencement of the battle. In a letter to the Secretary of State for War Lord Kitchener on 6 March, General Rawlinson stated:

> We want...better 4.7 shells. We have had several driving bands strip (4.7), which drop the shell 3,000 yards short of the target and the other day we killed some of our own men in this way. Then again, we burst a 4.7 gun three days ago owing to the shell exploding in the gun.[27]

It remained a fact that many of the British artillery pieces, particularly the 4.7 inch guns had seen service in the Boer War and some even before that, at the Battle of Omdurman in the Sudan in 1898.

4.7 inch Field Gun in action
(Image courtesy of Canada, Department of National Defence/Library Archives of Canada)

Rawlinson's continuing correspondence with Lord Kitchener was carried on behind the back of Field Marshal Sir John French and at best could be described as an effort by Rawlinson to protect his position in the event of him coming under pressure due to events on the ground and at worst duplicitous. To continue with the assault with faulty artillery was a great risk and is indicative of the pressure the British were under to mount an offensive. The dire straits which the British found themselves in with regards to artillery ammunition is evidenced by the fact that following the battle General Haig was encouraged to go back to England for a few days by Sir John French as there was not sufficient ammunition to resume offensive operations for two to three weeks.[28]

It could therefore be argued that the issues which needed to be addressed following Neuve Chapelle were; planning with realistic objectives, effective battle-field communications, a means of pinpointing and neutralising machine gun posts, and quality artillery pieces with an adequate quantity of suitable ammunition. It remained to be seen if these issues would be addressed for the next offensive.

Almost as soon as the dust had settled at Neuve Chapelle and impressed by the efforts of the British, General Joffre enquired if the British would be prepared to assist in a joint offensive around the beginning of May 1915. A detailed plan was forwarded to Sir John French on 6 April outlining the French plan of a combined offensive with the French Army attacking towards the plain of Douai, whilst the British were to attempt to seize Aubers Ridge, with the added bonus to the French of tying down potential German reinforcements in that area. Although conscious that he had neither suitable stocks of artillery ammunition, or enough seasoned troops, General French again felt obliged to accede to the request, no doubt reassured by the perceived breakthrough at Neuve Chapelle. Detailed planning for the second battle of 1915 in this area, which became known as the battle of Aubers Ridge commenced in earnest in early April. The British First Army under the command of General Sir Douglas Haig were again nominated for this attack, over much the same ground with the same conditions as existed on 10 March.

Following the battle of Neuve Chapelle, the Inniskillings reverted to their pre-battle routine of periods in the trenches at Cuinchy and Festubert, alternating again with the 2nd Ox and Bucks LI. On each of these trips to the trenches, there was a small, but constant attrition rate of casualties with one or two men being killed on each rotation, usually as the result of German artillery fire. On St Patrick's Day 1915, 19-year-old Joseph Kelsall was killed. Born in Oldham, Lancashire, he lived with his parents at New Dock Street, Belfast. Prior to the war, Joseph was a rivet boy in Harland and Wolff shipyard. In this work he was part of a close-knit team of four or five and his job would have been to catch the red hot rivets and place them before the riveters hammered them into place. It was dangerous work carried out whatever the weather. Army life must have seemed an easy option by comparison. In all likelihood, Joseph would have worked on the construction of the *Titanic*, having worked in the shipyard from 1910. Following his death, his mother received a letter from his Commanding Officer Lieutenant Colonel Wilding which stated; 'Dear Madam, I am deeply grieved to have to tell you your dear son was killed in action this afternoon. The doctor who attended him tells me that he could not have suffered at all. He will be properly buried tomorrow. The Bishop of Khartoum will read the funeral service.'[29]

Two days later on 19 March, 20-year-old Private Peter Kirwan, a native of Dublin was killed. He had been with the battalion since they had arrived in France in August 1914. On 27 March, as the battalion returned from a period of rest to the trenches, Private Joseph Donnelly, a member of the Irish National Volunteers from Grosvenor Place, Belfast was killed. He had two brothers also serving. On 29 March, Private Francis O'Neill was killed. A native of Coagh, County Tyrone, he left behind a wife Annie at their home at Ballygrooby between Magherafelt and Moneymore. On 2 April, Private Daniel John Joyce was killed. A native of County Carlow, (his father Patrick was the postmaster at Bagnalstown in the county), he has no known grave and is commemorated on Le Touret Memorial to the Missing.

Private Joseph Kelsall

Photograph of headstone from author's collection

The following day, Private Samuel Foster of Ballymagowan, Clogher, died of wounds in a base hospital in Boulogne. He had previously been wounded before Christmas when he had been shot in the head, necessitating periods at hospitals in France and England to recuperate. He left a wife Annie and is buried in Boulogne Eastern Cemetery. This cemetery is unusual in that the Commonwealth War Graves headstones are laid flat instead of standing upright. This is due to the sandy soil in the area. On 15 April, 25-year-old Private John Jones, a native of Southampton was killed and the following day Private Peter Murphy of Swanlinbar, County Cavan was killed, leaving a widowed mother and two younger brothers. This constant drip of fatalities must have focused the minds of the soldiers on the reality of the constant daily danger that they faced.

For the young soldiers of the battalion, most of whom had little experience of life outside their village or town, whilst there was constant danger, there was also a feeling of great adventure and excitement. This comes across in a letter written by another soldier from Dungannon, 22-year-old William Richard Dickson, from Derrygortrevy. The letter, sent to unnamed friends was published in two local papers, the *Mid Ulster Mail* and the *Tyrone Constitution*. In it Private Dickson gives a somewhat graphic account of his experiences which may have been embellished slightly for the benefit of the recipients, and urges others to follow in his footsteps:

> *I and some of my company have had terrible experiences for the last 7 months,*
> *particularly one night when we got an order to go back under heavy fire for the*
> *company's rations. The road we traversed was under heavy shell fire all that*
> *evening. On our return journey when we were within about 600 yards of our*
> *trenches, we were met by a company of Germans who had rifles and Maxim*
> *guns with them, and just as we came forward a shell bust amongst us and I was*
> *the only one of our party who was hit and would have got a nasty wound only*
> *for a watch in my breast pocket. Our company made a gallant bayonet charge.*
> *You could see the Germans who were bayoneted just covered with blood. My*
> *bayonet was bent with twisting it in the Germans to get it out, it would make you*
> *sick to see the slaughter, but our duty must be done. We are the boys that can*
> *do it, especially with the Huns who have destroyed Belgium. It would make the*
> *great generals of years ago rise from their long rest and wipe the Germans out*
> *from the face of the earth. But with God's help and our great leaders and gallant*
> *Inniskillings, we will make them feel the rifle never mind bullet and bayonet and*
> *Germany will pay for every drop of innocent blood that has been and is being*
> *sacrificed in this terrible war. Men of Dungannon, take advice from me and for*
> *God's sake wake up and take the 1s 9d a day or you will have the Huns in the*
> *Market Square soon. We have a few Dungannon chaps here and they are a credit*
> *to our gallant town for taking steps and coming to the front to represent the city*
> *of the volunteers. It is better to beat the Germans here than having them come*
> *over to Ireland to destroy everything as they have done in Belgium, which you all*
> *know is in ruins. Northern France and Belgium looks like some wild country, not*
> *like a civilised place at all. I hope all the boys at home will join the colours and*
> *help our gallant fellows out here to smash the Germans.*[30]

Somewhat ironically this letter was published on 15 May, the day of the battle of Festubert.

When relieved, the Inniskillings would march to billets in the hamlet of Gorre, some two miles behind the front line and three miles from Bethune. Here, life was relatively peaceful. The chateau stood untouched in the hamlet and it was used as an officer's mess and headquarters for troops billeted in the area. In addition the grounds of the chateau contained an improvised rifle range, a parade ground and perhaps more importantly from the point of view of the men, a football pitch. There were hints of other distractions available too. In a letter to his mother dated 23 March 1915, Lieutenant Alexander stated:

> *As the men have got so many smokes and as Harland and Wolff are sending out 20,000 cigarettes as a gift it would be wise for you to spend the 30 Shillings on footballs (about 7/6 each) or a little on notepaper and envelopes (they have a fair supply at present). The footballs would always be gladly received... Don't on any account send any bodybelts, mufflers or balaclavas as we don't know what to do with them and the men would only sell any more for drink as the weather is getting better!*[31]

The 20,000 cigarettes gifted by Harland and Wolff, (who had many former employees in the ranks of the 2nd battalion), ensured that each man received a reasonable share. For those non-smokers in the battalion they became a useful bartering tool for other luxuries such as chocolate, which was also in plentiful supply. The shipyard was not the only benefactor, however, as the regimental journal *The Sprig of Shillelagh* records thanks from Lieutenant Colonel Wilding passed to the Grove Weaving Company, Belfast, for cigarettes and tobacco forwarded to the battalion.[32] These gifts illustrate the popularity and respect with which the local soldiers were held from those left at home.

The rotations continued until 19 April, when the battalion were relieved in the trenches at Festubert by the 1/17th (County of London) Battalion – a territorial battalion known as the Poplar and Stepney Rifles. The Inniskillings marched to Bethune where they were billeted at Montmorency infantry barracks in the town. The next two weeks were spent at rest and recreation and in preparation for the forthcoming offensive. As part of these preparations, battalion-sized practice attacks were organised by 5 Brigade at a farm specifically requisitioned for the purpose. Referred to as Vertbois farm by the British, the Ferme du Vert Bois is situated around four miles north-west of Bethune and the Inniskillings would have marched there from their billets in the town. The 5th Field Company Royal Engineers, attached to 5 Brigade were responsible for the construction and upkeep of breastworks and bridges across ditches on the farm to simulate the ground which lay in front of the British lines. This remains a working farm to this day, although no evidence remains of any construction carried out by the engineers.[33]

Original outbuildings at the Ferme du Vert Bois
(Photograph from author's collection)

Whilst at rest, Lance Corporal John McIntyre of Derrygortrevy, Dungannon, took time to write to a friend at home. Letters such as this were frequently passed on to local newspapers to educate the community as to the wellbeing of soldiers. The letter, published in the *Tyrone Courier*, highlights a number of other local men who were all doing well, including John's brother William and a friend William Dickson, already mentioned above. The respect with which the Germans were held is also evident and interestingly, with no sign of animosity:

> *We have seen a lot of the country and a lot of the Germans. We have met them on several occasions. They are a great nation and there are some fine shots, especially the snipers. They never finish firing. They are very dangerous to us going into the trenches and out of them. As regards their Artillery they are not much good now, but they used to give us hell with their big shells at the beginning, but I think they have run short of ammunition or guns. Thank God for it too as they used to play our trenches up greatly.*[34]

Unbeknown to Lance Corporal McIntyre, following Neuve Chapelle the Germans had not been idle either. The German command realised how close they came to being overrun by the British and they vowed that such a breakthrough would not happen again. Almost immediately reinforcements were brought to the line, perhaps fearful of an immediate repeat of attack. An extra Division of VII Corps under the command of General Eberhard von Claer bolstered the front line troops – an extra 17,500 men. However, the extra troops were not there solely in case of a repeat attack, but to ensure that any repeat attack was not successful. For the next six weeks the Germans toiled night and day to make their defences impregnable. Deep ditches were dug in front of the parapet, with the earth removed filling countless sandbags which, due to the high water table were used to build up the parapet to a height of around seven feet. Coils of barbed wire were then placed in the ditches and in front of that lines of heavy gauge barbed wire wrapped round wooden trestles. The width of the parapet was increased to between 15–20 feet and within the parapet at regular spaces were built in large wooden boxes, designed to hold two riflemen. With the sandbags on top, these offered excellent protection. Every 20 yards or so, a large 'V' shaped wooden box was built into the parapet, again covered with sandbags. These boxes had steel loopholes to the front and were used to site the machine gun teams.[35] German faith in the power of the machine gun in this type of warfare had been enhanced following their Neuve Chapelle experience where their use greatly slowed the British advance on the flanks. Now, great care was taken to ensure that the spacing of the machine guns complemented each other and where there was a bend in the line, a machine gun was sited there, to ensure that any attacking troops would be subject to enfilade fire. Each machine gun was pre-registered on particular locations in the British front line and sited at ground level so as to be able to sweep the ground in front. Such was the professionalism in construction, it was maintained that only a direct hit from a howitzer shell could put the machine gun out of action.

A system of communications trenches led back from the front line and further machine gun posts were sited in strongpoints as far as 200 yards behind the front line to utilise as rallying places should any breakthrough be attempted. Deep dugouts known as 'wohngraben' were constructed behind the front line to enable troops to shelter during bombardments, but to be within easy access of the parapet to repel any assault. Some of these dugouts remain today such was the effort put into their construction. A visit to one in March 1915 described the conditions:

Some of the trenches have two stories and at the back of many of them are

subterranean rest houses built of concrete and connected with the trenches by
passages. The rooms are about seven feet high and ten feet square, and above the
ground all evidence of the work is concealed by green boughs and shrubbery.[36]

Such was the care taken in the construction and concealment of the workings
that little trace of them could be observed by aerial reconnaissance. One obvious
sign that work had taken place though was the sandbags. British sandbags were
khaki, whereas the Germans used both black and white sandbags, giving their
defences viewed from the British lines, the appearance of a giant chess board. The
enhanced defences were virtually completed by the end of April, just in time for
the next British offensive.

Whilst the Germans were well protected in their trenches and dugouts from
both shell fire and the elements, the British were not so fortunate. An account
from that time gives some idea of the conditions the Inniskillings had to endure:

We were on our own at Festubert- the terrain was too wet for trenches. We took
enough scrapes to fill the sandbags for a low wall. It was impossible to stand
erect. Many German dead were buried in the floor, and as it began to dry out the
shape of the bodies became clearly visible. We were in and out (mostly in) the
trenches at Givenchy, they were quite deep, especially in the mud.[37]

In addition to the dreadful weather conditions making it nigh impossible for the
British to improve their trenches, there was another reason why they remained
in such a poor state. As the British perceived themselves as the attacking force,
the trenches were never going to be anything but temporary. Creating fortified
structures similar to the Germans would have presented an image of permanency
and would have had an adverse effect on the offensive spirit of the troops.
Similarly, the British officially did not recognise no-man's-land, that area between
the British and German trenches. The front line was at the German wire, giving
the impression, officially at least, that when an attack was launched the British
were constantly advancing.

As the Inniskillings were practising their assault techniques at the Ferme du
Vert Bois, planning in fine detail was taking place for the forthcoming offensive.
The initial French plan was to advance and seize Vimy Ridge which would provide
excellent observation over the plain of Douai and the industrial centres of Lens
and Douai. The second part of this plan was to advance to a line between the

towns of Douai and Cambrai. The initial advance to Vimy was around three miles, with the secondary advance comprising a distance of 13 miles. The meeting point between the British and French armies was just south of the village of Cuinchy, which was held by British. The British line then ran north past the villages of Festubert, Aubers and Neuve Chapelle towards the Belgian border. Vimy Ridge was situated about 12 miles south east of Cuinchy.

Nothing much had changed for Field Marshal Sir John French since the planning for the battle of Neuve Chapelle. He was still awaiting the arrival of the new divisions and he was still desperately short of artillery pieces and suitable ammunition, an issue he reinforced at every opportunity with the Secretary of State for War, Lord Kitchener in London. However, he was buoyed by the gains made at Neuve Chapelle and believed that if all the conditions were right, a breakthrough could be made at Aubers Ridge. Precisely because there had been an initial breakthrough at Neuve Chapelle, there was a level of expectation from the French that the same could be done again. The response to the French proposal was delivered to General Foch by Sir John French on 9 April. An attack would be planned utilising ten divisions, 600 artillery pieces and would have in reserve five cavalry divisions. The plan was to break the enemy's line north of the La Bassée canal and reach the La Bassée-Lille road between La Bassée and Fournes. This attack would seize Aubers Ridge and provide the British with a commanding position over the low lying countryside beyond. Once this was achieved, the plan was to advance across the plain to a line between the villages of Bauvin and Don on the Haute Deule canal.[38]

The making of this offer indicates that Sir John French was possibly so blinded by the limited success at Neuve Chapelle, that he refused to acknowledge any negative facts or limiting factors, such as the wealth of intelligence reports and reconnaissance reports from the Royal Flying Corps that the German defences had been much strengthened. It may be that he felt obliged to match the thrust of the French Army, but he ignored the fact that he was doing so from a much weaker position in terms of men and materiel. The extent of the advance at Neuve Chapelle – with the element of surprise – was 1,200 yards or three quarters of a mile. In his proposal the phase one objective for the forthcoming battle was the La Bassée road, two and three quarter miles from the closest position of the British front line beside the wood known as the Bois du Biez. The second objective on the Haute Deule canal was six miles from the British front line at that time. It is prudent to assume that by including five cavalry divisions in his proposal, Sir

John French was reverting to type and envisaged the masses of cavalry sweeping down from Aubers Ridge and routing the fleeing Germans.

The attack was planned for Saturday 8 May 1915, and the British agreed to be ready by then.

Commander of First Army, General Sir Douglas Haig was again in charge of detailed planning for this battle and when the plan was briefed to his commanders it had changed slightly, so that the first objective of Aubers Ridge would be seized by a pincer movement. The Indian Corps and 1 Corps were to attack from south of Neuve Chapelle on a frontage from a local landmark known as Chocolate Menier corner (named after an advertisement hoarding on the side of a house) to Neuve Chapelle. IV Corps were to attack on a frontage north from Neuve Chapelle village with the intention that both attacks should converge at La Cliqueterie farm, astride Aubers Ridge. If successful, this pincer movement would isolate large numbers of German troops and equipment, which could be dealt with by reserves and flanks of the Indian and IV Corps. As a plan it was militarily sound, but it depended on the advance being able to take place and for this to happen, the German defences needed to be overcome.

Chocolate Menier corner in 1915
(Image courtesy of Imperial War Museum, Q17325)

Here the methods employed by the French Army and the British Army diverged. The French had realised from their battles in the Alsace region in 1914, that whilst a short bombardment retained an element of surprise, it was ineffectual at demolishing all but the most rudimentary of defences. For this reason for their planned attack on Vimy Ridge they planned to have a six day bombardment utilising 1,252 artillery pieces. The rationale being that the defenders would be so demoralised by the bombardment that the infantry should be able to breach the lines with ease. The British, however, favoured a short bombardment on this occasion planned for 40 minutes, but utilising 637 artillery pieces – nearly twice the number employed at Neuve Chapelle. To some extent, in planning the bombardment the hand of the British was forced. They simply did not have sufficient ammunition to sustain a longer bombardment. In addition, the situation regarding the artillery pieces themselves had not improved. Of the 637 field guns and howitzers, General Sir Martin Farndale in *History of the Royal Regiment of Artillery, Western Front 1914-18* points out that:

> *Of the field guns, 84 were obsolete 15 pounders, 20 of the field Howitzers were obsolete 5 ins, only 33 of the heavies were the effective 60 pounders, 28 4.7 ins guns were now so worn that the driving bands stripped off the shell at the muzzle resulting in extreme inaccuracy.*[39]

It is beyond doubt that the deficiencies in the artillery were known to the British High Command prior to the battle of Aubers Ridge, simply as they had not been remedied after Neuve Chapelle. It was known that the 4.7 inch guns particularly were seriously defective and had a disturbing habit of spraying shells in every direction, many falling short, and causing casualties amongst the troops packed tightly in the front line breastworks. The artillery plan for this attack was for 4.5, 5 and 6 inch howitzers and 18 pounders to bombard the German front line trenches and for 9.2 inch and 15 inch howitzers to concentrate on selected strongpoints to the rear of the German front lines.

Despite these known deficiencies, the planning proceeded. It would be charitable to suggest that General Sir Douglas Haig believed that the extra artillery pieces would make a difference, but he can rightly be castigated for failing to appreciate that the German defences had been improved so substantially that the artillery available was never going to make a difference. Reports of improvements in the defences had been forwarded to Haig throughout April from the Royal

Flying Corps. Lieutenant Colonel Hugh Trenchard, (later marshal of the Royal Air Force, the 1st Viscount Trenchard) was in charge of the Royal Flying Corps First Wing and was highly regarded by Haig. Aerial reconnaissance had been carried out of the German defences and these made into maps to brief the infantry but, as at Neuve Chapelle, the aerial photographs could not show the machine gun positions concealed from above and built into the parapets. Military intelligence had also reported on the Germans' strengthened defences. Cognisant of and perhaps blinded by the achievements at Neuve Chapelle, Haig appears to have ignored the facts and believed that with increased numbers of troops and the extra artillery, the objectives could be seized.

Whilst this planning was going on the Inniskillings continued their rest, recuperation and planning at Bethune. In between time on the rifle ranges and practising advances, there was plenty of time for relaxation. In two letters to his mother on 1 and 3 May, Lieutenant Alexander describes Mondays in Bethune as market day with the town being just like Dungannon, with fowl, stalls of boots and clothes and a large sale of vegetables, eggs being plentiful too. He also described attending the final of a football competition. This competition had been organised by the Right Reverend Llewellyn Gwynne, Bishop of Khartoum. Bishop Gwynne was an Army chaplain, and also a keen footballer, having turned out for Derby County before the war. The final featured the Inniskillings versus the 1/9th Battalion Highland Light Infantry, (a territorial Battalion also in 5 Brigade.) The Inniskillings team included Private William Henry Kelly in goals. The previous year he had won an Irish League champions medal with Linfield, with whom he had played for three years.[40] The match ended 0-0 after 90 minutes and a replay was arranged for 3 May which the HLI won 1-0. Like many a young officer, Lieutenant Alexander expressed his frustration with his job as transport officer, which kept him away from the action. Commenting that an Army Service Corps officer was to take over his post he stated, 'When I go to the company, I will go to Capt. Crawford's 'A' company, the one I always used to be in.'[41]Luckily for Lieutenant Alexander, the replacement was not to arrive for some time and he was to remain in his post. The officer referred to, Captain James Norman Crawford had commanded 'A' company from its arrival in France. An experienced soldier, the 41-year-old native of Dublin had also served in the Boer War, and had been wounded in September 1914, returning after recuperation in December 1914. He was to survive the war attaining the rank of Lieutenant Colonel and was awarded the Distinguished Service Order.

For the Inniskillings, their rest came to an end all too soon and prior to taking up position as reserves for what became known as the Battle of Aubers Ridge, they went into the front line at Cuinchy on 4 May relieving the 1st Battalion King's Royal Rifle Corps, close to where the British and French armies met. The KRRC had been in the trenches since 1 May and they had sustained a number of casualties from '*minenwerfers*', literally mine launchers, designed to fire a substantial charge a short distance with the intention of destroying defensive structures. In their four-day stay in the trenches, the Inniskillings were to suffer similar misfortune, sustaining five killed and six wounded, although the casualties could possibly have been much worse. On 4 May, the 2nd Battalion Worcestershire Regiment, who were alongside the Inniskillings in the front line breastworks, detected signs in front of them that the Germans were digging in a mine. Co-operation with the artillery ensured that the position was shelled with howitzers and sandbags and pit props were seen to fly into the air. This prompted retaliatory shelling from the Germans which killed Private Martin Moran from Cowie, Stirlingshire, Scotland. He had been with the battalion for a month. At 4.30 am the next morning the Germans detonated the mine, leaving a crater 20 yards wide and 15 feet deep, 50 feet short of the British breastworks. It was estimated that 4,000 pounds of explosives had been used. The mine itself caused one fatality with the Worcesters.[42] This was followed up by heavy shelling from the German artillery which caused further fatalities in the Inniskillings lines. Corporal Patrick King was the most senior of those killed, a native of Dublin, he is buried at Cuinchy Communal cemetery. Also buried in this cemetery were: Private Martin Moran, Private Charles Kelly, 25 years from Stranorlar, County Donegal who left a wife Madge and Private Joseph Taylor, a 48-year-old Boer War veteran from Coolreaghs, Cookstown, County Tyrone, who left a wife and daughter. Twenty-five-year-old Private John Goligher from Aubrey Street in the Fountain area of Derry, died of wounds on 7 May and is buried at Fosse 7 Military Cemetery, Mazingarbe, some six miles from Bethune.[43]

Relieved from these trenches on 7 May the Inniskillings returned to billets in Bethune.

In the early days of May the plans for the attack were finalised. However, once again the weather was to influence proceedings. In the last days of April and the beginning of May, the weather had improved significantly with several days of hot sunny weather from 1 May. This changed however on 4 May when there was a violent thunderstorm accompanied by heavy rain, followed by several days of hot humid weather interspersed with prolonged showers. This had the effect of reverting the ground to a glutinous morass. The rain of 6 and 7 May accompanied by humid conditions ensured that thick mists prevailed in the mornings. This interfered with the French artillery bombardment as the fall of shot could not be observed and also with the reconnaissance programme of the Royal Flying Corps, and as a result the joint offensive was postponed for 24 hours until 5.00 am on 9 May.

As previously mentioned the British 1 Corps was to form part of the advance. Its 1st Division under the command of Major General Haking was to lead the assault and its 2nd Division under the command of Major General Horne was to be the reserve, situated behind the 1st Division and ready to exploit any gaps in the German line. The Inniskillings were part of the 2nd Division reserve.

The 1 Corps operational order dated 7 May, states that the '1st Division will attack from its breastworks in front of the Rue du Bois.'[44] For orientation purposes, the Rue du Bois was a paved country road connecting Bethune to Neuve Chapelle. The British front line at this point ran parallel to it and about 300 yards south east of it. About half way along the 1 Corps attack frontage was a cinder track which led to the Ferme du Bois (Wood Farm) which was held by the Germans. This cinder track is of immense importance to the focus of events of the next week. From the junction of the cinder track with the Rue Du Bois to the British front line was around 350 yards at this point, with the German front line being around 200 yards further along the cinder track. The ground comprising no-man's-land was intersected by drainage ditches filled with water, the largest of which was around fifteen feet wide and about twenty yards in front of the British breastworks. The 1st Divisions' 3 Brigade were allocated a front line position with their right placed at the cinder track. The battalion nominated to attack from this position was an Irish battalion, the 2nd Battalion Royal Munster Fusiliers.

In addition to the preparations made by the assaulting troops in practising attacks over similar ground the Royal Engineers were busy, most importantly in the case of the Munster's constructing makeshift footbridges to enable them to cross the widest ditches. The Inniskillings left their billets at Bethune around midnight on 8/9 May and marched the four miles to their lie up point at the hamlet of Le Hamel where they would await news of progress. After the poor weather of the previous week, Sunday 9 May dawned fine and bright. If the British troops needed any incentive before the battle it arrived as they prepared to go over the top with the news of the sinking of the *Lusitania*. The Cunard liner en route from New York to Liverpool was torpedoed and sunk with the loss of 1,200 passengers on the afternoon of 7 May by the German U Boat *U20*, off the Old Head of Kinsale, County Cork. For the waiting troops the news provided more evidence of the moral degradation of a supposed civilised nation and the cry 'remember the *Lusitania*' accompanied the advance of many of the front line troops.

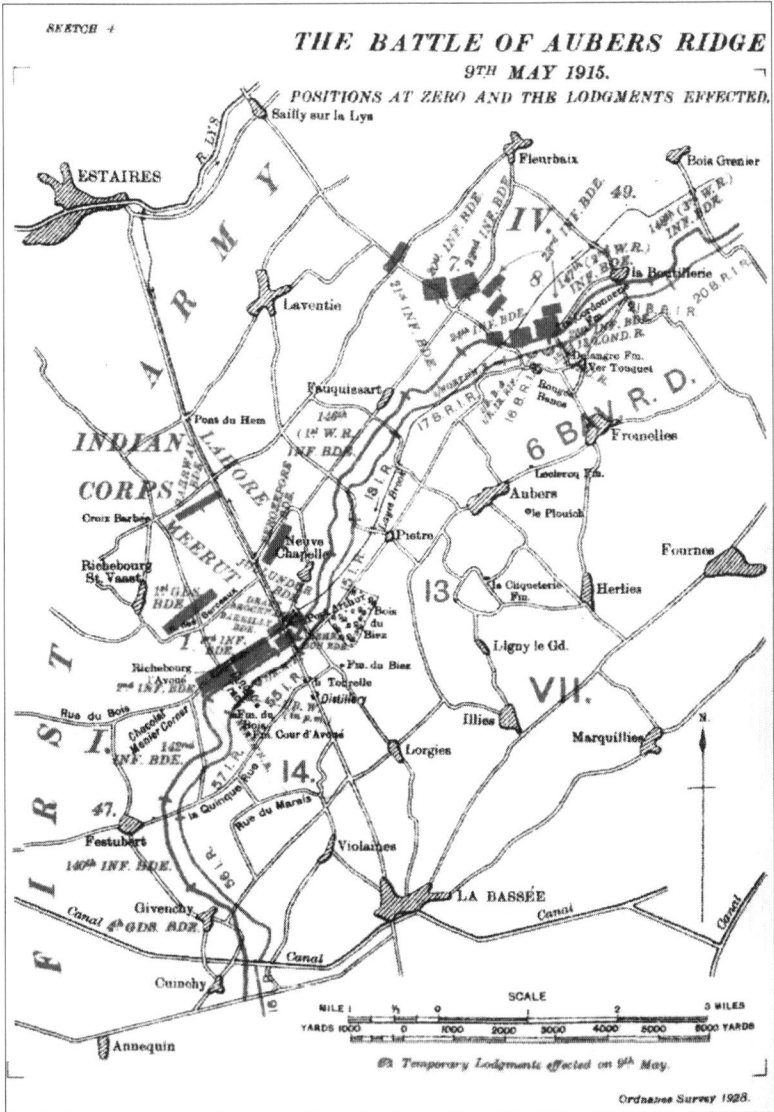

The Battle of Aubers Ridge[45]

At 5.00 am, nearly an hour after sunrise, the British bombardment commenced. At 5.30 am the rate of fire was increased and was concentrated on the German parapets. At this point it is of interest to view this bombardment from those on the receiving end. The trenches opposite were manned by nine companies of the 1st and 3rd Battalions of the 55th Infantry Regiment (Graf Bulow von Dennewitz), a regiment recruited from the north west of Germany. It is fortunate that a first-hand account exists from that time. Major Schulz, the commanding officer of the 55th Regiments' 2nd Battalion was in command on the right of the German line, nearly directly opposite the Munsters. His account is in the official history of the 55th Regiment:

The nightly trench work was ended. Drinking coffee, those exhausted through watch duty and trench-digging enjoyed the delicious warmth of the sun.

Shortly before 5 in the early morning an English flight squadron flew in a lengthy and staggered formation over the German positions. In the hinterland the barking of the aircraft-defence cannons could be heard, then dull explosions from bombs dropping. At 5.20am four heavy shells howled over. One hit the du Biez Farm, one the pumping station at Lorgies, a third went all the way to the Marquillies Station, and the fourth hit a fortunately temporarily empty dugout of the 3rd Company. Thereafter complete silence once again. Without having made us aware of a nearing attack, the enemy were once more testing the firing situation of their heavy artillery.

At 5.55am[46] the enemy unleashed a firestorm. The battle of La Bassée and Arras, which raged for many weeks until the end of July, had begun. All the gun barrels hurled their iron hail at the German positions. The explosions of the bursting shells followed, one after another, without cease. It was no longer possible to distinguish one strike from another; the thunder and crashing blurred into a dreadful symphony of rumbling, breaking and rattling. A wall of smoke and dust no longer penetrable by the eye rose above the German position.

At the beginning the telephone set had still just been able to report that the heaviest fire of all the guns was falling on all sections of the frontline; then the telephone connection between the trenches and the battle headquarters was broken. Running absolutely fearlessly, messengers delivered orders and reports. …The sandbags on the parapets had been torn to shreds, pulled apart by the rapid fire of the flat-trajectory artillery; within a short time the trenches were nothing but hollowed dips and so the garrison had to seek shelter in the support trenches which had not suffered to the same extent.[47]

By all British accounts the bombardment was an abject failure. The same issues which had been identified at Neuve Chapelle prevailed; faulty ammunition, difficulties with ranging the artillery pieces and observing the fall of the shells, and the condition of the artillery pieces themselves. However, for those Germans in the front line it was nonetheless a terrifying experience. Whilst the sandbags on the parapets may have been torn to shreds and some trenches collapsed, it appears that this was the exception rather than the norm. The wire appears to have been cut in a few places, but not to any great extent. What is certain, however, is that the bombardment failed to concentrate effective fire on machine gun positions and consequently, few if any of the machine gun positions were put out of action.

As the bombardment intensified for its final ten minutes the Munsters, along with the other front line battalions made their way over the parapet and out into no-man's-land, the Munsters immediate objective being a ditch about 150 yards from the British front line and within 80 yards of the German trenches where they were to lie down and await the cessation of the bombardment. The Munsters deployed B and A companies leading the advance with C and D companies following behind. The premise was that the bombardment would have driven all the Germans into deep underground bunkers and the infantry would have had a 'head start' in the advance. The artillery bombardment was also to cut two gaps in the enemy wire, one on the cinder track and the other to the left, the location of which had been agreed with the officer commanding A company. The experience of the Munsters was similar to that of other battalions in the advance. As they climbed over the parapet they saw the Germans watching them from their breastworks, such was the feebleness of the bombardment. As previously stated, the German machine gun posts required a direct hit from artillery to put them out of action and this had failed to occur.

Consequently, the Munsters were met with a hail of machine gun and rifle fire as soon as they rose from their lie up position. Their commanding officer, Lieutenant Colonel Victor George Howard Rickard, who was characteristically leading from the front was killed almost instantly, shot through the neck. However, the Munsters pressed on with exceptional bravery through a storm of steel now led by Captain Campbell Dick, commanding B company and about 100 men managed to find a gap in the wire and of these around 50 made it to the German parapet. Here, Captain Dick was shot dead as he cheered the men on.[48] As they crossed the parapet, one of the men was seen waving a green flag, (each company had been presented with a green flag emblazoned with a harp and the word 'Munsters' above it by a benefactor) and then they disappeared. The official history, *Military Operations France and Belgium, 1915*, states that, 'the survivors went on beyond the trench, but were held up by a broad dyke and mostly killed by the second British bombardment'.[49] The problem for the Munsters was that they were isolated with no support on either side. In addition, the Munsters' war diary recounts how the advancing troops were met with machine gun fire which 'undoubtedly came from our left and appeared to be almost parallel to the lines of trenches'.[50] This enfilading fire almost certainly came from a machine gun in a concealed position in a bend in the German front line. An alternative view of the reasons for the Munsters progress and their fate is provided by Major Schulz in his account:

> *Only in very few places had the enemy made it into the German trenches and here a bloodbath now began. The close-range fighting raged worst on the left flank of the regiment. The third platoon of the 55th's 11th company had been completely annihilated by the morning's heavy bombardment. Its brave leader, Acting Officer Vesting, also fell to a direct hit from a shell. The first enemy attack at 6.30am was here bloodily pushed back by two groups of the first platoon under Lance Corporal Prüßner who had been speedily hurried with his men to the position in danger. Now the overwhelming superior force of the enemy had allowed them to force their way into the troops of Infantry Regiment 57 and from there to entirely surround the 11th Company. Around 50 English stormed against the flank and back of the company. Yet the Lippe men, under their daring leader, Oberleutnant Herbert Reuter, showed themselves well-matched to the task......*
> *Of these, eight were made prisoner, all the remainder completely killed. In this battle Bugler-Lance-Corporal Ziegenbein of Hiddesen distinguished himself. He was constantly at the side of the company's leader; none of this most able guard's defensive acts failed his superior. He fell with the words: "Herr Oberleutnant, the English, from behind!*[51]

The truth of the fate of the Munsters is lost in the fog of war but suffice to say, none of those that made it into the German trenches returned. The bombardment mentioned in the British official history account was ordered by Major General Haking to assist a fresh attack timed for 7.00 am, however, this bombardment basically annihilated the survivors of the first attack sheltering near the German wire, or lying wounded in no-man's-land. It also failed completely to deal with the machine guns. Any survivors of this who were able to make it back to the British breastworks found it completely congested with dying and wounded men, preventing fresh troops going forward and as a consequence the 7.00 am attack, such as it was, met with the same fate as the first. As the assault rapidly turned into a debacle, Major General Haking reported the situation to 1 Corps headquarters. In reply to a question on the chances of success, he gave it as his opinion that, 'even if the whole 2nd Division was put in, it would not in the situation be successful.'[52]

All along the front being attacked by 1 and Indian Corps the story was the same. The failure of the artillery sealed the fate of thousands of men who were slaughtered, in many cases as they climbed over the parapet to begin the advance. The account from Major Schulz in the German front line graphically illustrates the scale of the massacre:

> Smoke was now flowing from the trenches like waves on the sea. Finally the enemy drew closer, facing up to the longed-for real fighting, man-to-man. Figures clad in earthen colours streamed forth from the English trenches, some with flat caps, others with burnoose hoods on their heads, and fell bodily on the defenders of the Flanders fort. In six strong waves the English 1st Corps and the 3rd Lahore Division of the Indian Army Corps started their attack. But the Westphalians and men of the Lippe, who, for three terrible hours, had huddled under the former parapets, greeted battle with naked arms as deliverance after the devastatingly heavy fire against which there was no defence. The fire ripped holes in the attackers in their dozens; every shot found its victim. Was there a surer target than this wall of human bodies? The rattle of the machine guns mixed itself with the chattering of the infantry fire. The cooling-water evaporated, the barrels glowing hot – shooting until they burst! The mountains of bodies piled up and, in this terrible surge, grenade met grenade and completed the hellish concert. The gunners at the artillery points in Halpegarbe, Lorgies, Illies, and Gravelin worked for their lives. The loading devices could not be tended to in quick enough time; sweat ran. The infantry and artillery leaders stand at the observation points. There are not so many orders to give in this crisis of the battle. Should they now want to alter the firing positions a little? Ridiculous! There is only one command: "Fire flat out from the barrels, until they explode!"
>
> Death reaps a terrible harvest from among the attackers. But new ranks storm up and over the bodies. The front attackers force forward, up to where in

the early morning along the front of the German position there was still a barrier
of barbed wire, erected with infinite care, but now only a pure tangle of wire and
stakes. They lie hanging in this former wire net. All others, if they have not fled
back to the safety of the English trenches, lie slaughtered on the battlefield.[53]

In their abortive assault the Munsters lost 19 officers and 370 other ranks,[54] by
no means the heaviest casualties in the 1st Division. In the sector to the north of
Neuve Chapelle attacked by IV Corps, the situation was no better. Another Irish
battalion, 1 Royal Irish Rifles attached to the 8th Division, attacked the German
trenches in this sector at Rouges Bancs. Like the Munsters they penetrated the
German trenches whilst under heavy fire and they managed to hold their position
until the morning of 10 May when they were driven out by means of bombs and
machine gun fire. In common with the Munsters, the failure of the battalions
either side of them to make progress rendered their position unsustainable. The
defenders were ironically, Adolf Hitler's regiment, the 16th Bavarian Reserve
Infantry Regiment. As all the Royal Irish officers were either dead, wounded or
missing they were led back to their original trenches by the Regimental Serjeant
Major William Carroll. RSM Carroll had several bullet holes in his clothing and
equipment, but was only slightly wounded in the hand. He was recommended for
the Victoria Cross for his actions in the attack and was subsequently awarded the
Military Cross. 1 Royal Irish lost 20 officers and 454 men on 9-10 May.[55] One of
those posted as missing, presumed dead, was 32-year-old Rifleman John Adams,
the eldest son of David and Cissie Adams of 12 Varna Street, off Belfast's Falls Road.
His younger brother Dominick was with A company, 2nd Inniskillings, only a few
miles away in reserve. The effect of the German machine gun fire was evidenced
in an account in Lyn MacDonald's excellent *1915: The Death of Innocence*. Private
Mitchell of 24th Field Ambulance recounted, 'I never saw an attack with so many
men who had bullet wounds as at Aubers Ridge. The Germans just mowed them
down and most of the bullet wounds were through the legs. We had a lot of
splinting to do, splinting, splinting, splinting.'[56]

By 7.00 am on 9 May, the advance as far as the British were concerned was over.
However, when the news reached Sir Douglas Haig in his headquarters, he refused
to believe it. Conscious of the fact that battlefield communications were anything
but reliable, he believed that the stalling of the advance was only temporary

Brothers Private John Adams Royal Irish Rifles, and Private Dominick Adams, Royal Inniskilling Fusiliers. (Image courtesy of Nigel Henderson)

and ordered a further advance for 12 noon. This, however, had to be postponed until 4.00 pm, due to the same problem which had affected the attack at Neuve Chapelle and had not been resolved – that the trenches were so clogged with dying and wounded men that reinforcements could not get into position. The attack at 4.00 pm met with the same results as the earlier attacks and simply resulted in further needless casualties. What irked Haig, was the news that the French had broken through and were advancing all along their front. Haig single-minded and obstinate, felt under pressure to succeed at any costs but in attempting to do so he sacrificed the lives of many men.

In a last desperate attempt to force a breakthrough, he ordered an attack to take place at 8.00 pm before darkness fell, using the bayonet. Fortunately, by this stage it was recognised that the roads leading to the front were so congested that the assaulting battalions would never be able to get into position in time. This included the Inniskillings who were still standing by at Le Hamel. This proposed attack was postponed until the morning of 10 May. However, when the full extent of the casualties became known, allied with the fact that artillery stocks were perilously low, Haig was forced to call off any renewed attacks. On this occasion, it is clear that Haig continued with the attack when it was obvious that no meaningful advance was possible and for this, as commander, he should shoulder the blame. It was left to those who were able, or could be assisted without drawing attention from the ever vigilant German machine gunners, to make their way as best as possible to the British lines. This took place over a number of days, with wounded men still being recovered until Friday of the following week. The Battle of Aubers Ridge, which had lasted just over 12 hours, had resulted in 11,619 British and Indian casualties for no gain whatsoever.[57]

After being observers to the debacle all day on 9 May, the Inniskillings were finally ordered into the reserve breastworks at 3.30 am on 10 May, to relieve the 2nd Ox and Bucks LI, who took over the front line along with 2 Highland Light Infantry. As a further British attack was proposed for 11.00 am, the Ox and Bucks and 2 HLI would have been the attacking troops with the Inniskillings, Worcesters and 9 Highland Light Infantry in support. At this time the Germans continued shelling the breastworks to prevent any British attempt at renewing the advance. Due to the realisation by General Haig that a further attack at 11.00 am was not feasible due to a lack of clarity of the situation, the attack was cancelled. The Inniskillings remained in the breastworks until 2.00pm on 10 May when they were relieved by troops from 6 Brigade and made their way to billets in Richebourg, just over a mile behind the front line. During their 11 hours in the trenches the battalion had seven men wounded by the shellfire. Of greater importance to the battalion, however, was the misfortune which befell the commanding officer, Lieutenant Colonel Wilding who had to be hospitalised after his horse fell and he injured his knee.[58]

This unfortunate accident robbed the Inniskillings of their commanding officer, just before their participation in arguably the most important battle in their history. Lieutenant Colonel Charles Arthur Wilding, a native of Shropshire was 56 years old when he took command of the battalion in September 1914, having been an Inniskillings officer for 26 years. He had served in the South African War as a company commander, and commanded the detachment of Inniskillings who first engaged with the Germans at Le Cateau on 26 August 1914.[59] Having served the regiment with distinction for so many years the events of the following week would have been the most important in his career and to miss them over a riding accident must have been devastating to him. However, unlike many of his contemporaries in the battalion he was to survive the war, retiring in 1922 with the rank of Brigadier General. He settled in Penbryn Hall, Montgomeryshire, Wales, and became a justice of the peace. In an interesting aside, it was reported in the press on 1 October 1923 under the somewhat sensational headline, 'A Beautiful Girl's Infatuation', that his daughter Carol had married – with the General's consent – a Reginald Davies, son of a Newport docker who was the General's valet.[60]

Leaving the misfortunes of Lieutenant Colonel Wilding aside, there was an able deputy waiting in the wings. Captain James Norman Crawford had been in charge of A company from the beginning of the war. He had been wounded in

September 1914 and had re-joined the battalion in December. Born at Palmerston, Dublin in 1874, his father Henry, was a major in the Regiment's 1st Battalion.[61] He was commissioned in 1893 and had served through the South African War. Widely experienced and respected within the battalion, he was tailor-made for the command.

In the days following the battle the reasons for failure to make any headway were examined. Realisation finally dawned on those at general headquarters that British artillery was not fit for purpose. This was reinforced by the knowledge that the French to the south had made a significant advance following their six day bombardment. That bombardment used over 2,100,000 shells of all calibres, quantities the British could only dream of.

This theme is borne out in the official history which gave the causes for the failure as follows:

1. The strength of the German defences and the clever concealment of machine guns in them
2. The lack on the British side of sufficient shells of large calibre to deal with such defences
3. The inferior quality of much of the ammunition supplied[62]

This is itself is an admission of failure in planning. Imagine the Germans having the audacity to cleverly conceal machine guns! How did this come as a surprise? The inescapable implication is that insufficient attention was paid to intelligence in relation to the siting of German machine gun positions. As has been mentioned above, the Germans had been carrying out construction for six weeks – not something that was thrown together at the last minute. The state of the defences seem to have surprised General Sir Douglas Haig though. In his diary entry of 9 May he stated:

> Bombardment began at 5am and our infantry advance to attack at 0540...Our bombardment seems to have been accurate, but the enemy had placed machine guns under his parapet to fire just above the level of the ground...the muzzles could not be seen or hit by shellfire. By 6pm it was clear that roads were so encumbered that fresh brigades for the attack at dusk could not be got forward in time, also enemies Artillery prevented rapid movement in rear of our line in the open. I therefore cancelled order for the attack.[63]

The British bombardment was anything but accurate, a realisation which Haig appears to have come to somewhat belatedly. In his diary entry of 11 May, he seems to have been convinced by the experience of the French, that a long bombardment was necessary:

The conclusions I arrived at are:

1. The defences in our front are so carefully (and so strongly made), and mutual support with machine guns is so complete, that (in order to demolish them a) long methodical bombardment will be necessary by heavy artillery (guns and howitzers) before infantry are sent forward to attack).
2. To destroy the Enemy's materiel – 60 pdr guns will be tried, as well as the 15 inch, 9.2 and 6 inch siege howitzers. Accurate observation of each shot will be arranged so as to make sure of flattening out the Enemy's strong points of support before the infantry is launched.
3. To destroy the physical power of the enemy, and shatter the nerves of the men who work his machine guns, the bombardment will be carried on during the night.[64]

Unfortunately it took the waste of many thousands of lives for Douglas Haig to arrive at this conclusion, which it could be argued had been evident since Neuve Chapelle. Aubers Ridge itself was not captured from the Germans until October 1918.

To add insult to grievous injury, on 11 May, the officer commanding the Munsters received a letter from Major General Haking commanding 1st Division, expressing the appreciation of the First Army heirarchy for their efforts. The letter contains a number of untruths. Firstly, 'that the attack was of the greatest value, because it drew away hostile reinforcements urgently required to repel the successful French attack to the south.' In fact, at 2.00 pm, nine hours after the battle had started the Germans 'stood to' two divisions in reserve in the area, but by evening sent them south to meet the French threat.[65] Secondly, the letter states; 'Aeroplane reconnaissance also report very heavy casualties in the enemy's line just in rear of his breastworks. The air observers state that these casualties alone exceed those of our men on both sides of his breastworks.'[66] In reality, German casualties numbered 1,551, around 14 per cent of those on the British side.[67] Whilst possibly wishing to bring some comfort to the Munsters following their ordeal, it is hard to believe that Major General Haking in his position of knowledge actually believed the information that he was conveying.

For their part, the Germans were initially surprised by the bombardment. They had been monitoring the French bombardment to the south, correctly believing that the main offensive would take place there. They were, however, quick to recover from the shock and, as is mentioned above, realised fairly quickly that their defences had held and that there would be no British breakthrough. They were free then, probably as they had intended, to send their reserves south as reinforcements against the French attack. In essence then, even the initial strategic objective in the planning of the attack on Aubers Ridge, that of tying down the Germans to render them unable to reinforce their line against the French attack had failed miserably.

Search parties braved German machine gun and shellfire to bring in those who lay wounded and were unable to make their own way back to safety, but the dead remained where they fell. On 10 May, the King's Royal Rifle Corps of 6 Brigade were in the British front line slightly to the left of the Munster's start position. In daylight they had the opportunity to view the ground over which the attack had taken place:

> This was quite flat and crossed by many ditches full of water. There were three lines of breastworks in addition to the front line which was half breastwork, half trench. These lines of breastworks all ran parallel to the Rue du Bois one about 100 yards in front and 2 behind it, There was a ditch about 12 feet wide running along with small wooden bridges placed there by 1st Div for their assault. It was possible from the position of the dead to form a fairly good idea of what had happened during the assault. A very few were lying close up to the German trenches, there were some at the bridges over the ditches 20 yards in front of our own parapet and a good many just in front of our own parapet, but the best majority were lying scattered over the cultivated ground between our 1st line and the 2nd line of breastworks.[68]

The positioning of the dead between the first and second line of breastworks indicates the pinpoint accuracy of the pre-registered aiming positions of the German machine guns and also the ferocity of the fire which met the advancing troops. The hopelessness of the cause indicated by the fact that many were killed before they actually crossed the British front line. Whilst every effort was made to locate the wounded, there were no men to spare to bury the dead. It was much too dangerous. So there they lay. These are some of the men whose names appear on Le Touret Memorial to the Missing.

The bodies of the fallen lying exposed to the elements gradually disintegrated, but the stench for those manning the trenches was all pervading. A graphic account of this process is given by Corporal Charlie Parke of the Gordon Highlanders in Richard van Emden's, *The Soldier's War*:

> *There was an overwhelming stench of death. The almost sweet but acrid smell of decaying flesh could not be compared to any other, but suffice to say that even someone new to this horror would know its source instinctively and immediately. In hot weather, corpses of horses and men would explode in about three days. The whole body would swell up, although different parts to different extents. Fingers inflated only slightly, whereas stomachs swelled the most and, in fact, it was at this point that the explosion would normally be expected to occur; in military bodies however, the extremely strong webbing belt held the stomach in, so bursting occurred in two places, just above the belt and just below, near the crotch. In that hellhole, one creature came out on top whatever the result of the skirmish; that creature was the rat. These vermin performed so well in stripping flesh from the corpses that they were a protected species, the standing order being that none were to be shot. I watched at first hand one of these monster rodents start ripping at the freshly felled German uniform, almost at the edge of the British parapet, fiercely searching for the prime Hanoverian flesh beneath. Rats were an extremely efficient demolition unit, usually starting at the peripheries, either head or toes; where there was an abundant supply of human flesh, which was usually the case, they would leave the stomach, the container of waste products, and start on a fresh corpse. Although they were an obnoxious sight, they performed a necessary duty in baring skeletons and I, from my own experience, found they never troubled live humans, not even when the men slept.* [69]

This was the environment in which the Inniskillings existed as they prepared for the battle of Festubert.

1   Sheffield G and Bourne J,(Eds) *Douglas Haig. War Diaries and Letters 1914-1918*, p122

2   Sheffield G and Bourne J,(Eds) op. cit, p.101

3   Sheffield G and Bourne J,(Eds) op. cit, p.107

4   Bridger G, (2009), *Battleground Europe, The Battle Of Neuve Chapelle*, Kindle ebook, Barnsley, Pen & Sword

5   Bridger G, Op. Cit.

6   Jones HA, (1969) *The War in the Air, being the story of the part played in the Great War by the Royal Air Force.* Volume 2 pps 90-92

7   Ibid p89

8   Farndale, General Sir Martin, (1986) *History of the Royal Regiment of Artillery. Western Front 1914-1918,* p1

9   National Archives, WO 95/1343/2 App 29 5 Infantry Brigade War Diary

10   Farndale, op. cit,. p.86

11   Bridger, G, op. cit.

12   Ibid. Lieutenant Colonel George Brenton Laurie, the Canadian commanding officer of 1 Royal Irish Rifles was killed by a sniper on the morning of 12 March.

13   Ibid.

14   National Archives. War diary of the 1st battalion Kings Royal Rifle Corps, WO/95/1358

15   www.cwgc.org

16   Authors records

17   www.cwgc.org

18   Ibid

19   www.census.nationalarchives.ie

20   www.cwgc.org

21   *Belfast Newsletter* 26 Mar 1915. The intimation from this letter is that Private Muldoon was killed by a British shell, one of the many which fell short, did not explode or went off course.

22   Swinton ED & Percy AIP, (1916). *A Year Ago. Eye-Witness Narrative of the war from March 30th to July 18th, 1915, pps 209-215*

23   Bridger, op. cit.

24   Ibid

25   *The Times* March 18 1915 p11, available online @http://www.thetimes.co.uk/tto/archive. Accessed 13 January 2014

26   Bridger, op. cit.. Lieutenants Albert Morgan and Aubrey Irving, 2 Squadron Royal Flying Corps were flying a BE2a and observing for artillery when they were struck by a large calibre British shell at 11.00 am on 10 March. Both were killed.

27   Ibid

28   Sheffield G and Bourne J (Eds) op. cit., p.122

29   Private Joseph Kelsall is buried at Woburn Abbey Cemetery on the outskirts of the village of Cuinchy

30   *Mid Ulster Mail*, May 15 1915, p.7, and *Tyrone Constitution* May 21 1915, p.7

31   PRONI D/4121/F/4/B/2/5/15 23 March 1915 CAM Alexander papers

32   *Sprig of Shillelagh*, May 1915 p124

33   The National Archives. WO 95/1330/2 5th Field Company Royal Engineers war diary. The farm is currently occupied by a very pleasant couple, M and Mme Carlier. At the time of its use by the Inniskillings, it was occupied by the present owner's grandfather, M. Albert Jacquemont. Whilst the farmhouse has been replaced, the outbuildings remain intact.

34   *Tyrone Courier*, 22nd April 1915 p.7

35   Edmonds, *Military Operations in France and Belgium 1915*, p14

36   Gailor, *Daily Mail* March 24 1915. Available online @ www.oldmagazinearticles.com accessed 23 November 2013

37   Jones N, (1983) The War Walk, a Journey along the Western Front, p48 description by Sgt John Larrad, 1st Batt, 18th London Regt, London Irish Rifles.

38   Edmonds, op. cit, p.4

39   Farndale, op. cit, p.103

40   *The Sprig of Shillelagh*, July1915, p162 & www.linfieldfc.com. Pte Kelly was to survive the war and in 1919 continued his football career with South Shields FC.

41   PRONI D/4121/F/4/B/2/6/1&2, 1 May 1915 CAM Alexander papers

42   The National Archives. WO 95/1343/2 5 Brigade war diary and Stacke, H, (1928) *The Worcestershire Regiment in the Great War*, Volume 1 p68.The Worcesters account indicates that the front line troops were withdrawn following the discovery of the mine.

43   www.cwgc.org

44   Edmonds, op cit, App 7 p.432

45   Edmonds, op cit, Sketch 4 page 6

46   Timings in the German accounts appear 1 hour later than that in British accounts as British accounts are based on Greenwich Mean Time.

47   Schulz D, (1928), *Infanterie Regiment Graf Bulow von Dennewitz, Nr 55 im Weltkriege* pps 87-88

48   Rickard JLM, (1918)*The Story of the Munsters at Etreux, Festubert, Rue Du Bois and Hulloch*, p.40

49   Edmonds, op. cit., p.22 note 2

50   The National Archives. WO 95/1279 2 Royal Munster Fusiliers war diary

51   Schulz D, op. cit., p.89-90.

52   Edmonds op. cit, p.23

53   Schulz D, Ibid

54   The National Archives. WO 95/1279 2 Royal Munster Fusiliers war diary.

55   The National Archives .WO 95/1730/4 1 Royal Irish war diary

56   Macdonald L, (1997), *1915: The Death of Innocence*, p.309

57   Edmonds, op. cit., p.39

58   Alexander, op. cit., p.43

59   Fox, Sir F. *The Royal Inniskilling Fusiliers in the World War*. p.41

60   'A beautiful girl's infatuation' *Lloyd's News* 1 Oct 1923. Available online @ www.trove.gov.au/ newspaper. Accessed 2 December 2013

61   www.ancestry.co.uk

62   Edmonds, op. cit., p.41

63   Sheffield, G and Bourne, J, (Eds) op.cit., p.122

64   Ibid p123

65 Edmonds, op.cit., p.43

66 The National Archives. WO 95/1279, 2 Royal Munster Fusiliers war diary

67 Bristow, A, (1995) *A Serious Disappointment. The Battle of Aubers Ridge 1915 and the Munitions Scandal* p.172

68 The National Archives. WO 95/1358 1 Kings Royal Rifle Corps war diary.

69 Van Emden R. *The Soldiers' War. The Great War through veteran's eyes*, Kindle ebook, London, Bloomsbury

··· CHAPTER 5 ···
MUNITIONS

Owing to the bungling and want of foresight at the War Office we only
have a very insufficient quantity of High Explosive. (Sir John French
C-in-C British Expeditionary Force following Aubers Ridge)[1]

Exasperated by the failure at Aubers Ridge, Sir John French realised that the
cause of the matter lay with insufficient artillery and poor quality shells. He
acknowledged that it was tantamount to murder to send men against machine guns
and well-protected defences without adequate artillery preparation. His concerns
were rooted in the failure of the British government to prepare adequately for
war. His subsequent actions set in train a course of events which led in part to
the fall of the Liberal government. Whilst many of the developments came much
too late to influence the situation facing the Inniskillings at Festubert, they are
symptomatic of the situation concerning artillery capabilities at the time and as
such they are worthy of examination to expose the parlous state of the British
ammunition holdings in the build up to the battle and the restrictive practices
which had inhibited British preparations for war.

As the battles of autumn 1914 receded and the opposing armies settled down
to trench warfare, Sir John French was acutely aware of the limitations of his
artillery. More shells had been fired in the brief battles of the autumn than in the
entire South African War and replacements were not coming fast enough. When
the Germans began to shell British positions it was often the case that the British
artillery had nothing to fire back with, or that such strict limitations to conserve
ammunition were placed on their 'daily allowance' of shells, that once it was
expended nothing more could be done.

Sir John began a long correspondence with the War Office and Lord Kitchener
Secretary of State for War, constantly requesting urgent resupplies of ammunition
and an increase in productivity. However, personalities again had a part to play
in how this episode unfolded. Kitchener was no friend of Sir John French and
regarded him as a mediocre soldier and definitely not one who should have
been in charge of the greatest British military adventure for a generation. It is
believable that he paid scant attention to the requests, regarding them as evidence
of French's inability to prosecute the war properly. He certainly did not discuss

the requests with members of the Cabinet Munitions Committee of which he was chairman. In holding this view, Kitchener had an ally in Major General Stanley von Donop, who held the grand title of Master General of the Ordnance. Fifty-five-year-old Von Donop was a career artilleryman, having held the titles of Chief Instructor at the School of Gunnery and Director of Artillery at the War Office. If anyone knew anything about artillery, it was him, and he wasn't going to be rushed into decision making by Sir John French. Prevarication and obfuscation characterised his dealings with the BEF Commander. In reply to one request for increased supply von Donop replied, 'the nature of the operations may alter again as they have in the past.'[2] In making this response he may have had a point, but the fact that both sides had dug trenches facing each other for nearly 500 miles should have been an indicator that there was to be no open warfare with chances to outflank the enemy for some time to come.

The vast majority of actual manufacture of ordnance was carried out by the Royal Ordnance Factories with a few accredited suppliers such as Vickers making up the difference. All of these institutions reported directly to the War Office and in this case Von Donop and Kitchener. The workers within these factories were proud of their skills which had taken many years to attain and were vehemently opposed to any dilution of the workforce, which the vast increase in supply demanded. In this they were supported by the unions, who had fought long and hard to achieve respectable pay and working conditions. They saw a threat in the imposition of new working practices and of unskilled workers and God forbid, women being recruited to take the place of those who had gone to the front. The workers were in a cosy position, which may have been suitable in peacetime but was a recipe for disaster in wartime.

Kitchener was in no mood to upset the status quo. The last thing he needed was industrial unrest when he was busy trying to create a new army from scratch. He paid lip service only to the Munitions Committee which should have been addressing the issue, citing the fact that he was too busy to attend – much to the displeasure of Lloyd George the Chancellor of the Exchequer, who foresaw the dangers ahead. The Munitions Committee was set up in October 1914 but due to Kitchener's intransigence, it withered on the vine and met for the last time on New Year's Day 1915. By this time, Kitchener would have been aware of a letter sent to him by Sir John French in which he outlined what ammunition he required for each gun on a daily basis. He requested 50 rounds per gun per day for 18 pounders, 40 for 4.5-inch howitzers and 25 for 4.7-inch howitzers. At the time (December 1914), he was receiving six, five and eight rounds per day respectively.[3] This had a drastic effect on operations at the front, with aArtillery batteries in the front line reduced to a miniscule daily allowance, sometimes as low as five rounds per day. Remarkably, the figures produced actually fell below this in January 1915 with this being attributed to the workers availing of their statutory Christmas and New Year holidays! Kitchener replied to Sir John French on 9 January 1915 in a classic stalling letter:

It is impossible at the present time to maintain a sufficient supply of gun ammunition on the scale which you consider necessary for offensive operations. Every effort is being made in all parts of the world to obtain an unlimited supply of ammunition, but, as you are well aware, the result is still far from sufficient to maintain the large number of guns which you now have under your command adequately supplied with ammunition for offensive purposes.[4]

As Kitchener stated, efforts certainly were being made across the world. The cargo manifest for the *Lusitania* en route from New York, contained over four million rifle bullets as well as over a thousand shell casings and crates of fuzes. Nor were the efforts from either at home or abroad successful. There had long been a problem with the quality of artillery ammunition, not only that manufactured in Britain, but also from other sources. This was an issue starkly highlighted in the account of Major Schulz in the German trenches at Aubers Ridge:

Very remarkable indeed were the duds from the British field artillery observed during the bombardment and found thereafter. A few missiles were opened. The filling consisted not of explosive but of sawdust – made in the USA![5]

In the early months of 1915, Sir John French kept up a steady flow of letters and telegrams highlighting the problem. Coincidentally, and totally unaware of the correspondence Sir John was conducting with Lord Kitchener, Lloyd George was embarking on a crusade to try and improve the output from the munitions factories. As a temperance campaigner, he identified drink as one of the main issues ailing the munitions industry. It was the practice for workers who had started early, to retire to the pub at lunchtime and in many cases fail to return, or return in an inebriated state where the quality of any work they would carry out in the afternoon would be questionable. The other issue he identified was that of strikes from workers anxious to protect their position. In a speech at Bangor, North Wales on February 28 1915, he addressed both issues, referring to strikes he stated that he 'found it intolerable that the life of Britain was being imperilled for the sake of a farthing an hour'. Referring to drink he stated that 'drink is doing us more damage in the war than all the German submarines put together.'[6]

On 9 March Lloyd George introduced the Defence of the Realm Amendment (No 2) Bill, which gave the government the power to take control for the duration of the war, all works capable of the production of munitions. Others shared Lloyd George's concerns over the detrimental effect excess drinking was having on the British war effort. He was visited at the end of March by representatives of the Shipbuilders Employers Federation concerned that increased wages were being spent by workers on drink. The depth of his concern over this matter is indicated in his reply to them:

The feeling is that if we are to settle with German militarism we must first of all settle with drink. We are fighting Germany, Austria and drink, and as far as I can see the greatest of these deadly foes is drink.[7]

Debates took place in parliament considering the shutting of public houses near munitions works altogether and amendments including the banning of the sale of spirits. Eventually legislation was introduced forcing all public houses in England to close in the afternoon. (For those of us old enough to remember, this legislation remained in place until the 1980s) This had an immediate effect on the sobriety of the workforce and although not the only factor, evidence indicates that quality and quantity of munitions increased from the spring of 1915. There were 91 artillery pieces manufactured in the whole of 1914, this rose to 3,226 in 1915 and increased throughout the rest of the war. [8] There were always those, however, who decided to chance their arm. A report in the *Belfast Newsletter* of 27 May 1915 highlighted a court case in Newcastle under the headline, '*Munitions Workers Fined for Drunkeness*' it continued:

At Newcastle upon Tyne yesterday several workers on war munitions were fined various sums for drunkenness. To two young men wearing war service badges who were fined at Gateshead, the chairman said, 'is that the way you expect to win the war? You are a disgrace to the service. There is too much of this sort of thing going on. You should have more sense of decency.[9]

The fact that those involved in munitions manufacture were making very good money grated with those who had given up good jobs to go to the front. Any indiscretions by these workers were pounced upon and broadcast widely by the local press. Another report in the *News Letter* highlighted the case of Samuel Gorman, a riveter at Armstrong Whitworth in Newcastle who was charged with being drunk on licensed premises. The prosecution indicated that:

> The trouble with the man was that he was making too much money. His conduct for the last fortnight or three weeks has been disgraceful. His wife and two children had to go away from him. The other night he lit his pipe with a one pound note rather than give it to his wife and family. He was making too much money.[10]

Following the battle of Neuve Chapelle, where the inadequacies of artillery support had been identified, the tone of Sir John French's correspondence grew more alarmist. In a letter to Lord Kitchener on 16 March 1915, he baldly stated, 'the object of His Majesty's Government cannot be attained unless the supply of Artillery ammunition can be increased sufficiently to enable the army to engage in sustained offensive operations.'[11] Kitchener again kept this correspondence to himself and maintained the facade that he was doing all he could to increase supply. Events, however, were about to undermine him.

The Prime Minister, Herbert Asquith was invited by trade unionists in Newcastle to address them. This he did on 20 April 1915 and caused great confusion when he stated as part of his speech that:

> I saw a statement the other day that the operations of war, not only of our army but of our Allies, were being crippled, or at any rate hampered, by our failure to provide the necessary ammunition. There is not a word of truth in that statement.[12]

He went on to state that there was no evidence of any lack of endeavour on the part of anyone in the munitions industry, contrary to what Lloyd George had been preaching for the previous four months. The speech must have also mystified Sir John French and perhaps given him an inkling that Lord Kitchener was being less than truthful in spreading the message at home. As it was, Asquith was furious with Kitchener for failing to reveal to him the true state of the problem which had made him look foolish and this period marked a cooling in their relationship. For Sir John French this episode impressed upon him that in the future, more ingenious methods may be required to solve the intractable problem.

He did not have long to wait.

The commander in chief had the opportunity, along with some invited guests (among them the then Winston Churchill MP), to observe some of the Battle of Aubers Ridge from a vantage point in a church tower at Laventie, a mile and a half behind the British attack by IV Corps north of Neuve Chapelle. Also with him was the military correspondent of *The Times*, Lieutenant Colonel Charles a Court Repington, with whom he was friendly. This personal friendship enabled access to *The Times* journalist and more importantly to the *Times* owner, Lord Northcliffe, who was no friend of Lord Kitchener.

As news of the failure of the attack began to filter through, Sir John French returned to his HQ with Repington. There awaiting him was the final indignity. A telegram from the War Office instructing him to send 2,000 rounds of 4.5-inch ammunition and 20,000 rounds of 18-pounder ammunition to the Dardanelles. Driven to exasperation by the inability of those in London to understand his position he undertook very contemporary action, more in keeping with issues of today – he went to the press.

Repington's presence was fortuitous and Sir John ensured that he was well briefed, taking the opportunity to send further briefing papers with his secretary Brinsley Fitzgerald and his aide de camp Captain Guest, for the attention of Lloyd George and the Conservative leader Arthur Balfour. Interestingly, this was the first information Lloyd George had had from Sir John French on the subject, due to Lord Kitchener retaining all previous correspondence himself. Somewhat fortuitously for Sir John French, personal tragedy also intervened. Lord Northcliffe's nephew, Lieutenant Lucas Henry St Aubyn King of the King's Royal Rifle Corps had been killed on 8 May during the preparation for the battle of Aubers Ridge.[13] Already grief-stricken, on receipt of the information from Lieutenant Colonel Repington regarding shell shortages, Lord Northcliffe held Lord Kitchener personally responsible for his nephew's death and had great delight in publishing anything which would be to Kitchener's detriment.

Repington's article, published in *The Times* on Friday 14 May was titled 'Need for Shells – British Attacks checked – limited supply the cause – A lesson from France. It continued, 'The want of an unlimited supply of high explosive was a total bar to our success.'[14] The full article can be read at Appendix I.

Publishing the article had the effect of bringing to the British public fed the usual jingoistic descriptions of battle, the true state of affairs. In addition it strengthened the hand of Lloyd George in his endeavours to establish a Ministry of Munitions. Whilst on its own, the publication of the article did not bring down the Liberal government, it created enough public disquiet over the management of the war that another blow to the cohesion of the Government may have proved fatal. As fate would have it, this duly arrived two days after the publication of Repington's article with the resignation of the First Sea Lord, Lord Fisher over the concept and implementation of the Dardanelles campaign. The Government duly fell on 19 May to be replaced by a coalition. Lloyd George got his wish to head the Ministry of Munitions and set about staffing it with hard-headed businessmen who knew how to get the job done. The output of munitions in both quantity and quality rapidly increased after this intervention and continued increasing for the duration of the war. By 1918, the ninety-one artillery pieces manufactured in 1914 had increased to 10,680.[15]

Kitchener meanwhile regarded French as having stabbed him in the back by going to the press and politicians over his head and never forgave him before his untimely death in 1916. Sir John French however, had brought the issue out into the open and forced change for the better. The price he was to pay was increased scrutiny of his performance which ultimately led to his enforced resignation before the year was out.

Whilst this issue was being played out, the Inniskillings were in their billets at Richebourg unaware that the greatest test in the history of the regiment awaited them. The resolution of the munitions issue was to come too late for them.

1   Holmes R, *The Little Field Marshal, A Life of Sir John French*, p286
2   Bristow, A *A Serious Disappointment. The Battle of Aubers Ridge 1915 and the Munitions Scandal* p 15
3   Ibid, p.18
4   Ibid, p.19
5   Schulz, p.86
6   Hammerton Sir JA, *A Popular History of the Great War, Volume 2, Extension of the Struggle: 1915.* p.204
7   Ibid p.206
8   Farndale, op. cit, p.341
9   *Belfast Newsletter* 27 May 1915 p5
10 Ibid, 24 June, p.7

11   Bristow, op. cit, p.20

12   Hammerton, op. cit p.207

13   *Belfast Newsletter,* 14 May 1915 p.7

14   *The Times,* 14 May 1915, p.8_

15   Farndale, op.cit., p.341

· · · CHAPTER 6 · · ·
COUNTDOWN: 11–15 MAY

The French have an almost unlimited supply of ammunition including high explosive and fourteen divisions in reserve so if they cannot get through we may take it as proved that the lines cannot be forced. (The less than optimistic view taken by Lord Kitchener in a letter to the Chief of the Imperial General Staff, Sir James Wolfe Murray, prior to Festubert.)[1]

Whilst the Battle of Aubers Ridge resulted in the attacking British forces being decimated, it did nothing to remove the threat of German reinforcements being sent south to engage in the ongoing struggle against the French at Vimy Ridge. Cognisant of this threat, and wishing to alleviate the pressure on his own troops, General Joffre exerted considerable pressure on Sir John French to renew the offensive without delay. This pressure was unfair, as although the French Army had on the day of Aubers made an advance of up to two-and-a-half miles, their inability to get sufficient reserves forward to consolidate this ground had led to the objective of seizing Vimy Ridge being lost. Therefore in essence, Sir John French and the British were being asked to pay the price for the organisational failures of the French Army.

This pressure placed Sir John in an invidious position and one which showed no signs of improvement, as the reserves of men and materiel had deteriorated consecutively from Neuve Chapelle through Aubers Ridge. Firstly, Sir John had another offensive to contend with – that of the Second Army engaged at Frezenberg Ridge near Ypres. The position of the Second Army was precarious, in that its left flank was exposed due to the withdrawal of two French divisions. General Foch's promises of a counter-attack to regain lost ground had come to nothing and Sir John was obliged to take action to ensure the security of the British forces. Secondly, the situation regarding ammunition, particularly artillery ammunition, had not improved. British artillery was desperately short of shells, a situation exacerbated by having to send precious supplies to Gallipoli. In May 1915, artillery ammunition received was 65 per cent of that requested for 4.5-inch howitzer and only eight per cent of 18 pounder. No other calibre of artillery ammunition saw a delivery percentage of over 50 per cent.[2] In addition, the reserves of rifle ammunition were down to 92 rounds per rifle.[3] Thirdly, and closely related to the second point, was the fact that the promised reinforcements from England had not arrived. The simple reason being that there was insufficient artillery and rifle ammunition for it.

However, Sir John knew where his duty lay and possibly in line with his obstinate nature, he agreed to a further offensive to rebut the French assertions that the British were not pulling their weight. Preliminary details for the planned offensive were discussed on 10 and 11 May, before a final conference to decide on the plan was held at 1 Corps headquarters on 12 May.

Contrary to the perception held by some that Haig was an unfeeling monster who blundered from crisis to crisis, there is evidence that having learned from the debacle of the artillery bombardment prior to Aubers, he decided to adopt the French approach of a prolonged bombardment with the fall of shells registered to ensure that everything that could be done was done, prior to sending the infantry over the top. Instead of the 40 minute bombardments of Neuve Chapelle and Aubers, it was planned that a 36-hour bombardment would take place, calculated to show the defenders no respite and gradually reducing their will and capability. This is the first time in the war that the British had adopted these tactics which were to become the norm for future offensives. Belatedly realising that the trench stalemate would not be overcome quickly, the British had decided on a policy of attrition.

Haig had also learned from the over ambitious plan which he had approved for Aubers. The plan for the forthcoming battle entailed a two pronged attack, similar to 9 May, but on this occasion the two attacking divisions, 2nd and 7th, were to be 600 yards apart as opposed to 6,000. The 2nd Division and a brigade of the Indian Meerut Division[4] were to attack from a base line of the Rue du Bois north of Chocolate Menier corner, whilst the 7th Division were to attack from the village of Festubert on a line north to Chocolate Menier corner. In realisation of the over ambitious objectives of 9 May, the objective for this battle was an advance of around 1,000 yards, or more specifically the road named La Quinque Rue, which ran parallel to the Rue du Bois.

In another departure from the norm and with a view to confusing the enemy, this two pronged attack was to take place in two stages, hours apart. In a ground-breaking manoeuvre, the 2nd and Meerut Division attack was timed to go in at night, with the 7th Division attack timed for dawn the following day. The plan was that the 2nd and Meerut Divisions would seize the German trenches and hold

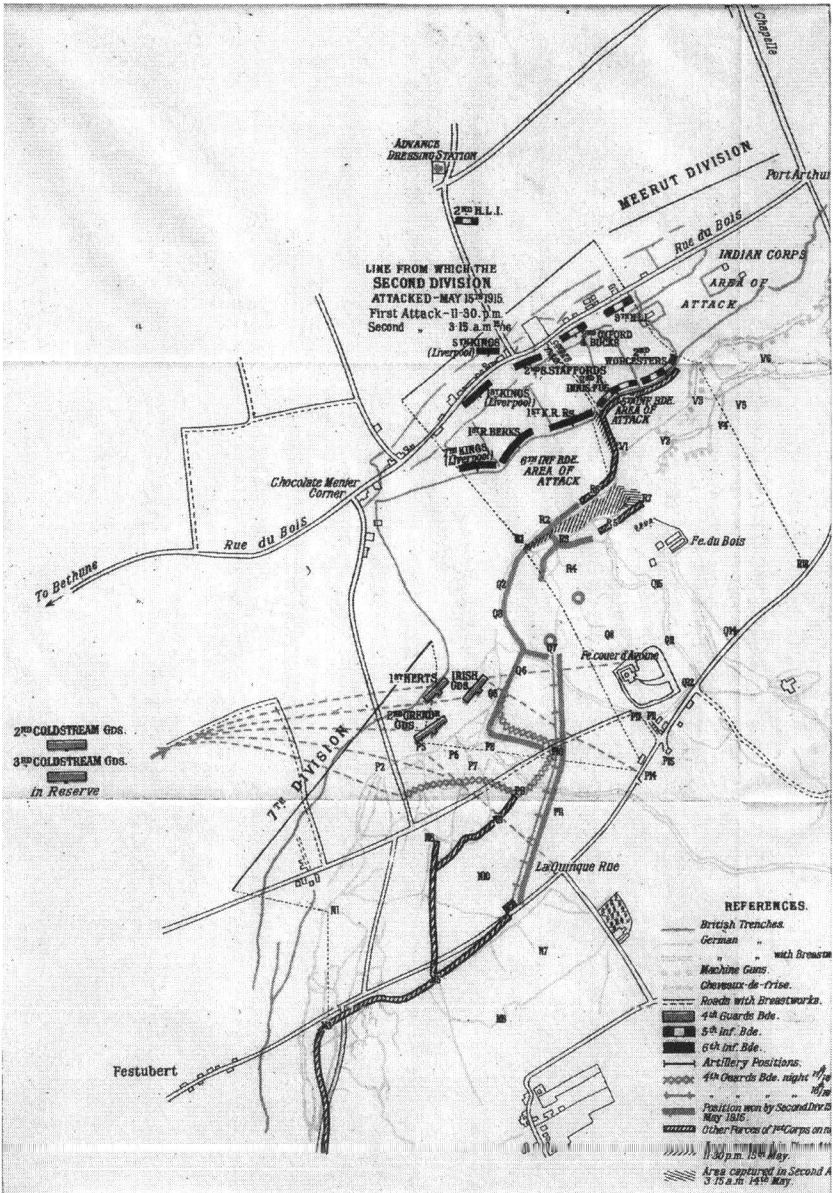

The battleground at Festubert[5]

them. Then as the 7th Division attack began the next morning, the 2nd and Meerut Division troops would advance with the benefit of daylight across country known to be pitted with ditches and water filled dykes with the goal that both attacking forces would meet on La Quinque Rue. So far so good and a quite audacious and innovative plan, completely divorced from what had gone before. The motivation for having a time difference between the different assaults was the fact that the 7th Division needed to attack in daylight as they had only recently arrived in the area and were unsure of the ground. (The 7th Division were transferred from IV Corps to I Corps on 11 May). It was Major General Harry Sinclair Horne, Commanding Officer, 2nd Division, who volunteered the 2nd Division to carry out a night assault, the reasoning being that the ground was well known to them.[6]

This claim bears further examination. As has been mentioned, the Inniskillings had been in and out of trenches in this general area from February, but that time was spent in trenches farther south around the villages of Festubert and Cuinchy, around three miles from Chocolate Menier corner, where the proposed 2nd Division line started. So although the Inniskillings were familiar with the general area and the topography was relatively unchanging, to state that the ground was well known is making a leap of faith. The decision to mount a night attack whilst innovative, was taking a serious risk. This form of attack had never yet been tried in this conflict, with dawn attacks being the norm – hence why battalions in the front line 'stood to' in the hours around dawn, to be in a position to repel any attack.

The Field Service Regulations, Part 1 (Operations) 1909 (revised 1912) – which General Haig had great input in compiling, was the army's bible and devoted 14 pages to the issue of night operations. The chapter begins on a cautionary note:

> *Night assaults, that is to say assaults delivered in the dark, should rarely be attempted by a force larger than an infantry brigade against a single objective unless the conditions are extremely favourable.*

On this occasion, the assault was planned utilising three Brigades, 5 Brigade (including Inniskillings) and 6 Brigade of the 2nd Division and the Garwhal Brigade of the Meerut Division, some 15,000 men in total. The regulations go on to state:

> *In the case of a force deployed on an extended front, several distinct objectives may be attacked simultaneously with advantage. The attackers should at*

once entrench the positions they secure. (Not that any attacking battalion commander would need any encouragement to carry this out!)

The regulations continue on a somewhat ambivalent tone:

> A night assault may then be justified as the only possible solution of a difficult situation, but when the conditions of the fire fight are likely to be favourable, it will be better to accept the inevitable casualties that must result from a struggle for fire supremacy in preference to the undoubted hazards of a night assault.[7]

The regulations were therefore hardly a ringing endorsement for a night attack in the best of circumstances. To compound matters, particularly in the area to be attacked by the Inniskillings and 5 Brigade, the ground had already been fought over the previous Sunday, was known to be intersected by dykes, water filled ditches and barbed wire obstacles, and was strewn with thousands of slowly decomposing bodies which it had proved impossible to recover.

The planning process continued, and in an attempt to reassure Haig following the reversals of 9 May, Sir John French wrote to him on 11 May regarding the forthcoming offensive:

> The strength of your Army is far superior to the hostile forces in front of you. The enemy has suffered heavy losses in the fighting near Arras, and he has few or no reserves other than local, which he can bring up.[8]

Whilst calculated to encourage, Sir John's words masked the fact that the German troops opposite had not changed from those who had wreaked such havoc against the attacking troops on 9 May. As such the 55th Infantry Regiment were confident in their defensive preparations and more importantly battle hardened, having already seen off the best the British could throw at them.

Whilst this planning was going on at staff level, the Inniskillings had moved from their billets at Richebourg where they had halted on 10 May, to bivouac on the Le Touret road, a short distance behind the front line on 11 May. At this stage, four out of the five 5 Brigade battalions were concentrated in the same area. The Inniskillings, 2nd Oxfordshire and Buckinghamshire Light Infantry and 2nd Highland Light Infantry would share responsibility for front line breast work duties over the next few days. 1/9th Highland Light Infantry (Glasgow Highlanders), were in reserve in the billets at Richebourg vacated by the Inniskillings, along with the 2nd Worcesters. On the morning of 12 May, the Inniskillings moved from their overnight location on the Le Touret road, to the billets at Richebourg, arriving around 8.30 am. There, they got some rest before relieving the Ox and Bucks in the front line breastworks in the evening, two companies being in the front line breastworks and two in reserve. In taking over the front line, the Inniskillings carried on the work of the Ox and Bucks in recovering wounded men from the 9 May attack, who had managed to struggle back unnoticed as far as the British breastworks. An account of this work was first published in the *Glasgow Herald*, and is almost certainly the account of an officer from 2nd Highland Light Infantry who were also in the front line breastworks at that time:

> At night patrols searched the front to bring in the wounded: the dead they left, the living must come first. Our patrols were not the only ones out, close to the enemy's lines the Germans were patrolling for the wounded and the dead. Many wounded we brought to our lines, some were able to crawl, some we found would have crawled in but they did not know which were our lines and which were the Germans. We showed them the way and off they started, helping one another. Until Friday night (13th) this went on, and then we were sure that none remained out except the dead, and from these we took discs and personal belongings to be sent to their relatives.[9]

On the night of 12 May, 600 men of the 1/9 HLI had been detailed to move from their billets to the ground to the rear of the Inniskillings in the front line, to dig trenches to be used as forming up points for the forthcoming battle – arduous work after spending the day dodging German shells in their billet dugouts.[10]

First Army instructions concerning the forthcoming attack were issued on 13 May. Derived from these, 2nd Division instructions were issued on the evening of the same date. These instructions are of a general nature and dealt with the broad outline of the operation. These would be complemented by operational orders, giving more detailed instructions when final refinements had been made, closer to the time of the battle. These instructions can be found at Appendix II.[11]

The 36-hour planned artillery bombardment commenced on the morning of 13 May on a front of 5,000 yards from Festubert in the south, north-eastwards to Port Arthur, just short of the village of Neuve Chapelle. In total 433 artillery pieces were employed. A combination of 4.5, 5 and 6- inch howitzers and 18 pounder artillery pieces concentrated on the German defences opposite the Inniskillings, with 9.2-inch howitzers concentrating on selected strongpoints in and around the German front line. This was a refinement of the bombardment pre-Aubers Ridge, perhaps in recognition of the need to concentrate on strongpoints in the German front line which may conceal machine guns. The instructions issued by 2nd Division on 13 May gave details of how the bombardment was to be carried out:

> *Howitzers – By day, deliberate bombardment of 1st and 2nd line trenches and certain strongpoints. By night, fire will be maintained at a reduced rate. Field Guns – By day, destruction of wire and parapets. By night, intermittent fire of shrapnel along 1st and 2nd line trenches to prevent repair of wire and parapets, and also of communicating trenches and approaches.*[12]

However, the situation regarding command and control of the various batteries had still not been resolved and therefore the Commanders' Royal Artillery attached to each of the divisions operated autonomously, with no one entity coordinating the overall effort.

More worrying was the fact that despite Haig's assertions that a long methodical bombardment was necessary, due to shortages in ammunition it was just not possible for this to take place. In reality, the bombardment consisted of three-two hour bombardments each day. Whilst the aspiration was for a storm of artillery fire to drive the Germans into their bunkers and render them incapable with constant explosions, the awful truth and ultimate slight was that the preliminary bombardment was so negligible that the Germans failed to recognise it for what it was until hours before the advance and believed it to be normal harassing fire designed to deter repairs to their defences.[13] This is confirmed by the war diary of 39 Brigade Royal Field Artillery, supporting the 5 Brigade attack. The entries for 13 and 14 May state simply, 'Intermittent fire kept up day and night on wire and destruction of parapets.'[14] The rate of fire for the planned 36 hours of the bombardment was 150 rounds per gun. Given that this was divided into two hour periods, this equates to 30 rounds expended every two hours, or one round every four minutes. Hardly an incessant barrage. This situation was compounded by the fact that considerable numbers of shells, particularly 4.5-inch shells, which were deployed against the communications and support trenches, were faulty and failed to explode.[15]

Observations of the bombardment and particularly the wire cutting attempts by the 18 pounders, indicated that at least there was some success in that area. This fire was particularly slow and deliberate, with the fall of every shot observed. The same difficulties of spotting the fall of shells remained, due to the lack of concealed elevated positions from which to safely observe. The results, accurate or not were conveyed to the officers of the attacking battalions. Reports from the observers indicated that many of the howitzer shells targeting the parapets failed to explode. Their effect was also reduced by the persistent rain of 13 May, which rendered the ground sodden and diminished the explosive effect of those shells which functioned correctly. The Royal Flying Corps assisted the artillery effort by observing targets to the German rear, with some success. A larger bombing programme was also planned concentrating on reserve billets, strong points, and known observation points again in the German rear. However, these efforts were also restricted by the weather, which curtailed flying hours.

Unfortunately for the Inniskillings in the front line breastworks, the bombardment from the British artillery ensured that there was little rest and more importantly, it provoked the German artillery into retaliation. This response from the Germans incurred casualties of one killed and nine wounded on 13 May. The soldier killed was 29-year-old Private John James Gilchrist, originally from Newtownstewart, County Tyrone. With the battalion in France since September 1914, he has no known grave and is commemorated on Le Touret Memorial to the Missing. The 2nd Highland Light Infantry, sharing the burden of the front line breastwork duties with the Inniskillings, fared worse on the 13 May having seven killed and fourteen wounded, their war diary describing the day as a 'very heavy artillery duel.'[16] The ferocity of the German artillery response is indicated by the fact that the Ox and Bucks LI who were the Brigade Reserve in billets in the village of Richebourg just over a mile behind the front line, suffered casualties of one dead and eight wounded.[17]

On the afternoon of 13 May, the commanding officer and adjutant of each of 5 Brigades' battalions attended a briefing at 2nd Division headquarters where an outline of the plan of attack was given. On return to their respective battalion headquarters, this was disseminated to the company officers. On the same date whilst fulfilling his duties as transport officer behind the front line, Lieutenant Alexander had time to write to his mother. In his letter he describes the battalion as being very fit and in the trenches and prepared for anything, including gas attacks. He goes on to state, 'You will be glad to hear I am still left on the Transport, there is no word on the ASC. The Colonel said I had better stay on as there is so much to do with all the moving about so often. We are not very far behind the battalion.'[18] The ASC referred to is the Army Service Corps officer who was to take over Lieutenant Alexander's post and free him for battalion duty with A company. Whilst reassuring his mother, he himself was unaware that the delay in his replacement in all probability saved his life.

The rain which had persisted all day on 13 May began to clear in the early hours of 14 May. With the planned advance around 12 hours away, erring on the side of caution and in a move that belied his perceived authoritarian persona, General Sir Douglas Haig gathered his divisional commanders and sought their opinion over the results of the bombardment in their allotted sectors. Major General Horne, 2nd Division stated that he was satisfied with the bombardment, but expressed an additional reservation, 'that the wet state of the ground might prove a serious obstacle'.[19] Major General Gough, 7th Division pronounced himself satisfied, but Lieutenant General Anderson Meerut Division, was unimpressed with the results of the bombardment particularly the wire cutting, which in his sector had not taken place owing to the batteries allocated for this task having to move position. In the circumstances and with an improving weather forecast, General Haig decided to postpone the attack for 24 hours. The benefits of this being that firstly, the ground may have dried out slightly and secondly, that the bombardment could continue for another 24 hours, thus improving the chances of destroying the German defences.

The morning of 14 May dawned dry and the weather steadily improved as the day wore on. A conference was held at 5 Brigade headquarters where the commanding officers were informed of the decision to postpone the attack for 24 hours. This meant an extra 24 hours to prepare, but also an extra 24 hours under the trajectory of the wholly unpredictable British bombardment and subject to retaliatory fire from the German artillery. Having been briefed that a night attack was to take place, battalion and company officers took great care to ensure that detailed reconnaissance was carried out of the start points, with the most beneficial ways of approaching the German lines whilst maximising cover and minimising obstacles such as ditches, being eagerly sought out and briefed to the attacking troops.

Contained in the 2nd Division Instructions issued on 14 May, were explicit instructions as to how the attack was to be carried out. 'The advance should be made in absolute silence and at a walk till close to the German line where a rush will be made and the enemy cleared out with the bombs and the bayonet'[20] This was emphasised in briefings of companies by their commanding officer. In fact the instructions issued by 2nd Division accurately reflected those contained within the *Field Service Regulations* relative to night attacks. Emphasising that the instructions were to be repeated two or three times to the men by company officers, the regulations continued:

1. Rifles should not be loaded, magazines should be charged, and cut-offs closed and no-one is to fire without a distinct order.
2. Until daylight, bayonets only to be used.
3. Absolute silence is to be maintained until the moment of assault. The troops will march as quietly as possible. Accoutrements must not be allowed to rattle.
4. No smoking is to be allowed, nor are matches to be struck.
5. If obstacles are encountered which cannot be readily traversed or removed, the troops will lie down until a passage has been cleared.[21]

Somewhat ominously regulations continue, 'If after the position of deployment has been left the enemy opens fire, all ranks should understand that it is their duty to press forward at once, cost what it may.'[22]

The issue of fighting with bayonets was one which every soldier would have received instruction on during basic training and with the forthcoming battle, hasty refreshers would have been carried out by serjeant-major's and company officers. In the case of the Inniskillings, this skill would have been practised in their training period in Bethune, but few if any of them would ever have previously been involved in a massed bayonet attack. The bayonet in question was the M1907 sword bayonet. As its name implied, the blade had a cutting edge, which some soldiers pre battle were keen to hone to razor sharpness. At 17 inches long it was a fearsome weapon. The *Infantry Training Manual, (1914)* gave the following instructions concerning its use:

A bayonet charge will normally be delivered in lines, possibly many deep, against a defending force also in lines, over rough ground, which may be covered with obstacles. Single combat will therefore be the exception, while fighting in mass will be the rule. This will make manoeuvring for an opening impossible. In a bayonet fight, the impetus of a charging line gives it moral and physical advantages over a stationary line.[23]

The implication from this instruction is that the sight of the advance utilising fixed bayonets by massed soldiers would prove more of a deterrent than the individual use of the weapon. The manual, published in 1914, anticipates the 'stationary line' to be of opposing soldiers, not of reinforced trenches with accurately sited machine guns.

For those in the Inniskillings and their sister battalions of 5 Brigade, 14 May must have been a very long day. Any form of relaxation would have been impossible due the British bombardment and the counter fire from the German batteries. On this day, the British artillery expended just over 14,300 shells.[24] The German replies were directed at the front line breastworks, but also at the billets to the rear. In the village of Richebourg St Vaast, just over a mile behind the front line, both the Ox and Bucks LI and 2 HLI were the brigade reserve and recorded heavy shelling on their billets. The Ox and Bucks had one killed and four wounded whilst 2 HLI were less fortunate, having seven killed and eight wounded, when their D company billets received a direct hit.[25]

The Inniskillings too manning the front line breastworks suffered their own share of misfortune, sustaining casualties of three killed and 17 wounded. Amongst the wounded were Second Lieutenant Victor Mattocks and Second Lieutenant John Blakeney. Second Lieutenant Mattocks was to recover from his wounds and rejoin the battalion. He rose to the rank of captain and remained with the battalion throughout the war. Second Lieutenant John Blakeney had been regimental serjeant major until he was commissioned in 1914. He had served with the battalion as a colour serjeant in the Orange Free State and the Transvaal in the South African War. He too was to recover and rejoin the battalion, also rising to captain and surviving the war. The three who died are fittingly all buried close to each other in the Rue des Berceaux Military Cemetery at Richebourg L'Avoue, just a few hundred yards from the British front line. The plot in which they are buried indicates that their remains were originally in other smaller cemeteries in the immediate area – some holding less than 20 graves and that they were reinterred in this cemetery as the war progressed.[26] The oldest of those who died was 22-year-old Private John Jordan. Private Jordan was a native of Moneymore, County Londonderry. His occupation prior to enlisting was a farm servant. A reservist, he joined the battalion at the front in September 1914 and in his will which he completed just over a month before his death, he left all his effects to his brother Duncan, a year younger and servant to another Moneymore family.[27] His older brother David had enlisted with him – they had consecutive regimental numbers and both were attached to the 2nd battalion. Both David and John had been hospitalised at the end of January 1915 with frostbite, the result of a period in the trenches in freezing winter conditions. Twenty-one-year-old Private Peter McGuigan was a native of Cecil Street, Newry, County Down. His widowed father also called Peter, was a blacksmith's helper in the town. Private McGuigan, a message boy prior to enlisting, had been with the battalion since they went to France in August 1914. In his will he left all of his property and effects to his elder sister Jennie.[28] The third Inniskilling to be killed was 19-year-old Private Edward Manning, from 11 Sultan Street off Belfast's Falls Road. He was the eldest son of Thomas and Bridget Manning. A labourer before enlisting, he had been at the front for just over six months when he was killed.

Privates John Jordan, Edward Manning and Peter McGuigan
(Image of Pte Jordan courtesy of Friends of the Somme Mid Ulster Branch.
Images of Pte's Manning and McGuigan courtesy of Nigel Henderson.)

The Inniskillings had another loss that day with the death of Serjeant Francis McGartland, B company, who died of wounds in a base hospital at Boulogne. Before enlisting he had been a farm labourer from Lisanelly, Omagh, County Tyrone. He was survived by his wife Catherine and four children, the youngest five years old.

General Haig had another innovative idea which he brought into play on 14 May and again on the 15th. Given that he believed that the element of surprise was lost due to the heavy bombardment (although from German records it appears that they were not aware that a bombardment was taking place until the 15 May), he decided on a ruse, or a series of feints to try and catch the Germans unawares. This ploy consisted of a heavy bombardment using all guns for a period of five minutes, between 9.55 and 10.00 am and 2.55 and 3.00 pm. This was accompanied by heavy rifle fire from the infantry. This was then followed by five minutes silence, then a heavy shrapnel bombardment and rifle fire on the German parapets. The intention of this was to lull the defenders into believing that an attack was taking place so that they would man the parapets and be caught in the second barrage. General Haig believed that this was a success, commenting in his diary, 'The enemy evidently expected us to attack because during the pause they manned their parapets and poured a heavy rifle fire against our trenches. Our shrapnel bombardment then suddenly started so it is hoped that a good many were hit!'[29] There is no mention in the German records of any recognition of this tactic on 14 May.

Detailed instructions concerning the prosecution of the attack were issued as 'Special Instructions' by 5 Infantry Brigade headquarters on the afternoon of 14 May. These instructions delegated responsibility to the Inniskillings for 250 yards of the front line straddling the cinder track, comprising 100 yards to the right of the track where they would meet with the 1st Battalion King's Royal Rifle Corps, and 150 yards to the left of the cinder track, where the Inniskillings would meet with the 2nd Worcesters. The Special Instructions can be found at Appendix III.[30]

During the hours of darkness, rest would have been hard to come by owing to the periodical continuation of the bombardment, but others were hard at work carrying out preparation. In an article in the *Belfast Telegraph* of 29 May 1915, the famous American war correspondent of Ulster descent Percival Phillips, described in further detail the work of the Royal Engineers prior to Festubert:

> *Part of the preliminary work of this attack concerned men who are scarcely heard of in the tumult of battle – the Royal Engineers. On them fell the task of making everything ready for the men who are to advance. They had to provide bridging, clear obstacles away from the ground to be traversed, build scaling ladders, dig trenches under fire and do a thousand and one necessary things at the risk of their lives. For this particular attack the field company had several night's dangerous duty. Between the German and British lines intervening ditches were spanned by plank footways, and marked so that the charging battalions might see them through the smoke of the bombardment.*[31]

The engineers of 5 Field Company Royal Engineers who were attached to 5 Infantry Brigade, were certainly experiencing a trying time. Directed to construct gun emplacements to facilitate the siting of artillery pieces, they were constantly called upon to reconstruct these under fire as they were destroyed by German counter battery fire. In addition, they were tasked with making exit points in the form of cuts in the parapets, to facilitate the movement of the infantry out into no-man's-land prior to the attack. Not only that, but to ensure that secrecy was maintained the cuts had to be disguised, so that they blended in to the breastwork parapets – no easy task. Remarkably, the engineers sustained no injuries in carrying out this work.

Dawn broke clear and bright on 15 May and the weather continued to improve throughout the day. The Inniskillings were still in the front line breastworks, alternating two companies in the front line with two in the reserve trenches behind. With the constant bombardment and counter fire from the German artillery, there was little difference between the two. Both the Inniskillings and the Worcesters on their left were tasked to observe the fall of British shells on the German line and to report where fire was required to be concentrated. The war diary of 5 Brigade records that both battalions made multiple reports. The Inniskillings were concerned with a German strongpoint where the German front line met the cinder track, the point identified at the time as V1, and the Worcesters with a strongpoint opposite them where the German front line trenches assumed a bend to the left, identified at the time as V3. This feature was of crucial importance for the defenders, as it would have enabled them to site a machine gun which would make it possible for them to pour enfilade fire into any attackers. Put simply, any German machine gun at this location would be able to fire in front of, and parallel to their own front line. Combined with machine guns sited facing the British front lines, they would have been able to have intersecting fields of fire through which progress of infantry would be nigh impossible. In the Official History, *Military Operations in France and Belgium, 1915*, Edmonds specifically mentions this hypothesis in relation to German tactics, 'In each of the regimental sectors (2,000 yards), one or more strongpoints had been built into salient or bends of the front line, and from them machine guns........could enfilade lines of enemy infantry advancing against the main position.'[32]

The reports by the Worcester's were primarily based on observations carried out on a patrol carried out on the night of 14/15 May by Second Lieutenant Douglas Tasker and a small party of men. The contents of the report which was compiled and forwarded by his commanding officer, Major Lambton to 2nd

Division headquarters prior to the battle should have set alarm bells ringing:

The officers' patrol reconnoitred ground between our front line and the German front line from V3 to 150 yards East. The salient of the enemy's line at this point was absolutely unharmed by our artillery and the Germans did a great deal of work on it in spite of our infantry fire. Every single shell fired by our howitzers on this salient failed to explode. I consider this matter ought to be investigated as it seems to me a very serious point. This strong point of the enemy's line is absolutely undamaged in consequence. The enemy opened fire during the night both with Machine Guns and rifles from this salient. The old trench in front of my right company's line is full of dead and the stench is dreadful. The German fire in front of this Coy seemed to come entirely from our right and swept the ground in front of our line particularly where our bridges cross our old trench.[33]

He went on to complain that the Worcester's company situated on the right beside the Inniskillings, had had one man killed as a result of wayward shrapnel shelling by British artillery.

If as Major Lambton suggested, there was a machine gun sited at the point identified as V1 and with the distinct possibility of one located at V3, the Germans would when alerted, have been able to instantly turn the area to the left of the cinder track occupied by the Inniskillings and the Worcester's into a killing zone. In addition, to the right of and opposite the Inniskillings frontage, the German front line again took a bend to the left. This bend would affect the advance of the Inniskillings D company on the right and B company of the 1st Battalion King's Royal Rifle Corps attached to 6 Infantry Brigade, who were on the Inniskillings right. Through reconnaissance, the KRRC were certainly aware of the threat, as their war diary indicates:

The German front line formed a very distinct salient from the bend mentioned as the left of our objective, and several of the enemy's Machine Guns were known to be placed on this salient so as to be able to enfilade any attack further west. The salient was given as their objective to the right battalion of the 5th Brigade, who happened to be the Inniskilling Fusiliers.[34]

British and German front lines and strongpoints[35]

With the assault taking place that evening there were a lot of tasks for the battalion to carry out. The cadre known as the LOOBs (Left out of Battle) were identified and warned off. These men were identified to be in a position to take key roles post battle – in effect to restructure the battalion should heavy losses be incurred. Lieutenant Alexander as transport officer, but with previous wartime experience with a rifle company, was identified as a member of this cadre. Although there is no mention of his feelings regarding this decision in any of his letters, he must have experienced mixed emotions. Relief that he would in all probability survive the battle and disappointment that he was not involved with the rest of his fellow officers and subordinates in what was the greatest engagement for the battalion of the war to date. The need for experienced officers and men to remain out of the battle was great due to the attrition that nine and a half months on active service had brought. In the May 1915 edition of the '*Sprig*', it was reported that less than ten per cent of those who had landed with the battalion in August 1914 remained on active service, indicating the heavy rate of attrition trench warfare created.[36]

The 2nd Division operational order was issued at 12.30 pm and outlined the general plan of the 2nd Division assault – to assault under cover of darkness and seize the German system of trenches to the right of the Indian Division and then at 3.15 am on 16 May to continue its attack simultaneously with that of the 7th

Division to reach the objective of the Festubert-La Tourelle road. It goes on to state that, 'The assault will be carried out tonight at 1130pm by the 6th and 5th Infantry Brigades under arrangements already notified.'[37] These already notified arrangements were contained in more detail in the 'Special Instructions' issued on 14 May and in 5 Brigade operational order no 29, issued by the commanding officer Brigadier General Chichester at 4.30 pm on 15 May. This confirmed that the 2nd Inniskillings and the 2nd Worcesters would carry out the assault supported by the 2nd Ox and Bucks LI and The Glasgow Highlanders of 9 HLI respectively. Fulfilling the role of battalion reserve was 2 HLI. The assaulting battalions – Inniskillings and Worcesters, were to be closed up in the front line breastworks by 9.00 pm. Prior to this, a representative was to be sent to brigade headquarters at 7.00 pm with two watches, in order that time could be synchronised between battalions and headquarters. This was a precaution to ensure that the issues over timings which had occurred at Aubers Ridge the week before would not be repeated. The operational order can be found in full at Appendix IV.[38]

Field Marshal Sir John French, despite personal disagreements he may have had with senior officers, was well thought of by the troops and on the eve of the battle, he took the opportunity to pay them a morale boosting visit. An account of this appeared post battle in both the *Belfast News Letter* and *Irish News*:

> *In the late afternoon, Sir John French rode out amongst the troops and was received with enthusiastic acclamation. He wished them good luck and addressed to all a few warm and inspiring words. No one knows better than he how to strike the right note in an appeal to soldiers and he had the pleasure of observing how keen the men were for a dash at the enemy, how confident they were in his leadership and how delighted they were that the hour had come at last for the attack.*[39]

The men of the Inniskillings were certainly keen for a 'dash at the enemy'. In a letter to a friend in Belfast, Private Robert Thornton, a former bakery worker from Bloomfield bakery in East Belfast described the preparations and the mood: 'During the week before and on Saturday afternoon, 15th ult, we had a lecture from our Company officer as to the coming advance. After that some of the boys had a sleep. Then we had tea about five o'clock. All the conversation was about the charge and the boys were as jolly and light hearted as if it was play, saying what they would give the Germans.'[40] The tea described by Private Thornton, would have been a good meal. It was often the case that the better the food got, the nearer the soldiers knew they were to the battle. There was always plenty of gallows humour amongst the troops of 'being fattened up for the kill'.

The comment that before 'some of the boys had a sleep', is an interesting one given the proximity of the battle and the ongoing artillery bombardment and German response. In addition there would have been a multitude of last minute preparations to be carried out. Perhaps the Inniskillings also engaged in a wholly practical if somewhat morbid practice described by the poet Robert Graves, who served in the same part of the line with the Royal Welch Fusiliers. He described how:

> Before a show, the platoon pools all its available cash and the survivors divide it up afterwards. Those who are killed can't complain, the wounded would have given far more than that to escape as they have, and the unwounded regarded the money as a consolation prize for still being here.[41]

It was also essential that all the troops were kitted out and equipped in the same way. The 7th Division (carrying out the dawn attack on 16 May) operational order gives directions about what equipment each man was to take. 'Troops will wear packs and will carry cardigan jackets, but no greatcoats. Greatcoats to be collected under Brigade arrangements. Every man will carry 200 rounds. Every man will carry one day's rations besides the remainder of the current days' issue. Every man will carry two empty sandbags.'[42] Collecting the greatcoats was another task for which Lieutenant Alexander was responsible, as well as other items not needed for the battle, including officers' valises containing all their personal effects which were either redistributed after the battle, or in the worst case scenario, went through the army postal system and arrived at their home address following their demise. The two empty sandbags referred to were to be used to shore up defensive positions to counter any German attempt to seize lost ground.

In terms of uniform, other ranks wore 1902 pattern service dress. This consisted of a thick khaki woollen tunic and trousers. The tunic had four pockets, one on each breast and one on each side at the waist. These could be fastened by buttons. The tunic was worn fastened to the neck by five brass buttons, in the Inniskillings case showing the regimental crest of Enniskillen castle. There was an internal pocket on the front skirt of the tunic which held a field dressing. A brass badge with the regimental name was on each shoulder. The trousers below the knee were wrapped in khaki puttees (from the Hindustani word 'patti' for bandage). These supported the lower leg and kept the lower part of the trousers from catching on objects and ripping. On their feet, the men wore what are still known today as 'ammunition boots'. Ankle boots with iron toecaps, iron plates on the heels and iron studded soles. The regulation service cap was worn, as steel helmets were not on general issue until 1916. On active service the stiffening wire was removed to facilitate carriage in the belt or pocket. Other equipment was carried on the webbing belt. At this stage of the war, the majority of webbing belts were made of khaki canvas, fastened at the waist and had braces which were secured by brass buttoned epaulettes on either shoulder. The webbing belt had pouches to the left and right, each containing up to 75 rounds of ammunition, a bayonet 'frog' or short scabbard, and an entrenching tool with a canvas pouch for the head and a water bottle. The rations referred to above were carried in a canvas haversack. One peculiarity on each soldier's uniform for this battle was a white patch worn on the chest and back as a distinguishing mark. It has to be asked, given that the attack was in the hours of darkness, would this not have identified the advancing soldiers to the Germans as well?

Each soldier in the ranks was armed with a rifle. Widely regarded as the best rifle of any of the combatant armies, the Short Magazine Lee Enfield (SMLE) was a formidable weapon. It was 3 ft 9 inches in length – hence the prefix 'short' and with the aforementioned bayonet attached was 4 ft 9 inches long. It had a bolt action and had a ten round magazine loaded by five round clips of .303 ammunition from the top. It had formidable stopping power, being able to penetrate filled sandbags at 200 yards, had an effective range of 550 yards and a maximum range of 3,000 yards. The British Army defined close range as anything up to 600 yards, effective range was between 600-1,400 yards and distant range from 2,000-2,800 yards. The army had spent considerable effort in training their soldiers in this weapon with the result that even a reasonable shot could fire 15 aimed rounds in a minute. British volley fire was so rapid that on occasion German defenders claimed they had come under attack from machine guns. All things being equal, his rifle gave the British soldier an advantage over their German foe who were armed with the 7.92mm Mauser rifle, which was longer and therefore less manoeuvrable in confined spaces, had a five-round magazine and a slower rate of fire.[43] In preparation for the battle, the soldiers, who normally carried 120 rounds of ammunition were ordered to carry an extra 100 rounds per man. This was carried in a cloth bandolier, slung across the shoulder.

Officers by contrast were dressed and armed differently. The uniform was the same colour, but that was where the similarities ended. The cloth was of a much superior quality, and the tunic was lined and tailored to fit the individual – only to be expected as officers were required to pay for their uniform. It was designed to be worn with a shirt and tie and had the regimental badge on each lapel. Rank insignia were displayed on the epaulettes, and instead of a webbing belt, the officer wore a 'Sam Brown' leather belt on which was a leather holster containing his service revolver.

As indicated, until the advent of the steel helmet, neither officers nor men had any form of issued protection from the storm of steel encountered when going 'over the top'. However, officers featured disproportionately in the casualty lists. There were a number of reasons for this. Firstly, the officer was expected to lead from the front. This meant being first over the top and in front of the men. Secondly, the Germans quickly realised that the officer was identifiable by his mode of dress and with the rationale that the following soldiers would falter and fall back, targeted the officer first in any attack. This is borne out by statistics in John Lewis-Stempel's excellent and aptly named, *Six Weeks: The Short and Gallant Life of the British Officer in the First World War*, which show that between 1 Oct 1914 and 30 September 1915, 14.2 per cent of officers were killed as opposed to 5.8 per cent of other ranks. The figures for the same time period those wounded show a similar imbalance, 24.4 per cent of officers were wounded compared to 17.4 per cent of other ranks.[44] The stark reality was that most junior officers knew that this was their fate, and that there was little that they could do about it. As the year 1915 ended, the realisation that officers were being targeted by the Germans permeated to the highest levels in the army and instructions were given that from that time, officers could wear the same uniform as the men going into action. This, however, was not a panacea, as the officer was still first out of the trench, was carrying a revolver and was the one who could be identified waving and encouraging the men forward.

At Festubert, both officers and men had an extra piece of equipment to carry – the gas mask. Ever since the first German gas attack near Ypres around three weeks before on 22 April, efforts had been made to provide some rudimentary protection should there be a repetition. At this stage the protection was at its most basic and consisted of an impregnated cotton pad secured around the head by cloth strips. Prior to the attack, the possibility of the use of gas by the Germans was a concern, which Lieutenant Alexander mentioned to his mother in a reassuring fashion in a letter written on 13 May, 'There are no signs of gas in this area, I think it was only at Ypres they are using it now. This does not seem a suitable place for it. The whole army is well prepared anyway for it.'[45] The precautions against gas are also mentioned in the preparations for the battle contained within the war diary of 9 Highland Light Infantry. 'The battalion is now complete in every respect with its requirements for the advance. Masks have been issued to all ranks, and lime water prepared, it is arranged that every third man shall carry this in his water bottle.'[46] Lime water was and is still used as an antidote to poisons. In the early days of gas attacks and in the absence of anything more scientifically recommended, it was believed, mistakenly, that lime water would counter the effects of gas.

Another innovation that the evolution of trench warfare had brought about was that of the grenade. Initially in 1914 such primitive grenades as were available were the preserve of the Royal Engineers, but it quickly became apparent that mass production of grenades was an imperative. However, until they became readily available (like much else with the British munitions effort, progress was painfully slow – a mere 70 per week were being manufactured in November 1914.[47]), the soldiers turned to improvisation. Favourite amongst the British was the 'jam tin' grenade, which consisted of a jam tin filled with explosives and packed with scrap metal or stones. Careful attention was needed to judge the length of the fuse, with it being generally accepted that an inch of fuse gave a second and a quarter delay. The fuse was lit by matches or cigarette end and the device thrown. Care had to be taken that the fuse was not so long that the Germans had time to lift the device and throw it back, or too short and the device exploded prematurely.

By the time of Festubert, the Inniskillings regimental journal *The Sprig* was able to report that, 'There are now 64 Grenadiers in the battalion who are armed with bombs which have been found very useful in trench warfare.'[48] The grenades they were armed with would be alien to what we are familiar with today. At the time of Festubert, two types of grenade were in use. The first was akin to what we would recognise as the classic German 'stick grenade'. It had a long wooden handle, to which were attached cloth streamers to ensure it was stable in flight and detonated on impact. A description of this novel method of warfare appeared in the local press of the time:

Each man in the bomb throwing party carries a certain number of bombs fitted into a wooden case which he carries round his waist. To each bomb is attached a wooden handle, much in the style of a rocket, and when the time for action comes the bomb is drawn out and thrown stick and all, with a high lobbing motion into the enemy's trench, in which if the aim be accurate, it causes great destruction.[49]

The second was a sphere, slightly bigger than a cricket ball and made of cast iron. An igniter had to be struck against the fuse prior to throwing. This grenade weighed just under two pounds.[50] The Inniskillings' 64 grenadiers were divided into teams consisting of two bombers, two bomb carriers and two bayonet men, under the command of a non-commissioned officer, (NCO). The officer in charge of the Inniskillings' grenadiers was 20-year-old Second Lieutenant Alfred Douglas Wingate. He was chosen for this demanding role due to his extraordinary drive and determination. Second Lieutenant Wingate was the son of a senior member of the Indian Civil Service, Sir Andrew Wingate and Lady Catherine. Born in Bombay, he was educated at Dulwich College where he was an enthusiastic member of the Officer Training Corps, (OTC). He entered the Royal Military Academy Sandhurst in 1913, was appointed the King's India Cadet and was commissioned as a Second Lieutenant in the Indian Army in August 1914. Whilst at Sandhurst he excelled as a member of the academy's revolver shooting team and won the academy's Silver Cup for revolver shooting. The outbreak of war found him in India, a backwater in the war where he was unlikely to see any action, so he volunteered for Imperial Service, joining the 4th Battalion Royal Inniskilling Fusiliers at Leenan Camp, County Donegal. From there he was attached to the 2nd Inniskillings, joining them in France on 24 November 1914. A natural leader, brave and keen to be in the thick of it, he was exactly the sort of officer required to lead the grenadiers.

For any offensive action, a crucial part of the battalion's armoury was the machine gun section. As we saw earlier the Inniskillings' machine gun officer was Lieutenant Ralph Hinds, who along with his team had performed splendidly at the forest of Compeigne in September 1914. In a normal frontal attack, the machine gun section was to provide supporting fire for the battalion and move forward to a new position when ground was consolidated. In this night attack however, where silence was the key, the machine gun section was to move forward rapidly with their machine guns after the front line had been seized and site their weapons on the German parapet to defend against any counter-attack. Lieutenant Hind's section comprised himself, one serjeant, one corporal and two six-man teams, one for each gun. They were all needed, as the gun tripod and spare barrel weighed around 51 pounds. In addition, each crew carried 11,500 rounds of ammunition in 46 250-round belts.

All in all, with the equipment each man had to carry for personal use, the extra ammunition, the specialist equipment such as grenades and machine gun belts, it is no understatement to say that the Inniskillings were heavily burdened and this before they had set foot on a no-man's-land that was a sodden mire.

On the evening of 15 May, final preparations were made prior to moving up to the attack positions in the breastworks. As the nominated attacking battalions, both the Inniskillings and the Worcesters had working parties attached to them. In the case of the Inniskillings this was three platoons, numbering around 150 men from across the company strength of the 2nd Ox and Bucks LI. In addition to their equipment, these men were carrying sandbags and shovels to assist in reinforcing any positions gained. The 2nd Division instructions issued on 13 May had been specific about their task once the German lines had been secured, 'Parties will be detailed at once to commence digging and preparing communication trenches… Flanks will be secured by demolishing a few traverses and utilising the material to form a barrier. This will leave a space which can be denied to the Germans by bombing.' In an optimistic and cautionary note it continued, 'Care must be taken to avoid bombing the men of the Meerut Division attacking on our left.'[51] In the case of the Worcesters, their support was provided by 9 HLI. As their war diary states, 'No 4 company detailed three working parties of 50 men each to act with the Worcesters, – these parties were handed over to that battalion at 5.30 pm, the whole of that company being thus employed.'[52]

In addition to the working parties from the Ox and Bucks, No 4 section, 5 Field Company Royal Engineers reported to the Inniskillings at 6.00 pm on 15 May. Specific sappers within this section were detailed to accompany the working parties with responsibilities in respect of the German first and second lines, once attained. Further sappers were detailed to assist in the construction of effective communications trenches. Accompanying the main assault were two, two man parties equipped with bangalore torpedoes.[53] The bangalore torpedo was invented by Indian Army Engineers around 1912 as a means of destroying barbed wire at minimal risk to infantrymen. The device consisted of a long narrow tube about two-and-a-half inches in diameter and six-and-a-half feet in length. A charge was at one end of the tube and a wooden firing handle and fuse at the other. Both these could be removed and additional tubes added to increase the length and minimise the risk to the user. The idea was to place the charge in the middle of a barbed wire defence and blow it apart, not to place it on the ground where the effect of the charge would be diminished.

Meanwhile, on the German side of the line, realisation had dawned sometime in the afternoon of 15 May that the British bombardment, which had been taking place for around 50 hours by that stage, was actually the prelude to an attack. There had been some suspicion on the part of the Germans on 14 May when Crown Prince Rupprecht, the commander of the German Sixth Army had commented on the unusual pattern of the bombardment. However Major Schulz of Infantry Regiment 55 noted the increase in severity of the barrage on the afternoon of 15 May, accompanied by numerous British aircraft which appeared to be concentrating on the observation of German positions. He then described how: 'After the arrival of darkness a sudden barrage of fire from the enemy infantry that lasted only a couple of minutes started up. After an hour the barrage of fire picked up again. Now we were warned.'[54] Indeed, there are two separate reports, one from the Inniskillings and one from the 2nd Battalion Leicestershire regiment of the Garwhal Brigade, that on the afternoon and early evening of 15 May the Germans had actually shouted across that they were waiting for an attack.

The disposition of the German forces facing the 5 Brigade attack had not changed since the attack on Aubers Ridge the previous Sunday. Directly facing the Inniskillings and Worcesters of 5 Brigade, and the Leicesters and Garhwalis of the Meerut Division's Garhwal Brigade, were Major Schulz's 55th Infantry Regiment. To their left and facing the attack of the 6 Brigade's 1st King's Royal Rifle Corps and the 1st Berkshires were elements of the 57th Infantry Regiment. Major Schulzs' 2nd battalion as we have seen was responsible for repulsing the attack of the Munsters the previous week, inflicting heavy losses. They were undoubtedly battle hardened and more importantly, they had confidence in their equipment, their defences and above all their ability.

In accordance with the operational order to be in the front line breastworks by 9.00 pm, the Inniskillings were in position at 8.30 pm. A and D companies were in the front line breastworks, with B and C companies immediately behind. The British front line for this attack was exactly the same as it had been for the abortive attack the previous Sunday. The line ran parallel to and about 375 yards on the La Bassee side of the Rue Du Bois. The Inniskillings' position was astride the cinder track which ran from the Rue Du Bois to the Ferme Du Bois which was behind the German lines. In fact, the cinder track was the dividing line between A and D companies. D company were at the extremity of the 5 Brigade attack. To their right were the 1st King's Royal Rifle Corps of the 6th Brigade, and beyond them the 1st Berkshires. To the left of A company were the 2nd Worcesters, and beyond them the 2nd Leicesters and the 39th Garhwali's of the Garhwal Brigade.[55]

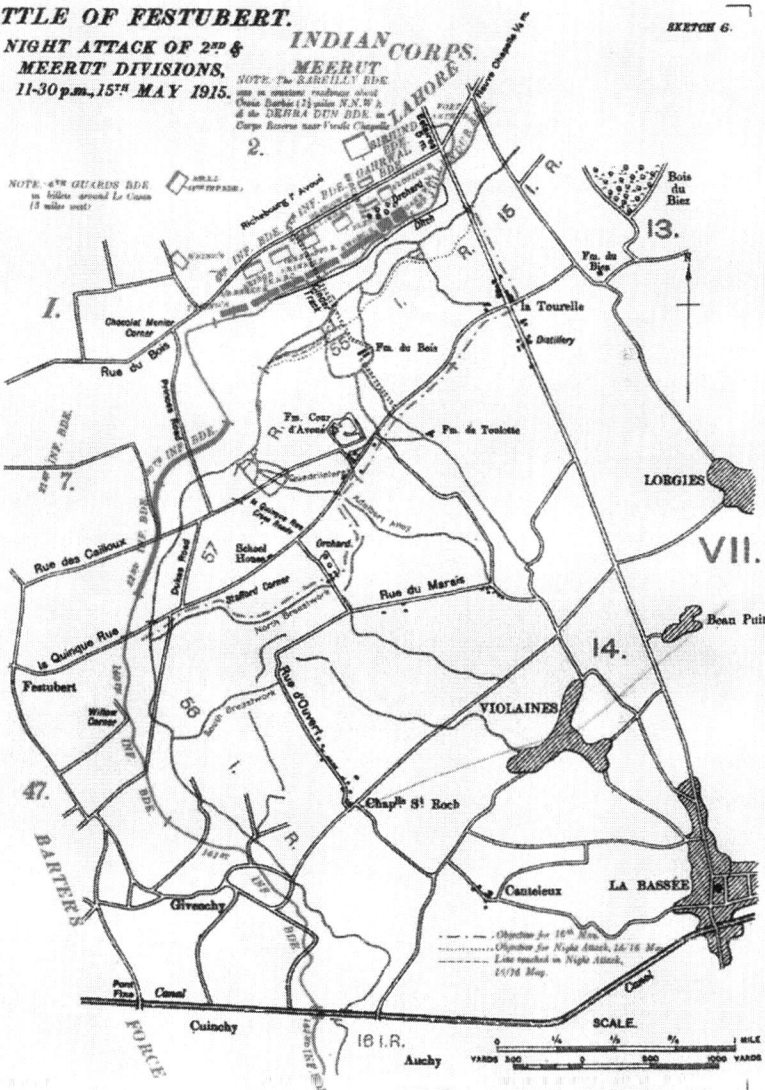

In position behind the Inniskillings were the 2nd Ox and Bucks LI and the Glasgow Highlanders of the 9th HLI were behind the Worcesters. With these troops deployed, 5 Brigade stretched back from the front breastworks, 200 yards towards the Rue Du Bois. The 2nd Highland Light Infantry, the Brigade reserve were situated on the other side of the Rue Du Bois, close to an Advanced Dressing Station. The 5 Brigade frontage for this attack was 600 yards and as the battalions moved into position, in this 600 by 200 yard area, there were in excess of 4,000 soldiers congregated. Casualties were inevitable due to the continued German response to the British bombardment. At this stage the Inniskillings had been manning the front line breastworks for 75 hours. For 60 of the 75 hours they had endured the British bombardment with the constant concussion of the guns firing a short distance to their rear and the ever present danger of rounds falling short. They also had to contend with the German counter bombardment, which before the scheduled time of attack, had resulted in five fatalities and 53 wounded.[56]

Once in the front line breastworks, this is where the enormity of the situation hit home with the Inniskillings. Having been in the same area since Aubers the previous Sunday, they would have been aware of the potential situation facing them. They could see the ground leading to the German front line, it was flat and ploughed in places before war took precedence over agricultural considerations. There was rough grass covering most of it, but this hid obstacles such as waterfilled ditches. They could also see and smell the sickly sweet stench of the bodies of the Munsters, Sussex and Welsh Regiment soldiers that remained unburied in their hundreds in no-man's-land. The British bombardment may have offered some reassurance, but the incessant German counter bombardment would have reminded them that the Germans were still active.

The final hours were spent checking equipment over and over again, tightening belts, buckles and webbing to ensure that there was nothing that rattled or made a noise, discarding anything that was not needed or likely to cause discomfort. There was the double rum ration, brought round by the quartermaster serjeant. Something to warm you, but also to take the edge off the anxiety. Then there was time for a personal moment. Taking longing looks at photographs of loved ones, checking a lucky charm was in the right place. A last minute consultation of a pocket bible, making your peace with God before placing it in the breast pocket over the heart. Private prayers with the bible or religious medals and always, always, obsessive clock watching. Watching the seconds tick by, each minute seeming like an age. This is where the skills of the officer came into their own.

This was a heavy burden on the subalterns of the Inniskillings. Lieutenant Oliver Stacke and Second Lieutenant Lionel Mordaunt-Smith of A company were 20 and 19 years old respectively, Lieutenant John Stewart was 19, Second Lieutenant Alfred Wingate in charge of the grenadiers was 20. Second Lieutenant John Morgan of D company was older at 27, however, he had been commissioned from the ranks of the Royal Irish Rifles, where he had been a company sergeant major. The Battalion machine gun officer, Lieutenant Ralph Hinds was 23. For all of them, this would be their first experience of a battalion assault on a strongly defended objective.

There were many things that an officer could do badly in carrying out his duties and get away with. Making a mess of drill commands, being useless at platoon administration, these could be sorted out, usually with the help of an obliging and competent serjeant. However, leading the men over the top and into battle was the officer's responsibility and his alone. As Lieutenant Talbot of the Rifle Brigade was told by his colonel prior to a 1915 engagement, 'Remember, you are responsible for fifty-two lives, your own doesn't count.'[57] Harsh words, but necessary in the situation. These men were born to be leaders, but the circumstances of leading fifty men into battle where the likelihood was that you would either be killed or seriously injured put intolerable pressure on 19 and 20-year-olds. They had the personal fear of what would happen to them, but the overriding fear was that of failure, of showing fear and of letting the men down, of letting their brother officers down and of letting the battalion down. This fear drove them and ensured that they carried on, when all natural reactions would be to run away. For the battalion and the wider army, the psychology of the situation was simple. The officer had to hide his feelings and lead the men with confidence, with nonchalance if they could, because if the officer showed fear, it would quickly transmit to the men. The men followed the officer for many reasons, out of respect, because it was expected, to appear brave amongst their peers and out of loyalty to their friends, their company and the battalion. If the officer showed fear or faltered, all these reasons could easily be undermined. The *Infantry Training Manual 1914* sums up the situation succinctly:

> The paramount duty of all leaders in the firing line is to get their troops forward, and if every leader is imbued with a determination to close with the enemy, he will be unconsciously assisting his neighbour also, for as a rule, the best method of supporting a neighbouring unit is to advance.'[58]

As was expected of them, the Inniskillings' officers in the final hours before the advance suppressed their fears and tried to busy themselves to banish the thoughts of what lay ahead. A final journey along the breastworks to check on the men in the platoon – difficult in itself to do as they were packed so tightly in. Dispensing words of encouragement, perhaps an attempt at a joke, checking that all equipment was secure, and all the time constantly checking the watch, until it was time to give the order, 'fix bayonets!

---

1   Edmonds, p.46. Full quotation, ' *Sir John French may possibly have 7 divisions in reserve-also a good supply of artillery ammunition which he thought would be sufficient, and 7,500 rounds a night increase to be kept up steadily. It may be doubtful whether this will enable him to break through. But the French have an almost unlimited supply of ammunition including High Explosive and 14 Divisions in reserve so if they cannot get through we may take it as proved that the lines cannot be forced.'*

2   Bristow, p.151. Some of these figures had actually decreased from previous months indicating the problems inherent in the British munitions industry.

3   Edmonds, op.cit., p.45

4   The Meerut Division were part of the Indian Corps attached to First Army. It consisted of three Brigades, Dehra Dun, Garwhal and Bareilly. The Garwhal Brigade was nominated for the assault consisting of 2nd Leicestershires, 39th Garwhalis, 2/3rd and 2/8th Gurkhas and 1/3rd Londons, a territorial Battalion.

5   Wyrall E, (1921) *History of the Second Division, Volume I, 1914-1916*, p202

6   Edmonds, op.cit., p.50

7   General Staff, War Office (1912) *Field Service Regulations, Part 1, Operations*, HMSO, London, pps176-183. A wonderful paper and very much of its time. It contains a chapter entitled 'Warfare against an uncivilised enemy,' which opens with the line 'In campaigns against savages.....'

8   Edmonds, op.cit., p.49

9   *Belfast Evening Telegraph*, 27 May 1915 p.8

10 National Archives. WO 95/1347 9th Battalion Highland Light Infantry war diary

11 Edmonds, Apps 10 and 11, pps 439-441

12 National Archives. WO 95/1285 2nd Division war diary

13 Sheldon J, *The German Army on the Western Front 1915* p.145

14 National Archives. WO 95/1249 39 Brigade Royal Field Artillery war diary

15 National Archives, CAB 44/20 Draft of Official History. Contains handwritten note from the then Field Marshal Haig to the effect that '*much of the artillery ammunition was very faulty until 1917*'.

16 National Archives. WO 95/1347 2nd Battalion Highland Light Infantry war diary

17 National Archives. WO 95/1348 2nd Battalion Oxfordshire and Buckinghamshire Light Infantry war diary

18 PRONI, D/4121/F/4/B/2/6/5A 13 May 1915, CAM Alexander papers

19   Edmonds. op.cit., p.55

20   Edmonds, Ibid, Appendix 11, 2nd Division Instructions p.440

21   Field Service Regulations, op.cit., p.187.

22   Ibid p188

23   General Staff, War Office, (1914) *Infantry Training (4-Company Organisation)*. The manual contains eight pages of exercises and manoeuvres to be carried out to ensure proficiency with the bayonet.

24   National Archives. CAB44/20 p.18

25   National Archives, WO 95/1348 and WO 95/1347

26   www.cwgc.org

27   www.soldierswills.ie

28   Ibid. It appears that Private McGuigan's will which was in his service pay book, may have been recovered from his body after he fell.

29   Sheffield G and Bourne J (Eds) *Douglas Haig. War Diaries and Letters 1914-1918*, p.124

30   National Archives, WO 95/1343/2 Appendix XLIV

31   *Belfast Telegraph*, 29 May 1915, p.6, Percival Phillips was born in Pennsylvania in 1877. His maternal grandfather was a Protestant Minister from County Tyrone. Pre-war, he had visited Belfast as a correspondent for the *Daily Express*, covering the Home Rule crisis. Although an American, he was one of only five correspondents approved by the British government to cover the Western Front.

32   Edmonds, op.cit., p.15

33   National Archives WO 95/1285 op.cit.

34   National Archives. WO 95/1358 1st Battalion King's Royal Rifle Corps war diary.

35   National Archives. WO 95/1285/2 2nd Division War Diary, p116

36   *The Sprig of Shillelagh*, May 1915, p.124. Of over 1,300 who embarked to France, 120 remained with the Battalion.

37   Edmonds, op.cit., p.442 App. 12

38   National Archives. WO 95/1343/2 5 Infantry Brigade War Diary, App. XLV

39   *Belfast News Letter*,18 May 1915 p.5 and *Irish News*, 18 May 1915 p.7.

40   *Belfast Evening Telegraph* 29 May 1915 p.8

41   Graves, R, *Goodbye to all that*. Kindle ebook

42   Edmonds, op.cit., p.446 Appendix 13

43   Bull S Dr, *World War 1 Trench Warfare (1) 1914-1916*, p.9

44   Lewis-Stempel, *Six Weeks: The Short and Gallant Life of the British Officer in the First World War*, p.183

45   PRONI, D/4121/F/4/B/2/6/5A 13 May 1915, CAM Alexander papers

46   WO 95/1347, op.cit.

47   Bull S, op.cit., p28

48   *The Sprig of Shillelagh*, May 1915, p.124.

49   *Irish News & Belfast Morning News*, 29 May 1915, p.6

50   Grenades at this time were still in the experimental stage and the 'Mills' type grenade were not put into mass production until August 1915.

51   Edmonds, op. cit., p.440

52   WO95/1347, op.cit. p199

53   National Archives. WO95/1330/2 5 Field Company Royal Engineers war diary. The remainder of number 4 section were detailed with the battalions in reserve.

54   Schulz D, *Infanterie Regiment Graf Bulow von Dennewitz, Nr 55 im Weltkriege*. p.93. From this it would appear that General Haig's 'ruse' actually had the opposite effect to that which had been intended.

55   Edmonds, Sketch 6, p48

56   Although the Inniskillings war diary indicates that one soldier was killed pre-battle on the 15 May, research has been unable to positively identify him, due to fatalities from the attack itself occurring on the same date.

57   Lewis-Stempel, op.cit., p.184

58   *Infantry Training (4-Company Organisation)* op.cit., P143

··· CHAPTER 7 ···
THE ADVANCE

The enemy's defences are now so strong that they can only be taken by siege methods – by using bombs and by hand to hand fighting in the trenches – the ground above is so swept by gun and machine gun and rifle fire, that an advance in the open, except by night is impossible. (General Sir Douglas Haig, Commander First Army, following the battle of Festubert.)[1]

The special instructions previously referred to and issued by 5 Infantry Brigade headquarters on 14 May, complemented the operational order issued by the 2nd Division, and indicated how the advance was to be carried out. The objective for the Inniskillings and the Worcesters was, 'the 1st and 2nd line of German parapets from R7 to a point NW of V5 and to get in touch with the Meerut Division at that point.' (See Special Instructions at Appendix III) In layman's terms, for 5 Brigade this was a frontal attack, designed to drive the German front line back some 400 yards over a frontage of 570 yards.

It was recognised that following the communications failures at Aubers Ridge the previous week that correct timing was of paramount importance. The attack was to be carried out by all units simultaneously. To ensure that this occurred, each unit involved in the advance was to send a representative with at least two watches to battalion headquarters at 7.00 pm on 15 May in order that the watches could be synchronised. The artillery bombardment was timed to lift at 11.30 pm to concentrate on the German rear areas to hinder any reinforcements being brought to the front. It was reinforced that the infantry would not perceive any change in the bombardment and therefore the attack must take place at the stated time to enable the troops to have a chance to reach the German front line with at least some element of surprise. The plan was that the attacking battalions would move out from the front line breastworks and take up a position in no-man's-land prior to the start time of 11.30 pm. As each platoon moved out of the front line breastwork, their position was to be taken by the succeeding platoon, so that a gap of 100 yards would be maintained between each successive line. It was stressed in the special instructions that, 'The attack will be carried out in absolute silence, and at a walk until the enemy's trench is approached, when it will be rushed.'² This was reinforced at briefings given by the Inniskillings' company commanders throughout 15 May.

At around 10.00 pm, the Inniskillings and the first ranks of the other attacking battalions started to move out of the front line. Despite the fact that the engineers had made gaps in the breastworks, in many cases they were too small and it proved a slow process, with soldiers opting to clamber over the parapet rather than wait and possibly delay the advance. An article initially published in the *Daily Sketch* newspaper and reproduced in the *Sprig of Shillelagh*, gave some idea of the task:

> *The 2nd Inniskillings were to lead the van in the principal sector, and the attack was to be made under cover of darkness. The space between the trenches was somewhere about 200 yards, and in spite of the pitchy blackness of the night it was certain that the German machine guns and rifles would take a heavy toll before the trenches were reached. But the Inniskillings mix brains with their bravery. So soon as night fell, about 8pm, they crept over the parapet one by one, and squirmed on their stomachs towards the German trenches. Slowly and painfully they crawled through a sea of mud, from dead man to dead man, lying quite still whenever a star shell lighted up the no-man's-land. By this method, platoon after platoon spread itself over the corpse strewn field, until the leaders were within a few yards of the German parapet. Then came the hardest task of all – to lie shoulder to shoulder with the dead, until at midnight a glare gave the signal to charge. But the Skins held on through all the alarms of the night. Occasionally, bullets whistled across the waste, and some who had imitated death needed to pretend no longer.³*

An examination of the war diaries of the battalions right across the line of attack, in the Garwhal Brigade and both 5 and 6 Brigades, indicate that this phase of the operation was carried out successfully and without raising any suspicions from the Germans and by shortly after 11.20 pm the vast majority of the attacking troops were in position in no-man's-land.

It was at this point that things began to go horribly wrong. As previously mentioned, part of General Haig's deception plan was for brigades not involved in the attack to have short, sustained bursts of rifle fire at appointed times to mislead the enemy. The Jullundur Brigade of the Lahore Division, roughly three-quarters of a mile to the left of the Inniskillings in the vicinity of Neuve Chapelle, was one of the battalions involved in this activity. Records indicate that they carried out this procedure in five minute bursts at 8.45 pm, 9.30 pm, 10.00 pm and 10.30 pm. This had the opposite effect to that intended, in that it alerted the Germans right along the front that an attack was imminent – a fact highlighted by Major Schulz in the history of the 55th Infantry Regiment. 'After the arrival of darkness a sudden barrage of fire from the enemy infantry that lasted only a couple of minutes started up. After an hour the barrage of fire picked up again. Now we were warned. In the trenches, observation posts, batteries, everything was ready for conflict.'[4]

It is agreed by the majority of the war diaries of the battalions involved in the British attack, that at 11.28 pm, two minutes before the time to advance, the Germans opened up heavy machine gun and rifle fire. This was preceded by flares of various colours which completely illuminated the battlefield. Major Schulz's account continued:

> Immediately after this, red flares rose from the first squadron of the 55th's 2nd Company, the arranged light signal for the beginning of an enemy infantry attack. What now played out on the line between La Bassée and Estaires cannot be described with words. Countless German batteries lying in range, as well as those of the neighbouring section, aimed their quick fire at this position. The earth trembled under the force of the fire.[5]

There is, however, another version of events contained within the *Worcestershire Regiment in the Great War*, the official history of that regiment which warrants critical examination. This history is widely regarded as one of the finest in existence, due to its detailed accounts of even minor engagements. The account of the battle of Festubert contains the following:

> The strain of that midnight deployment was great, and no adequate arrangements had been made between the different units for a simultaneous assault. (synchronization of watches had not been instituted). The watches of the Worcestershire officers were still several minutes short of the 'zero' hour – 1130pm, when suddenly the Inniskilling companies on the right flank rose to their feet and with a chorus of wild Irish yells, charged forward through the darkness.[6]

The implication in the above account is that the Inniskillings compromised any semblance of surprise and indeed were the architects of what followed due to indiscipline. Of interest is that fact that no claims of this nature are contained in the war diary of the 2nd Worcesters, which states, 'At 11.28 pm the enemy opened a heavy fire with rifles and machine guns.'[7] Nor is anything resembling this allegation made in the war diaries of any of the other three 5 Brigade battalions, nor of the King's Royal Rifle Corps to the right of the Inniskillings, nor the 2nd Leicesters of the Garwhal Brigade to the left of the Worcesters. The war diary of 5 Infantry Brigade itself contains no mention of this allegation, nor does the German history indicate that this occurred. Also of interest is the fact that the Worcester's official history is erroneous in stating that watches had not been synchronised, when this is clearly stated as a prerequisite in 2nd Division operational order No 29, issued on 15 May 1915.[8] It is incomprehensible as to why such an allegation was made against fellow comrades in adversity, unless it was an effort to deflect criticism from, as we shall see, the subsequent failure of the Worcesters to make any meaningful advance. In a remarkable coincidence, and one which makes the allegation even more baffling, the Worcester's official history was compiled by Captain Henry FitzMaurice Stacke, whose younger brother Lieutenant Oliver Stacke was one of the officers leading the Inniskillings A company – the very unit the allegation is levelled against.

With the sending up of flares by the Germans, night turned into day on the battlefield and any element of surprise was lost. For those soldiers out in no-man's-land, there was no going back. The only option was to press forward in a perfect hail of rifle, machine gun and shell fire, in an attempt to reach the German lines. Accurate German shell fire was now concentrating on the British front lines, destroying the bridges over the dykes and creating massive shell holes to be negotiated by the attackers.

The Inniskillings A company, commanded by Lieutenant Charles Henry Daniels who had been with the battalion for four years and were attacking to the left of the cinder track, bore the brunt of the German defensive effort. They were simply mown down by the accurate, pre-set machine gun fire of the defenders. Research by the author has positively identified over 80 men – nearly 50 per cent of the company – who were killed in the initial advance. Included in this number was the 20-year-old Lieutenant Oliver Stacke, who had had such a daring escape from the Germans in August the previous year, and the author's great uncle James. It seems miraculous, but some members of A company managed to reach the German line. However, they were unable to hold this position, primarily due to the severe losses they had sustained in the advance, but also due to the fact that deep dykes ran either side of the cinder track, effectively cutting them off from their D company colleagues. An attempt was made by B company commanded by Captain Rupert Caesar Smythe, an experienced officer who had been with the battalion since the Boer War, to support them. However, due to the heavy machine gun and rifle fire they were unable to reach the German line, sustaining heavy casualties in the attempt. Any A company members who reached the German lines were either killed there or had to seek shelter from the murderous machine gun fire in some of the many shell holes in no-man's-land. On the other side of the cinder track D company, commanded by Captain Charles Hewitt, fared a little better. They were able to occupy the German front line and seizing the initiative pushed forward to occupy the German second line. In doing so they suffered heavy casualties – research by the author has identified 64 D company members killed in this attack. They received support from C company, commanded by Captain Samuel Duffin and then from the supporting battalion, the 2nd Ox and Bucks LI, but had to consolidate their position because no advance had been made left of the cinder track – rendering their position vulnerable to counter-attack and enfilading fire from the defenders. At this time it is believed that the Inniskillings held 120 yards of what had been the German front line.

Private Patrick McKenna from Dungannon, County Tyrone, was attached to D company and in a letter home to his sister Eliza, he vividly describes his experience, including a lucky escape:

We had a rough time since I sent you my last letters. I sent you all the letters as I did not know whether I would be alive or not next day. We went into action that night at half past eleven, so I wrote as it was a thousand to one whether I would come out safely or not. But I am now both safe and sound, only a little bit shaken. Dear Sister, I was thinking of you all at home when I was outside the trench, and I was wondering if you knew the position in which I was, would you sleep. It was an awful fight. No one could believe what it was like as the shells were bursting over us in fours and fives, and machine guns were mowing us down. We had four hundred yards to go to the German trench and our company was in front leading the attack. Well, it was awful. The boys fell around me in dozens. I don't know under God how I escaped, for they fell on each side of me and I still kept going on. I don't know, but I think above all times in my life I had no fear. It was just like going for a walk until I got to the German trench. Then I came to my senses, for the Germans were there, and I had to use my rifle. I was sitting in a gap in the trench when I saw two Germans. They also saw me, but I played to win and I shot both. It was their lives or mine, so I did not want to die just yet. Our Company took the trench but at an awful cost. We went into action with 280 strong all told, and at roll call there were only 80 of us all told. Dear Sister, your prayers for me must have been heard or I would never have come out of it safely. You could compare it to nothing else but all the devils in hell let loose. The two McIntyre's were wounded, one on the side and one on the foot. We had to get this position at all costs. The fight is still going on, and we are lying back off the firing line at present. We get the news from the wounded who are brought back. There were 300 wounded Germans surrendered this morning, so we are doing fairly well. I only hope to God that the Germans were driven back out of the trenches, then we would have a show for our lives. They would be in the open as well as us. It is hard facing the guns in the trenches. One cannot hit back until he has got up to them. I was nearly knocked over by a piece of shell which hit me on the right side. As God would have it, my pouches caught it. There were 30 rounds of ammunition in them, and it tore the pouches off me and my strap caught fire. The ammunition went off and I was sent on my back about 10 yards. I was nothing the worse of it. I had some Woodbine cigarettes in my pocket. I will send them to you. They were riddled, and I had some holy pictures and they were also riddled, but I am keeping them. I lost my beads that night, and I want you to send me ones, also a pair of blessed scapulars.[9]

Obviously a deeply religious man, Patrick was lucky to survive the battle unwounded and indeed served for the duration of the war.

Another who had a lucky escape was Lance Corporal George Owens from Marlborough Avenue in Derry. In a letter to his wife shortly after the battle, Lance Corporal Owens stated:

I can with the greatest confidence say that God heard all the prayers you offered up, and the Masses that were said for me, as He guarded me through what I am sure is one of the greatest battles in history. I lost two of my pals, but I thank God that He has spared my life. I got the rifle broke in my hand with a bullet, which also pierced some of my equipment and went right across my breast. The Germans are fed up, they are putting up their hands in all directions and crying for mercy.[10]

The experience of others in the advance is also captured in letters written home and are an important record of the advance. Private William Sheppard, in a letter to a friend in Londonderry, described the advance:

> *The Inniskillings were ordered to take a part of the enemy's lines which other regiments had failed to take, as the enemy had it full of machine guns. Our regiment lined the front trenches about 1,200 strong about 1130 that night. Other regiments were on our right and left, and we were to take the centre of the enemy's lines. We got the order to go over our front line and our men went over the breastwork just as cool as if they were in parade in Derry. We were ordered to form up in line and advance at walking pace. Just then the enemy sent up what we call flare lights which show up all the ground. We were seen at once. Our officers gave the order, 'Advance Inniskillings'. The enemy opened a terrible fire with rifles, machine guns and all sorts of Field guns. Our men went on, their ranks never wavered. Many were falling, but come what might the Inniskillings continued their advance to the German lines. At last we got to the German barbed wire and then charged the German trenches. Nothing could stand against what was left of our brave regiment. Not one of the enemy was left in a few minutes, and we also took their machine guns. Nearly all our brave officers had then fallen. Our men formed up and went right on to take the next German line in great style. Few if any of the enemy got away alive.[11]*

Private Robert Thornton, who had earlier commented on his colleagues having a pre battle sleep, was wounded in the thigh. In a letter to a friend from hospital, he stated:

> *At 8.30 pm we went to our trenches, and an hour later we were ordered over the parapet and lay in front of the trench until 1130pm when we got the order to advance. We started very slowly so as not to let the Germans know, but had only gone 100 yards when the enemy sent off some rockets, but I think they were so much surprised they could hardly believe it was us. They then sent up hundreds, and made the night as clear as day. They could see us quite plainly, and opened a terrific shell, rifle and machine gun fire. We began our rush amidst this shower of hail and shrapnel, the men falling in dozens. The KRR were luckier than we were meeting with very little opposition. They gained the first line and started for the second. The Worcester's who were beside us could not advance at all. Our fellows, shouting and yelling, rushed on but were pushed back. They came a second time and by this time we were all mad and angry at our losses and*

thinking of nothing rushed the front line of the enemy with bomb and bayonet.
As soon as we gained the front line we rushed off to the second, and had a good
deal of fighting to get them out of the second trench. At one time half the trench
was full of Germans and us, but we soon cleared it.[12]

Another account from an observer – believed to be a Lieutenant in the 2nd
Battalion Highland Light Infantry who were 5 Brigade reserve is of interest, in that
as an observer there is little deviation from that of the soldiers who were actually
involved in the assault:

Here the regiments attacking were the Worcesters, Royal Inniskilling Fusiliers,
the Kings Royal Rifles and the Kings Liverpool Regt. Soon after ten o'clock along
this front there were four lines of men lying in the open in front of the breastwork
with more behind waiting to support. At 1130 in pitch darkness they rose with
one accord to the attack. In perfect quietness they went forward at a walk. They
had hardly started when a flare rose from the German trenches, on they went
still walking. The flare had apparently discovered them, for other flares went
up, then a hail of lead was poured into the advancing troops who then started
to charge. The sharp bark of the machine guns and the crackling of rifles firing
rapid were deafening. For some reason, most opposition was met on the left of
our line by the Worcesters and Inniskillings. The KRR and the Kings on the right
soon obtained their trench and went on to their second. On the left, nothing
daunted by the sheet of lead that they had to penetrate the Worcesters and the
Inniskillings went on bravely. Numbers fell and the Worcesters found their task
impossible, but the Irishmen, knowing no fear, pushed on line after line and
after terrible losses of officers and men obtained their section of trench and
immediately made for the second line. A rush through another hail of lead, and
the second lines fell to them.[13]

It is mentioned in two of the above accounts that the 1st Battalion King's Royal
Rifle Corps were successful. This battalion, to the right of the Inniskillings, were
able to advance to the German lines without any direct fire from in front of
them. However their Adjutant, Major Armytage had a grandstand view of the
Inniskillings attack:

Then a burst of fire broke out mostly on our left and the enemy began to send up lights in all directions. One could then see silhouetted against the lights our front line which appeared to be quite close to the German trench. The whole space between the lines was dotted with men, some lying on the ground, but the majority still advancing. As our front line reached the German trenches, the lights from that part ceased to go up but it was possible to get glimpses of what was going on when the enemy fired lights further to our right of behind their front line. All this time a very heavy machine gun fire had been coming across from the salient on our left and sweeping our fronts and this did not seem to diminish much as time went on. Rifle fire also continued from this direction.[14]

The last two sentences of the above account are of great importance in understanding what had happened to the Inniskillings.

The concentration of German defensive fire was on the portion of the front line being advanced across by the Inniskillings and Worcesters of 5 Brigade and the Leicesters and Garwhal Rifles of the Garwhal Brigade. As previously mentioned, it is believed that the Germans had a machine gun emplacement in the bend of their front line opposite the Worcesters, providing enfilading fire across the ground through which the Worcesters and Inniskillings were advancing. When the German sent up their flares and opened fire, the Worcesters advanced with the Inniskillings, with D company on the left and B company on the right. As their war diary indicates:

At 11.30 pm the advance commenced, but the left Company, D could make no progress due to the enemy's heavy fire. B Company supported by A went forward with great dash, but suffered so heavily that only three officers and a few men got near the German line.'[15]

The Worcesters D company soldiers who were not wounded, eventually made their way back to the original front line, to reorganise for a planned renewed attack at 3.15 am, 16 May. However, the failure of the Worcesters' attack ensured that the machine gun in the bend of the German line was able to operate unhindered as evidenced by Major Armytage of the KRRC.

This left the Inniskillings in an invidious position. Those who had breached the German line had only finite supplies of bombs and ammunition. The persistent machine gun fire prevented reinforcements and fresh supplies reaching them, rendering their position precarious.

The problem that had bedevilled the British attack at Aubers Ridge – lack of effective communication, now reasserted itself. Once the Inniskillings left the front line breastworks, no one in the supporting battalions and certainly not at brigade headquarters had a clue as to how the advance was progressing. Any telephone wires carried forward by signallers were cut by shell fire and repairing them under heavy shelling was impossible. By arrangement, the Inniskillings carried yellow flags (issued to all attacking 2nd Division units), with which to signal when an objective was taken. Given that the night was pitch black, perhaps a wiser course of action would have been to emulate the initiative shown by the King's Royal Rifle Corps, who carried forward two motor lamps to signal their success.

The 2nd Ox and Bucks LI, supporting the Inniskillings were keen to do their bit in pressing the attack. As the last of the Inniskillings advanced over the British front line, they were replaced by the leading companies of the Ox and Bucks. It is fortunate that not only the battalion war diary exists, but also the diary of their commanding officer, Major Archibald Eden.[16] The entries in this diary and particularly the documentation of the exchange of messages between Major Eden and brigade headquarters, provide an invaluable insight into how the battle unfolded and the confusion caused by the lack of credible information and are detailed as follows:

> To Bde HQ – 1155pm. Commanding Officer and last line Inniskillings just leaving now. German Infantry fire apparently from their second line.
> To Bde HQ – 12mn. I believe first line taken.
> To Bde HQ – 1245am 16th. Half this battalion now in first line.
> To Bde HQ – 0108am. We are being shelled from La Tourelle. Have only two companies left in breastwork.
> From Bde HQ – 0115am. Can you report further on the situation? Do you know where left of Inniskillings rests? Have you sent forward Grenadiers?
> To Bde HQ – 0122am. Cannot say for certain where left of Inniskillings rests. My grenadiers have gone forward. Shelling of the breast work now less. Am holding back my last Company to cooperate with the Worcesters attack at 0130.
> From Bde HQ – 0130am. Worcesters will not attack again until 3.15am after bombardment from 2.45am. Find out definitely where Inniskillings left rests, so that artillery fire can be arranged.

To Bde HQ – 0210am. I now feel pretty certain we have not got front of German line from V1 eastwards. Shall Royal Engineers therefore dig forward to cinder track?

To Bde HQ – 0220am. Inniskilling Officer just returned. Reports we are in occupation of German second line trench about R7. Am sending two platoons to reinforce them.

From Bde HQ –0230am. 6th Brigade attack has been successful. Inniskillings have captured front line. At 0245 artillery will bombard German first and second line trenches. The assault will be carried out by the Glasgow Highlanders.

[Author's note: The Worcesters were deemed unable to carry out this fresh assault, due to casualties sustained, congestion in their trenches with dead and wounded and an inability to reorganise in time.]

To Bde HQ – 0305am. Have definitely found out that V1 is our left. I believe Maxim's [Machine Guns] still untouched between V1 and V2.

From Bde HQ – 0310am. Are you in touch with the front line? Do they require further support?

To Bde HQ – 0321am. Not yet in touch by wire with front. Heavy shellfire by enemy now proceeding.

To Bde HQ – 0415am. Yellow flags are being waved at V1. Not much sign of life East of V1. Possible Maxim still hidden. Good line of approach for supporting troops is west of cinder track. Considerable shelling still continues.

From Bde HQ – 0445am. Am out of touch with Glasgows. Please report their position. Send orderly to find out. Did they attack?

Given today's expectation of and reliance on effective communications, the above exchanges indicate the difficulties in ascertaining even the most basic of information. It should be remembered that the brigade headquarters was not situated miles away, it was actually in a house on the Rue du Bois, around three hundred yards behind the British front line. The brigade headquarters was trying to control the activities of five infantry battalions – over 5,000 men, but they had no coherent method of doing so. They were responsible for making life or death decisions concerning those under their command but, as is seen in the message at 1.30 am, they were reliant on the commanding officer Ox and Bucks to make a life or death decision concerning artillery support. Indicative of the difficulties in ascertaining progress are evidenced in the message at 2.20 am – the only credible information received thus far, three hours after the advance. The fact that an Inniskillings officer instead of a battalion runner returned with the information, indicates the importance of the message. It is not recorded who the Inniskillings officer was, but it is known that Second Lieutenant John Joseph Morgan, D company, was engaged in several perilous trips back to the British lines with messages and to organise reinforcements, before he was mortally wounded on one such mission. The clarity of understanding of the situation exhibited by brigade headquarters does not improve with time. The second attack which took place at 3.15 am, to coincide with the attack of the 7th Division farther east, involved 9 HLI, who had replaced the 2nd Worcesters. However at 4.45am, one and a half hours after this attack took place, Brigade headquarters were unaware whether the Glasgow Highlanders had attacked or not.[17]

The problem with communications was what it was. There was no panacea for this problem, as a portable battlefield radio had not been developed at that time. The tried and trusted methods of laying telephone wires quickly after an advance endured, but these were susceptible to enemy shellfire and counter-attack. In the case of the Inniskillings attack, the Engineers responsible for communications were not deployed as it was deemed too dangerous. The other option then was to utilise runners. Second Lieutenant Morgan fulfilled this role for the Inniskillings, but more often it was a young private soldier, considered fleet of foot. The drawback with this method was that that the person sending the message could never be sure that it had arrived, as the runners job was one of the most dangerous, involving countless trips back and forward across bullet and shell swept ground.

The situation after the night assault at 11.30 pm on 15 May then, was that progress had been made to the right of the cinder track, in that the Inniskillings D company had taken the German first and second lines and were now supported by the 2nd Ox and Bucks. To their right, the King's Royal Rifle Corps had made similar progress. To the left of the cinder track, no progress had been made. The majority of the Inniskillings A company lay dead or wounded in no-man's-land. The Worcesters to their left were back in their original trenches and to the left of them, the 2nd Leicesters had been unable to advance at all. This now left the German front line with a sharp bend to the right of the cinder track. The imminent danger was that the Germans would attempt a counter-attack to restore the integrity of their line. However, members of D company Inniskillings were unaware as to the fate of their A company colleagues and the accepted tactic was to attempt to join up with them in the German front line. To this end, attempts were made by Inniskillings supported by Ox and Bucks soldiers to advance by use of bombs along the German trench. This was intense and bloody trench fighting at its worst with many casualties on both sides. Among those killed was the officer in charge of the Inniskillings bombers, 20-year-old Second Lieutenant Alfred Douglas Wingate, who had joined the Inniskillings from the Indian Army seeking action. He was last seen alive at about 3.30 am on the parapet of the German front line under heavy fire, directing his bombers. His body was discovered just beyond the German parapet on 20 May by soldiers from the Highland Light Infantry and he was buried where he lay. His grave was subsequently lost and he is commemorated on Le Touret Memorial to the Missing. The regard in which he was held is evidenced in a letter sent to his parents immediately after the battle when his fate was unknown:

He was last seen alive and unwounded fighting hard at 3.30am on 16 May, and I am afraid that he was such a brave boy and was always anxious to be in the thick of everything. I feel certain that it is extremely unlikely that he was taken prisoner. He was a good soldier and his bravery was an excellent example to his men. It will be impossible to replace him, for his duty of leading the bombers requires exceptional courage.... A splendid youngster. Another officer wrote, his bomb throwers were much attached to him, as indeed everyone was.[18]

2nd Lieutenant Alfred Douglas Wingate
(Image courtesy of DeRuvigny's Roll of Honour)

The Germans were eventually able to establish a block in the trench to deny any further advance by the Allied troops, leaving the British in control of the area to the right of the cinder track, that is still controlling the old German first and second lines. Acting-Serjeant John Hollinger of the Inniskillings bombers was awarded the

Distinguished Conduct Medal for his part in this action, the citation reading, 'For conspicuous gallantry since the start of the campaign. On one occasion he led a section of bombers on the left of the captured enemy trenches, completely breaking up their attempts at recapturing them.'[19] Wounded in the action, Acting-Serjeant Hollinger was unable to return to active duty, transferring to the Labour Corps. The ferocity of the fighting by the Inniskillings D company in an attempt to consolidate their position is reflected in the award of the Distinguished Conduct Medal to Serjeant Thomas McFarland. The citation reads, 'For conspicuous gallantry and ability in leading his platoon and carrying out under heavy fire, the duty allotted to him until all his platoon had been killed or wounded. He has invariably shown great courage and zeal in his work and has always been ready to volunteer for dangerous duty.'[20] Serjeant McFarland was a native of Tattynure outside Omagh and had completed nine years' service with the Inniskillings before emigrating to Canada. At the outbreak of war he returned and rejoined the battalion. He was to survive the war, gaining a bar to his DCM for gallantry in October 1918.

Whilst the Ox and Bucks provided ten platoons – roughly 500 men, to assist the Inniskillings in consolidating their position in the German lines, the three platoons designated to go forward as a working party with the initial advance were in a perilous position. Due to the ferocity of the German fire, they were halted about 100 yards short of the German front line and had to seek what cover they could until they were recalled to the British breastworks on the morning of 16 May. Notwithstanding the circumstances of this working party, it was imperative to establish some permanent means of communications with those in the captured German front line. At around 12.30 am on 16 May, a party of one hundred men from 2 HLI, the brigade reserve, under the control of a small party of Royal Engineers, were detailed to attempt to construct a communications trench from the British breastwork to the German front line – a distance of some 200 yards. Given the constant machine gun, rifle and shell fire sweeping no-man's-land and the position of the original working parties, this was an extremely hazardous proposition. It was quickly discovered that the course of the proposed trench led to a part of the enemy line still held by the Germans, so the location was changed to run parallel to and to the right of the cinder track. By daylight on 16 May, despite their best efforts, only one hundred yards of a shallow dip which would enable a man to crawl along had been dug – the digging having to be done lying down.[21] This attempt cost 2 HLI 16 killed and many wounded.

The original plan for the battle envisaged that the 2nd Division, including Inniskillings, would having attained the objectives of the German first and second line, resume the attack at 3.15 am to coincide with the attack by the 7th Division further along the line in the vicinity of Festubert village – the aspiration being that both 2nd and 7th Division troops would complete a pincer movement and meet each other at La Quinque Rue. However, the events since the advance at 11.30 pm on 15 May rendered this impossible. The Inniskillings and the Ox and Bucks were fully engaged in securing the foothold they had won so dearly and were unable to advance at the stipulated time. To their right, the King's Royal Rifle Corps were similarly engaged. To the left of the Inniskillings, the Worcesters were being withdrawn and replaced by 9 HLI, the Glasgow Highlanders, but this process was carried out so slowly due to congestion and disorganisation in the Worcesters' trenches that the Glasgow Highlanders could not meet the start time. To the left of them the Leicesters, having been badly mauled in the 11.30 pm advance had been withdrawn and replaced with the 3rd London Regiment and the 2/3rd Gurkhas. Their attempted advance at 3.15 am met the same fate as that of the Leicesters and led to some timely and humane decision making by the Garhwal Brigade Commander, Brigadier General Charles Guinand Blackader,[22] as he described in a post battle report:

> 0245 – bombardment of enemy's trenches – it was not possible to launch the assault from the enemy's side of the ditch, as men could not reach that position unseen. At 0315 the assault was launched. As soon as the first line surmounted the parapet the enemy opened heavy rifle, machine gun and artillery fire, and the assaulting troops were unable to reach the enemy's trenches, the majority being shot down as they crossed our own parapet.
>
> In the circumstances it appeared to me that in the face of intense rifle, machine gun and artillery fire directed against our parapet and on the ground immediately in front of it, any attempt to renew the assault would not meet with success and would only lead to a great and useless loss of life. I therefore directed the 3rd London Regiment and the 2/3rd Gurkhas to hold the line and reorganise in case they should be required to make another attempt.'[23]

The attack of the 7th Division went ahead as planned and met with more success, but still the gap remained between the 2nd and 7th Divisions.

For those Inniskillings holding the captured German lines, dawn on 16 May brought a realisation of the extent of their success, but also of the precarious nature of their position. Although they were awaiting a potential German counter-attack, they were spared the attentions of the German artillery – possibly as the Germans could not be sure of the exact position of their own troops. Resupplies of bombs and ammunition were urgently required and 2 HLI undertook this arduous task throughout the day – complicated by the fact that the German artillery concentrated all their fire on the old British front line, reasoning correctly that the British would be attempting to move up further resources.

This artillery fire also had serious implications for the evacuation of the wounded. As dawn broke on 16 May, a vision from hell must have greeted those Inniskillings lying wounded in no-man's-land. Countless bodies and body parts of their comrades lay strewn about and the ground had been transformed into a moonscape by both British and German artillery – although this did have the benefit of providing some shelter in the many shell holes from the incessant machine gun fire. An additional threat came from the German lines. There are separate accounts from soldiers in the Innniskillings and other attacking battalions of the Germans throwing what is described as 'vitriol' from their lines, setting the ground and in some places the wounded on fire. This is commented on with outrage by the Inniskillings as further evidence, after the use of poison gas and attacks on passenger liners, of German barbarity. One witness who commented on this was the Inniskillings Private Thornton:

> The Germans were firing on our wounded and setting fire to them by firing vitriol or some other stuff for their cowardly purpose.[24]

In their war diary the 2nd Leicesters to the left of the Inniskillings, also commented on this phenomenon:

> The enemy threw from their parapet some kind of fire grenade which burst into fire on impact with the ground.[25]

Paddy Griffith in his excellent 'Battle Tactics on the Western Front, The British Army's Art of Attack 1916-1918,[26] describes the development by both sides at this time of primitive incendiary grenades containing phosphorous. As the weapons used were definitely not flamethrowers – according to Wyrall, (1921), 'the projection of burning liquid'[27] was first used by the Germans on 30 July 1915. It is highly possible that incendiary grenades may have been what was witnessed.

The wounded then faced the problem of getting back to the British lines. Those that could walk or at least crawl, were able to attempt to get back through the shell holes, the churned up ground and the dykes, all the while fearful of the Germans noticing movement and opening up with machine guns again. One of those caught in this position was Lance Corporal John McIntyre from Dungannon. In a letter home he described his predicament:

> I can nearly swear that out of the thousand men of the Inniskillings who made the great charges on Saturday and Sunday, there were 700 or 800 killed or wounded. I don't know how young Joe Cunningham of Dungannon got on as I had no time to see. I got wounded and fell beside two of my chums, and we lay under heavy fire until three o'clock on Sunday morning. We were too bad to crawl out of danger. One of my wounded chums got killed by a bullet as we lay there, so we had a close shave. The shellfire was terrific and the shells burst all round us as we lay waiting on our turn. I never saw such fire from the big guns, rifles and machine guns, and the latter mowed down our men like grass. On Sunday morning when I revived, I tried to make my way back to the trenches with the German bullets cutting the ground around me. I took cover behind a dead comrade, and on looking into his face I thought at first to my horror that it was my own brother, but on creeping into our trenches he was the first man to speak to me, as he had reached it before me, and had had his wound dressed. I was obliged to stop all that Sunday in the front trench and German shells nearly did for the lot of us. I saw a dozen of our men killed and wounded by one shell from the enemy's heavy guns. Another killed three of our wounded not more than two yards from where I was lying. It was an awful Sunday.[28]

In common with other units, the battalion utilised members of the regimental band as stretcher-bearers, identified by an armband and these were supplemented by members of the Royal Army Medical Corps attached to the battalion and members of No 5 Field Ambulance. Theirs was a job of unimaginable danger throughout 16 May. Firstly, a number of accounts indicate that the British breastworks were heavily shelled all day on the 16th without pause. This was the start and end point for any venture by the stretcher bearers out into no-man's-land. Secondly, once out in no-man's-land the bearers had to identify those in need of the most urgent assistance – a manner of battlefield triage and then get those wounded back to the British breastwork, all the while whilst under fire from the German front line trenches. The physical effort required was described succinctly in an account by a stretcher bearer involved in the battle and later killed at the Battle of Loos in September 1915:

> *I gave a hand with my party of six and between us we carried down two: you have no idea of the physical fatigue entailed in carrying a 12 stone wounded a thousand odd yards across muddy fields. Oh this cruel mud!*[29]

For those wounded who were lucky enough to be collected, it must have seemed that they had been rescued from the brink of death, but in many circumstances it was a case of 'out of the frying pan and into the fire', as the danger in what shelter existed in the British breastworks exceeded that in no-man's-land.

Major Armytage of the KRRC, having been wounded in the thigh in the German front line managed the journey back to the British lines. In an account he described the situation there:

> *It was very slow work getting along the trench as besides its garrison it was packed with wounded. I got dressed by our stretcher bearers and then tried to make my way out by the communication trench; it was, however impossible to do this as it was now daylight and the enemy were plastering the communication trench with high explosive shrapnel and whizz bangs* – they were also giving our front trench a very sound shelling with every sort of gun.....It was very difficult to move down the communication trench which was badly damaged by shelling and blocked with dead and wounded.*[30]

For the Inniskillings, it was certainly the case that many of those retrieved from the battlefield were killed on arrival at what should have been a place of relative safety. One such casualty was an NCO from D company. Corporal William John Brolly, a talented footballer originally from Ballymoney but married and living at Pittsburg Street off Belfast's York Road, was wounded in the assault on the German trenches and on being carried out of the firing line a shell exploded a short distance away, killing him outright. Private Thornton of the Inniskillings described the scenes he witnessed on the evening of Sunday 16 May:

> *Our stretcher bearers when carrying the wounded back were killed, and the*

wounded buried alive, with the trenches being blown in on top of them. It was
terrible to see, some fellows sitting with their backs against the side of the trench,
with their head, arms and legs blown off.[31]

Corpl. WM. BROLLY.
2nd Batt. Royal Inniskilling Fusiliers, late
of Distillery Football Club, killed in action
on May 15. His wife resides at 4 Pittsburg
Street, Belfast.

Corporal William Brolly
(Image courtesy of Nigel Henderson)

Serjeant Langford, attached to battalion headquarters and wounded himself, also commented, 'Many of our wounded were buried by shells in the dugouts where they had been placed for safety.'[32] In reality the task facing the stretcher bearers was immense, and there were some areas and wounded that were impossible to reach. Those unfortunates had to fend for themselves as best they could. One of these was Private William McCaffrey from Chapel Hill Cookstown, who, shot in two places in the initial advance, lay on the battlefield for four days before he could be rescued. That he was able to reach a base hospital in Boulogne after that trial, gives some indication of his physical and mental fortitude. Interestingly, he may have been rescued due to a personal initiative by the adjutant of 2 HLI. He had called at the No 5 Field Ambulance headquarters on the afternoon of 19 May to inform them that a large number of wounded men still lay on the battlefield from the initial advance of 15 May. Bearer teams were immediately organised and directed to the area and recovered over 20 wounded men.

That the stretcher bearers and medical staff were able to rescue so many, is testament to their dedication to duty, a fact recognised by Lieutenant Alexander, who commented, 'The devotion to duty displayed by the regimental stretcher bearers (mostly bandsmen) was most commendable.'[33] For his outstanding work at this time, Corporal John McNeill of the Royal Army Medical Corps, attached to the Inniskillings, was awarded the Distinguished Conduct Medal. His citation stating, 'For conspicuous gallantry on the night of May 15-16 1915 near Rue du Bois. He repeatedly went out and brought in wounded men under heavy fire, and showed the greatest bravery and devotion to duty.'[34]

The wounded were taken along communication trenches back from the British front line, initially to the battalion aid post on the Rue du Bois and then taken to the dressing station of No 5 Field Ambulance, about a quarter of a mile farther back in the hamlet of Richebourg. Their war diary records that extra stretcher bearers had to be brought in due to those on duty, 'being worn out due to the hard work.'- understandable when the prolonged physical exertion was taken into consideration. In the twenty-four hours up until 9.00 am on 16 May, their war diary indicates that they processed 700 wounded. The diary goes on to explain that their stretcher bearers worked all day and night on 16 May collecting wounded and that no figures of those dressed and wounded were collected – the implication being that there were too many to keep accurate accounts.[35] Sterling work was however carried out at the dressing stations which enabled many soldiers to make a complete recovery. One of those fortunate was A company's Serjeant James Bradley. From Lowry Street in East Belfast he was seriously wounded in the advance having part of his ear and neck blown away. However, he made a full recovery and continued to serve for the rest of the war, being awarded the Military Medal and Distinguished Conduct Medal. He was discharged from the Army in the rank of Company Serjeant Major in 1930.

Some of the wounded Inniskillings at least, had the good fortune to be treated by a doctor from their home city. Captain Arthur Clarence Turner, Royal Army Medical Corps was a 48-year-old native of Londonderry. His family resided at 28 Foyle Street and his father Walter, was a Justice of the Peace in the city. In a letter to his father Captain Turner described that, 'He had professionally attended at least fifty wounded soldiers from Derry, all belonging to the Royal Inniskilling Fusiliers.' He went on to mention that the soldiers, who had relatives in the Lecky Road, Long Tower district, Rossville Street, Fountain Street and Waterside had recognised him and appeared pleased to be in his care. Commenting on the battle they had been engaged in he stated, 'All these Derry boys fought with a splendid courage and determination and are a credit to the city they came from.'[36] Captain Turner was an experienced military surgeon, having served as a civilian surgeon with the British forces in the South African War where he was mentioned in despatches for his outstanding work.

As early as the morning of 16 May, faced with the failure of the initial attack of the left of 5 Brigade and that of the Meerut division, and the subsequent failure to deliver the 3.15 am attack, General Haig made the decision that the left of the position gained by the Inniskillings would be the left boundary of the offensive front. Therefore, in essence the cinder track became the offensive boundary, with the troops to the left of this remaining on the defensive, whilst all offensive efforts were concentrated to the area on the right where ground had been gained. As this decision was disseminated down to 5 Brigade headquarters, the decision was made to relieve those troops involved in the initial advance. It was realised that the Inniskillings had suffered exceptionally heavily and efforts were concentrated in effecting their relief. In reality, what remained to be relieved in the captured German first and second lines was the remnants of D and C companies, perhaps 200 men at most. Their relief was initiated by a request from 5 Brigade headquarters to Major Eden of the Ox and Bucks LI around 4.00 pm on 16 May, to ascertain if he could hold the captured position with his own troops allowing the Inniskillings to withdraw. He answered in the affirmative provided that he was resupplied with bombs and ammunition. This done, the Inniskillings began the slow and poignant withdrawal past so many of their fallen comrades to the reserve breastworks from where they had begun their advance less than a day before. They held these breastworks until midnight on 17 May, when they were relieved by the 1/1st Gurkhas and marched the short distance to the hamlet of Le Touret. For the Inniskillings at least, the battle of Festubert was over.

For those Inniskillings who had taken the German first and second lines, the extent of the defensive work the Germans had carried out over the winter came as an unwelcome surprise. Compared to the pathetic, makeshift structures that the British had in the marshy Flanders mud, the German defensive structures must have seemed like something from a different planet. An account in the *Irish News* shortly after the battle, detailed the extent of German preparedness in the area between Festubert and Richebourg:

> These trenches, battered by our shell fire, were wonderful constructions in concrete. They were fitted with electric light and fans and with mechanisms worked by electric power for draining them. The necessary power was obtained from the electric plant of the coal mines in the La Bassee area. In one trench our men profited for several hours by the electric light, but eventually the enemy severed the wires, and so cut off the current. Most of the trenches were provided with machine guns embedded in concrete casemates.[51]

It was little wonder that the ineffectual pre-battle bombardment had failed to destroy the enemy defences.

The ground which the Inniskillings D company had won at such great cost remained a deadly place. On 18 May, one of four Victoria Crosses awarded during the battle was won by Lieutenant John Smyth of the 15th Ludhiana Sikhs attached to the Lahore Division. He volunteered along with ten of his men to carry forward boxes of bombs and ammunition to troops in the area of the second German line captured by the Inniskillings. Under fire for the entire journey, he was the only one to reach the destination alive.[38]

The advance at 3.15 am on 16 May focused mainly to the right of the Inniskillings and involved 20 and 22 Brigades of the 7th Division. Substantial progress was made by 22 Brigade, led by the 1st Queens Regiment and the 1st Royal Welch Fusiliers. By 7.00 am they had advanced over 600 yards and had reached the battle's objective of La Quinque Rue however, the casualties sustained in this advance against the spirited defence of two companies of the German 57th Infantry Regiment meant that the advance stalled. Twenty Brigade to their right did not fare so well. The leading companies of the 2nd Battalion Scots Guards and the 2nd Border Regiment, in their eagerness to advance ran into the British bombardment, with severe losses. On the night of the 16/17 May, the Germans in assessing their situation, voluntarily withdrew their troops to a better defensive position around three quarters of a mile to the rear. Ironically, a fact not recognised by the British for two days. On 17 May the gap between the 2nd and 7th Divisions was finally joined when the 1st Battalion King's (Liverpool Regiment) of 6 Brigade met with the 2nd Battalion Royal Scots Fusiliers of 21 Brigade on the afternoon of 17 May. Ironically, meeting this main objective of the battle was almost denied by British artillery. The artillery of the 2nd Division supporting the attack of 6 Brigade, shelled the British 21 Brigade troops, particularly those of the Royal Scots Fusiliers, causing considerable casualties – the Fusiliers having 28 men killed on this date.[39] This fiasco occurred as there was still no centralised control of British artillery, despite the implications of the issue being repeatedly identified and led to a humbling apology from the commander 2nd Division, Major General Horne, himself an artilleryman.[40]

Further attacks to maintain momentum were carried out over the next week and in this time both the 2nd and 7th Divisions were relieved by the 51st and Canadian divisions respectively. A further advance took place on 25 May involving the Canadian and 47th Divisions in which around 400 yards of ground across a frontage of 1,000 yards was taken. That was the final action in this battle. A map of the final position of the opposing armies shows that the German front line

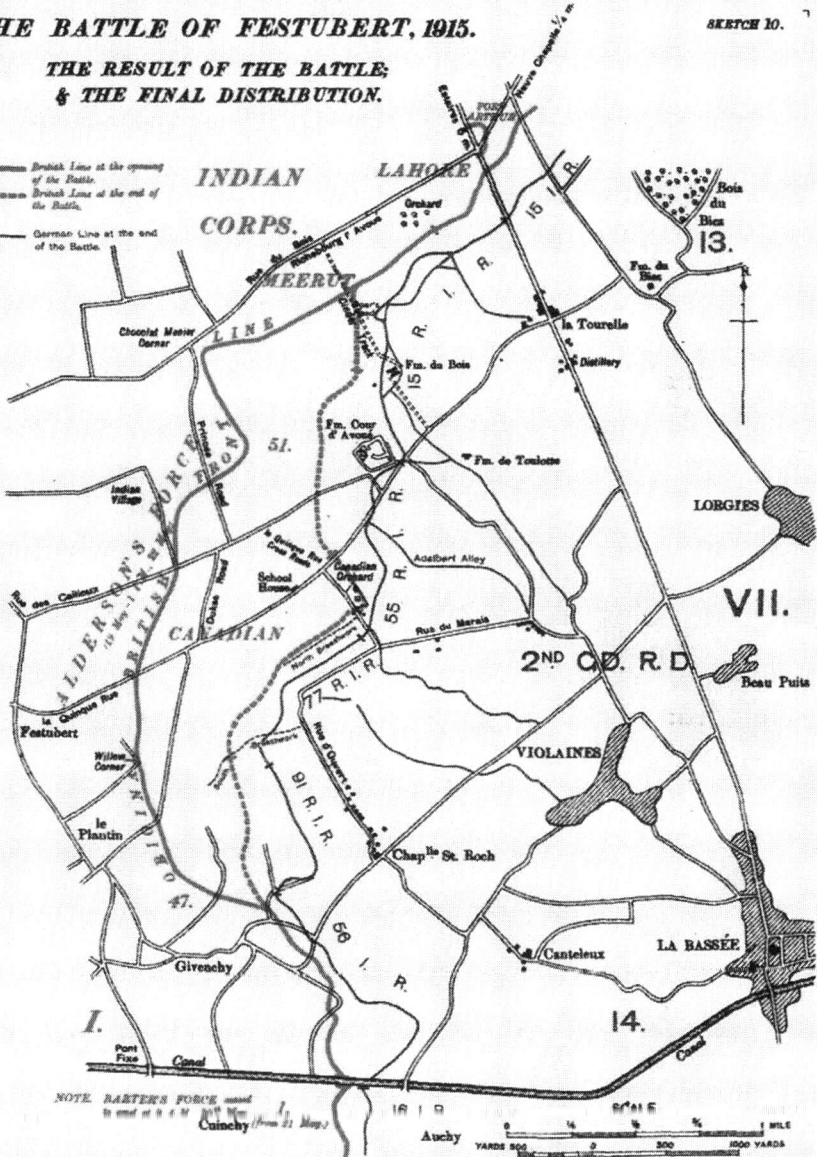

THE BATTLE OF FESTUBERT, 1915.

THE RESULT OF THE BATTLE;
& THE FINAL DISTRIBUTION.

to the left of the cinder track, attacked by A company Inniskillings on 15 May remained exactly the same on 27 May. The ground gained and held by D company in the earlier hours of 16 May had not advanced in the subsequent 11 days.[41]

1   Sheffield G and Bourne J, (Eds) *Douglas Haig. War Diaries and Letters, 1914-1918*.p.129. After his third set piece battle of Spring 1915, Haig comes to the inevitable conclusion.

2   National Archives. WO 95/1343/2, 5 Infantry Brigade, Special Instructions, 14 May 1915

3   The *Sprig of Shillelagh*, January 1916, p.274

4   Schulz, D. Infanterie Regiment Graf Bulow von Dennewitz Nr 55 im Weltkriege, p.91

5   Ibid, p.92

6   Stacke, H FitzM, *The Worcestershire Regiment in the Great War*, Volume 1, p.71

7   National Archives. WO 95/1351, 2nd Battalion Worcestershire Regiment war diary

8   National Archives. WO 95/1343/2, 2nd Division war diary, Appendix XLV

9   *Fermanagh Herald*, 5 June 1915, p.5

10   *Derry Journal*, 28 May 1915, p.8

11   Ulster and the War, *Belfast Newsletter*, 9 June 1915

12   *Belfast Evening Telegraph* 29 May 1915, p.8

13   Ibid p.8

14   National Archives. WO 95/1358, 1 King's Royal Rifle Corps war diary

15   National Archives. WO 95/1351, 2nd Worcesters war diary

16   Major Eden's diary available online @ www.lightbobs.com/1915-battle-of-festubert.html Accessed 2 November 2013.

17   National Archives. WO 95/1347. 1st/9th Highland Light Infantry (Glasgow Highlanders) war diary. The situation remained that the Glasgow Highlanders had not attacked as they could not occupy the front line in time due to the fact that it was completely blocked by the Worcesters who did not vacate it until 04.30 am.

18   UK DeRuvigny's Roll of Honour, available online at www.ancestry.co.uk Accessed 27 November 2013

19   *London Gazette*, 11 March 1916

20   *London Gazette*, 30 June 1915. Serjeant McFarland was awarded a bar to the DCM for further acts of bravery in March 1916.

21   National Archives. WO 95/1343/2. 5 Infantry Brigade war diary. Work was continued on this communications trench by one hundred men of the 107th Pioneers, attached to the Meerut Division, but by the morning of 17 May, it was still forty yards short of the German line.

22   General Blackader was later sent to Ireland following the Easter rising of 1916. He was the chairman of the courts martial which sentenced to death five of the seven signatories to the Proclamation of the Irish Republic. After sentencing Patrick Pearse he stated, 'I have just done one of the hardest tasks I have ever had to do. I have had to condemn to death one of the finest characters I have ever come across.' www.minerva.mic.ul.ie//vol1/pearse.html accessed 6 August 2014

23 National Archives. WO 95/3945/2. Garhwal Brigade war diary. After action report by Brigadier General CG Blackader

24 *Belfast Evening Telegraph,* 29 May 1915, p.5. Vitriol is another term for sulphuric acid.

25 National Archives. WO 95/3945/2, 2nd Battalion Leicestershire Regiment war diary

26 Griffith, P. *Battle Tactics of the Western Front. The British Army's Art of Attack 1916-18.* p.113

27 Wyrall, E. *The History of the 2nd Division, 1914-1918. Volume 1 1914-1916,* p.215

28 *Mid Ulster Mail* 29 May 1915 p.7

29 Chapin H, *One Man's War: Letters from a soldier killed at the battle of Loos.* (Kindle eBook). Chapin was attached to No 6 Field Ambulance, working with 6 Brigade at Festubert. The fact that six men only managed to retrieve two casualties gives some idea of the effort involved.

30 National Archives. WO 95/1358, King's Royal Rifle Corps War Diary.* 'Whizz bang' was the term given generically to German artillery shells, but was originally said to refer to the German 77mm field gun.

31 *Belfast Evening Telegraph* 29 May 1915 p.8

32 *Sprig of Shillelagh,* September 1915, p.211.

33 Alexander, CAM. *With the 2nd Battalion Royal Inniskilling Fusiliers in France, 1914-1916.* p.48

34 *Sprig,* op.cit., p.209

35 National Archives. WO 95/1337/2, No 5 Field Ambulance war diary

36 *Derry Journal* 24 May 1915 p.5. Arthur Clarence Turner was in medical practice in Levenshulme, Manchester at the beginning of the war, and immediately volunteered for the front. He survived the war, returning to Manchester where he died in 1927. Twenty-one men from the city of Londonderry have been positively identified as having been killed in the battle.

37 *Irish News and Belfast Morning News,* 27 May 1915, p.5

38 Batchelor P and Matson C, *VC's of the Western Front 1915,* p.157. Lieutenant Smyth was recommended for a bar to his VC on the North West Frontier in May 1919, but was awarded a Military Cross for that action.

39 www.cwgc.org

40 National Archives. WO 95/1285/2, 2nd Division War Diary. This incident was deemed so serious that a report was compiled by the commander 2nd Division, Major General Horne in which he states, ' First of all I wish to convey to 7th Division and 2nd Royal Scots Fusiliers in particular, how deeply we deplore that they should have suffered loss at the hands of 2nd Div Artillery.' He concludes by stating, ' I am afraid that the case now reported, offers another instance of the great difficulties to be overcome in co-ordinating the action of artillery on a wide front.'

41 Edmonds, Sketch 10, p72

· · · CHAPTER 8 · · ·
AFTERMATH

Mrs Beattie of 29 Kenilworth St, Belfast, is very anxious for news of her son, Private Robert Beattie 3350, 2nd Inniskillings, of whom she has heard nothing since the engagement at Festubert on 15th May. (Ulster and the War Column, *Belfast Newsletter*, 21 June 1915)[1]

Having left the battlefield at midnight on the 17 May, the Inniskillings marched the short distance – around a mile – to the hamlet of Le Touret where those unscathed were able to get a few hours' rest. At that time the rest of 5 Brigade was relieved by the Sirhind Brigade of the Lahore Division and on the afternoon of 18 May the entire brigade relocated to billets in Gonnehem, a small village north west of Bethune and ten miles behind the front line. It could be argued that a ten mile march for those having just left the hell of the battlefield was one way of focusing the minds of the survivors and not letting them dwell on what had just taken place. But it would have been the case that many of those marching must have been in a state of shock at what they had just witnessed and experienced. There was to be no lengthy rest period at Gonnehem however, as the Inniskillings relocated again on 29 May, marching the seven miles to billets in the village of Burbure where they were to rest, recuperate and reorganise for the next seven days. At this time, the Inniskillings were in a relatively peaceful area of French countryside, some 20 miles behind the British front line.

It was at this time that the important work of trying to establish the exact number of casualties and the whereabouts of those wounded and missing began. Company roll-calls were held and the survivors asked for information and last sightings of their colleagues who they had witnessed being killed or who may have been wounded and still lay on the battlefield. Field Ambulance records were also checked, to establish exactly who they had treated and where they had been sent to. This information was required urgently for a number of reasons. To enable the next of kin of those killed to be promptly informed. To identify those who were missing so that further enquiries could take place as to their whereabouts. To identify how many replacements were required and how much billeting and food would be required, and of course to provide statistics up to command level so that the effectiveness of the attack could be analysed.

There is no doubt that the Inniskillings suffered grievous losses, but exactly how many casualties were sustained? Sadly, there is no definitive answer to this question. Various totals have been given over the years, but few are in agreement. One reason for this is battlefield confusion and the failure to keep exact records – unsurprising when one considers the mayhem of the dressing stations and Field Ambulances who, as described in the previous chapter were often overwhelmed. The term 'casualty' is agreed as those who are dead, wounded or missing from a battalion's strength. With the passage of time it should be possible to have an absolute figure of those dead and missing, those wounded might be slightly more problematic as there is no clear definition as to what constituted a wound. Was it someone who had their identity recorded as passing through the hands of the military medical services? What then of those who may have sustained a minor wound which they dressed themselves and remained on duty – should they be counted? This ambiguity could explain some of the differences in figures.

Another complicating factor is that the exact strength of the Inniskillings going into the battle is unknown. A British infantry battalion's active strength was 1,000 which was to be maintained whilst on active service. Obviously with leave, sickness, wounded, courses etc, there would be fluctuations in this number, but at that stage of the war we can assume that for the battle, the Inniskillings should have been putting 1,000 men in the field. The only official figure we have comes from Lieutenant Alexander, who in his book, *With the 2nd Battalion Royal Inniskilling Fusiliers in France 1914-1916*, states, 'On 31st December 1914, the Battalion strength was 28 Officers and 995 other ranks.'[2] As seen in the previous chapter, Private William Sheppard in a letter home after the battle stated, 'Our regiment lined the front trenches about 1,200 strong about 1130 that night.' – in all probability a rough estimate. If the active service strength benchmark of 1,000 all ranks is used then, the following estimates of casualties indicate the severity of the Inniskillings' losses.

It is of interest to look at the various estimates chronologically, as it could be expected that initial estimates, due to the confusion post battle may be less accurate. Firstly, the Inniskillings war diary for 15/16 May indicates the casualties sustained as, '39 killed, 371 wounded and 239 missing in action'.[3] This gives a total of 649. On 21 May, 5 Brigade war diary records in a post action report furnished by the Brigade Commander, Brigadier General Chichester to 2nd Division, that the Inniskillings sustained casualties of 18 officers and 650 other ranks.[4] On 22 May, the 2nd Division war diary indicates that the Inniskillings losses were 670, including 432 missing in action.[5] On 24 May, possibly as some of those who may have got mixed with other units in the confusion of the battlefield returned, the 5 Brigade war diary records the Inniskillings losses at 649, including 251 missing. Of note is the fact that this document also records the casualties sustained by the other battalions in the Brigade:[6]

2nd Battalion Worcestershire Regiment – 305
2nd Battalion Oxfordshire and Buckinghamshire Light Infantry – 370
2nd Battalion Highland Light Infantry – 378
1/9th Battalion Highland Light Infantry (Glasgow Highlanders) – 209

These are the only figures which exist from the immediate aftermath of the battle.

In *The Royal Inniskilling Fusiliers in the World War*, published in 1928, Sir Frank Fox puts the Inniskillings casualties at '19 Officers and 652 other ranks.'[7] However, published in the same year, *Official History of the War, Military Operations in France and Belgium, 1915*, by Brigadier General Sir James Edmonds states, 'On this day, mostly in this attack, the 2/Royal Inniskilling Fusiliers lost 19 Officers and 630 other ranks.'[8] This coincides with and may even have been taken from 5 Infantry brigade reporting of 24 May 1915. These figures are also quoted in Thomas Johnstone's 1992 book, *Orange, Green and Khaki. The story of the Irish regiments in the Great War, 1914-18*. These are the main publications which quote total casualty figures. As both the Inniskillings' war diary and the official history settle on the figure of 649 for total casualties, it may be that this should be the accepted total.

To offer a comparison, on the first day of the Battle of the Somme, the Royal Inniskilling Fusiliers had five battalions in action. They sustained total casualties as follows:[9]

1st Battalion – 549
2nd Battalion – 162
9th Battalion – 477
10th Battalion – 418
11th Battalion – 592

Whilst none of these casualties exceed that of the Inniskillings at Festubert, the collective effect on such a small geographic area of origin was understandably devastating.

Concerning the Battle of Festubert, in his 2009 book, 'Belfast Boys. How Unionists and Nationalists fought and died together in the First World War' Richard Grayson states that, 'the death toll for the battalion eventually reached 245 other ranks.'[10] From the author's own research, this is a conservative estimate. Utilising information gleaned from the Commonwealth War Graves Commission, and cross referencing it with the Soldiers Died in the Great War 1914-1919[11] details, 264 members of the battalion who were killed or died of wounds in the period 15-26 May have been positively identified.[12] In Mitchell and Smyth's (1931), The Official History of the War, Medical Services, Casualties and Medical Statistics, it is stated that throughout the First World War, the ratio of total killed to total wounded across all ranks was 1:5.19.[13] If we accept the total casualties as 649 and the number of dead at 265, the proportion of dead to wounded soldiers in this battle for the Inniskillings was a much more severe 1:2.44. This can be partly accounted for by the fact that as the war progressed beyond 1915, protective measures and battlefield medicine had advanced considerably, leading to a better chance of survival. However, it is of no consolation to the Inniskillings that in 1915 the British Army was still learning the art of trench warfare.

Of the 264 that research has identified as having been killed, the breakdown by company very much tells the story of the battle. It should be stated at the outset that research has not been able to positively match all of the fatalities to a particular company or role, but sufficient numbers have been identified to illustrate the course of events. It is probable that each rifle company would have gone into the battle with a strength of around 200. Of the two companies in the initial assault, A company, to the left of the cinder track sustained at least 81 identified fatalities. D company, who captured the German first and second lines, sustained at least 65 identified fatalities. B company supporting A company, sustained at least 39 fatalities and C company in support of D company suffered at least 21 fatalities. The machine gun section and bombing sections also suffered considerably.

Nevertheless, quoting figures of numbers of casualties does not illustrate the extent of personal suffering that took place. Not just for the soldiers themselves, but for their families waiting at home, dreading the knock on the door from the telegram boy or postman, for it was the case that officer's next of kin received a pro-forma telegram, whilst those of other ranks received a pro-forma letter, both from the War Office.[14] Or they were anxiously scanning newspaper articles and casualty lists in the newspapers to try and construct a picture of what had happened to their loved ones. It is the personal details and stories that best illustrate the Inniskillings' experiences of those crucial three days of May 1915. Whilst it is not possible for reasons of space to include biographical details of each of the Inniskillings killed, hopefully what follows will help to illustrate the background of those who made the ultimate sacrifice.

Within infantry battalions of the British Army the Company Serjeant Major, (CSM) is the senior non-commissioned officer attached to each of the companies. These were career soldiers, men who had joined probably as boy soldiers and had worked their way up through the ranks to a position of vital importance to the smooth running of the company. This ascent through the ranks earned them the respect of the other ranks within the company. A wise company commander trusted the judgement and advice of his serjeant major. In battle, whilst the company commander led his company by his side would be the serjeant major, exhorting the men to greater efforts, but always ready to dispense practical advice to the commander. This was a high-profile job, but in a battle situation one of the most dangerous as they led from the front. The exemplary dedication of the Inniskillings' CSMs is illustrated by the fact that three of the four were killed in the advance, a grievous loss to the battalion.

Company Serjeant Major Joseph Crilly was attached to A company, and typified the image of the experienced soldier. A Dublin man, he had 20 years' experience in the ranks and had received medals for his service in the Punjab, India in 1897 and had fought throughout the South African War in the Transvaal and the Orange Free State in 1902. Another Dublin man was D company's 33-year-old Company Serjeant Major Mervyn James Williams. A native of Blackrock, he left all his effects in his will to his younger sister Eleanor, who looked after his widowed father John.

Company Serjeant Major Mervyn Williams
(Image Courtesy of Nigel Henderson)

Londoner, Company Serjeant Major Alfred Ernest Jackson of B company was another soldier with 20 years' experience in the battalion, having also served in India and during the South African War.

None of the serjeant majors have a known grave, with all being commemorated on Le Touret Memorial to the Missing. In common with many of their subordinates, it may be the case that these serjeant majors were buried on the battlefield and their graves, marked or unmarked were later lost or destroyed by shellfire, as the ground the Inniskillings advanced over was contested until 1918. Two accounts exist which attest to this practice of battlefield burial. Soldiers of the Sirhind Brigade who relieved 5 Brigade commented:

> The dawn displayed a scene of complete desolation. Bodies, British, Indian and German – lay sprawled in the mud, trenches had collapsed and where they had not, parapets had been blown down or dug away. The carnage was made worse by British shelling having unearthed German makeshift graves. Bodies and bits of bodies in varying stages of decomposition added their cloying smell to that of the rotten overmanured mud, burnt lyddite and overflowing latrine pits. The HLI alone buried 104 bodies of a variety of nationalities and Regt's during the night of 18 May.[15]

On 19 May in a situation report to the 2nd Division, Brigadier General Lord Cavan of 4 Guards Brigade stated, 'One Company 3rd Coldstreams ordered up to bury dead about old British and first German line where work can be done by day.'[16]

Those Inniskillings killed had a wide age range. There were career soldiers such as those highlighted above who had seen the world and reservists who had experienced life outside the army before being recalled to the colours at the start of the war. There were also teenagers keen to take part in a great adventure. The oldest soldier identified as having been killed was 46-year-old Private John McGee[17] from Belleek, County Fermanagh. A member of A company, he had been in France for exactly a month to the day that he met his death. He was survived by his widow Maria. By contrast, three 17-year-olds lost their lives. Private John Armstrong was born in Lisburn, but prior to enlisting resided with his parents at Oldcastle, County Meath. He was attached to B company. Attached to D company was Private William McCreadie Stewart. The eldest son of John and Mary Stewart, he was from Newmarket Street in Coleraine, County Londonderry and was survived by two brothers and three sisters.

Attached to A company was the author's great uncle, James. Born in 1897, he was the fifth son of William and Sarah Nugent. He was born and brought up in the maze of close knit streets which run between the Shankill and Falls Roads close to Belfast city centre. As he was growing up, the home rule crisis dominated the political environment and with many of his contemporaries he was a signatory to the Ulster Covenant, signing on 28 September 1912 as a 15-year-old at the Albert Hall, which houses the Shankill Road Mission. A message boy prior to enlisting, he was killed three days before his 18th birthday having been at the front for six months. In all, five of William and Sarah's sons served, with James and his elder brother Robert being killed.[18] At first James was one of the many reported missing and it was a year of agonised waiting before the family had confirmation of his death. The notice below appeared in the *Belfast Evening Telegraph* of Monday, 22 May 1916:

NUGENT—Missing since the 16th May, 1915 (now reported killed), No. 11162, Pte. James Nugent, 2nd Royal Inniskilling Fusiliers, aged 18 years, dearly-beloved son of William and Sarah Nugent.
His warfare o'er, his battle fought;
His victory won, though dearly bought;
His fresh young life could not be saved,
He slumbers now in a soldier's grave.
Deeply regretted by his loving Father, Mother, Sisters, and Brothers.
31 Percy Street, Belfast.

(Image courtesy of Walter Millar)

All three 17-year-olds are commemorated on Le Touret Memorial to the Missing.

Across the battalion, death was no respecter of rank or social status. One of the first over the top with A company, leading his platoon was Second Lieutenant Lionel St George Mordaunt-Smith. He was the eldest son of a prominent military and banking family from Rugby in Warwickshire. After his father's death, his mother remarried a Major Mathew, who was attached to the Inniskillings 4th Battalion. Educated at Elstree school and Charterhouse public school, he entered the Royal Military Academy, Sandhurst in 1913, being commissioned as a second lieutenant in the Inniskillings in October 1914. He joined A company of the battalion in November 1914. A report in *The Times* roll of honour stated, 'he was killed leading his platoon in the charge against the German trenches, which he almost reached and died heroically.'[19] Second Lieutenant Mordaunt-Smith was killed three weeks after his 19th birthday. In common with the majority of his men, he has no known grave. He is commemorated on Le Touret Memorial to the Missing and also on the Laugharne War Memorial, Carmarthenshire, Wales, where his mother and stepfather were residing. Many other 19-year-olds within the ranks also lost their lives. One of them, attached to B company was Private Richard Anderson who prior to enlisting lived at Edith Street, East Belfast. He had joined the battalion in France on 14 May – 2 days before his death.

2nd Lieutenant Lionel St G Mordaunt-Smith (Image courtesy of De Ruvigny's Roll of Honour)

As the military authorities followed strict protocols to definitely establish the fate of a soldier before notifying the next of kin, numerous cases arose where colleagues with good intention, ended up unwittingly being the bearers of devastating news. One such case was that of Private Joseph McCart, attached to A company, of High Street in Gilford, County Down. On 26 May, Mrs McCart received a letter from a colleague of her husband Lance Corporal Fred Lindsay, stating that, Joseph had been wounded on 15 May and had died on 16 May. By the middle of June, no official confirmation of his death had been received, evidenced by a *Belfast Newsletter* article about Joseph and his siblings serving at the front which indicated that 'a third son, Joseph McCart, Royal Inniskilling Fusiliers, who was unofficially reported killed in action last month has not been heard of since.'[20] The anguish of Mrs McCart, who had two children under the age of six, can only be imagined.

Not surprisingly given the mayhem of the battle, in very few cases does an account exist of a death having being witnessed. The death of B company's Private William Dickson from Derrygortrevy, Dungannon, County Tyrone, who had previously written to the local press outlining his experiences, was witnessed by two of his colleagues. Private John Johnston of the Inniskillings machine gun section in a letter to a friend describing the battle stated, 'Of course it meant the loss of some brave men, but when the Germans saw the steel, it was enough for them. I never saw the like of the fighting, and I hope I never will again. I was actually talking to Dickson when he fell, hit by a shell, which went on and burst about 200 yards distant.'[21] Also close enough to witness the death was Lance Corporal John McIntyre, who stated in a letter to his mother, 'We were lucky as nearly all the regiment were killed. Young Dickson was killed and Joe Cunningham is wounded. Joe and I may be home in a month or so. Young Dickson was killed beside me, and I took a wee box from him to bring home to his mother.'[22] In this tragic case similar to that of Private McCart above, the situation arose that the letters sent home by well-meaning colleagues reached Dungannon before any official notification that Private Dickson was in fact a casualty. The *Mid Ulster Mail* article went on to report:

> On hearing of the intimation, Rev TJ McEndoo MA visited the house and broke the sorrowful news to the parents. Mr Dickson afterwards wired for information to the War Office and received a reply that the name did not appear in the casualty list furnished. This was some consolation, but it is feared that the information contained in the two letters may be accurate.[23]

The information was accurate, with the family receiving official notification from the War Office on 31 May 1915. Private Dickson is another with no known grave. In addition to Le Touret Memorial, he is commemorated on the family headstone at Castlecaulfield, County Tyrone.

In addition to describing the death of Private Dickson, Private Johnston also touched on the losses suffered by the machine gun section:

> We lost our Machine Gun Officer and all the men, so I am now full corporal, having got the second stripe in the field.[24]

The officer referred to was Lieutenant Ralph William Gore Hinds, killed whilst advancing with the machine gun section to support the gains made by D company. Lieutenant Hinds was the eldest son of Lieutenant Colonel William Hinds, a retired surgeon from the Royal Army Medical Corps. Born at Kildare in 1891, by 1905 the Hinds family resided at Royal Terrace, Kingstown, County Dublin. Ralph was educated at St Columba's College Rathfarnham, Dublin and then by private tutor, before entering the Royal Military Academy Sandhurst in 1910. He was commissioned as a 2nd Lieutenant in the 2nd Battalion Royal Inniskilling Fusiliers in March 1911. A young man with an interest in all things mechanical and with a strong sense of adventure, in October 1913 he attended the Great Britain Royal Aero Club school at Brooklands, where he attained a certificate of competence in flying, piloting a Bristol biplane.[25] He applied for and was selected for the embryonic Royal Flying Corps, pending successful completion of a course of instruction at the central flying school. On 12 June 1914 however, he withdrew his application citing private reasons. It is possible that with war looming on the horizon, he realised that he was better off with his colleagues in the battalion. He was appointed machine gun officer before the battalion left for France and remained in that post until his death. He was certainly highly regarded within the battalion and he received a 'Mention in Despatches' on 5 April 1915. Following his death a fellow officer commented:

> When I was wounded at the Aisne he came out under heavy fire and bound my wound up and helped to carry me to the dressing station. No-one could have shown greater devotion than he did. During the whole time I knew him, he was the keenest man I ever served under in work and in sport.[26]

Lieutenant Hinds was also a close friend of Lieutenant Alexander the transport officer who, in a letter to his mother on 19 May described how, 'Poor old Hinds got killed on Sunday doing well…… I was more sorry about Hinds than anyone else as he was my best friend in the Regiment.'[27]

Unlike many of his colleagues, it is believed that Lieutenant Hinds does have a grave, however, the location of it was disputed and was the subject of correspondence between Lieutenant Hinds' father and the War Office. On 17 May 1915, the family received the standard pro forma telegram from the War Office with the following text:

> Deeply regret to inform you that Lt RWG Hinds, Royal Inniskilling Fusiliers reported killed in action 15th to 16th May. Lord Kitchener expresses his sympathy.[28]

On 9 September, Lieutenant Colonel Hinds received a letter from the War Office indicating that Lieutenant RWG Hinds was buried in a small cemetery at Orchard

Farm, Givenchy. However, this contradicted information already forwarded to Lieutenant Colonel Hinds by the Headquarters Graves Commission (forerunner of the Commonwealth War Graves Commission), on 23 August 1915, which stated that Lieutenant Hinds had been buried at Richebourg L'Avoue, south of Rue Du Bois. In his reply, quite reasonably Lieutenant Colonel Hinds stated, 'As Orchard Farm, Givenchy stated in your memo is some distance from Richebourg L'Avoue, Rue Du Bois, I shall feel obliged if you will kindly inform me, which is correct?[29] On 6 October a reply was received which stated that the exact location is, 'Richebourg L'Avoue south of Rue du Bois (West of Cinder path).[30] This meant that the grave was on the battlefield, although Lieutenant Colonel Hinds may not have been aware of this. It is now believed that Lieutenant Hinds is buried in the Guards Cemetery, Windy Corner, Cuinchy. This cemetery contains the graves of four identified Inniskillings from the battle and a number who have not been identified, these gravestones being inscribed with the regimental crest and the inscription, 'A soldier of the Great War, Royal Inniskilling Fusiliers.'[31] Beneath the crest is inscribed, 'known unto God.' There are 3,444 graves at Windy Corner, 2,198 of whom are not identified.[32] This is due to the fact that over 2,500 bodies were brought to Windy Corner cemetery for interment after the war from smaller cemeteries in the surrounding area and from graves on the battlefield itself. It appears that this was the case with Lieutenant Hinds. The author had the opportunity to visit Lieutenant Hinds' grave in March 2014. The headstone bears the inscription, 'believed to be buried in this cemetery', which gives rise to some ambiguity still existing over the exact location of the grave.

The Hinds family were fortunate on two counts. Firstly, that Lieutenant Colonel Hinds was a military man and was aware of military systems and the administrative processes. He knew where to go to get the right answers to his questions. This could be contrasted with the Dickson family mentioned above who were able to send a telegram to the War Office, but had no other means of finding out any details save waiting for the witnesses, Lance Corporal McIntyre and Private Johnston to contact them, if and when they returned from the front. Secondly, the Hinds family were fortunate that their son was an officer. Throughout the British Army there was roughly one officer to every 40 other ranks. This made it manageable to focus on obtaining details of officers. In keeping with the circumstances of the time, class and social standing also decided how much effort was put into dealing with death in action and subsequent provision of information and assistance.

Photograph of Lt Hinds courtesy of De Ruvigny's Roll of Honour.
Photograph of headstone from Author's collection.

One example of this is how the personal effects of those deceased soldiers were dealt with. All soldiers on active service completed a will to take effect on their death and numerous examples of these still exist. The will of Private Richard Anderson, mentioned above states, 'In the event of my death I give the whole of my property and effects to my cousin, Mrs Kate Mulholland, 18 Edith Street.'[33] In reality, property and effects related to items that were left at home. For the soldier in the ranks, the army provided everything in terms of clothing and equipment, so personal items were few and may have consisted of photographs of family, a pocket bible or some other personal mementoes. As in the case of Private Dickson above, these would have been despatched in the post by comrades or physically brought home by colleagues when going on leave.

For deceased officers, however, a company was contracted to deal with personal effects. It should be remembered that officers paid for their own uniform and personal equipment, so perhaps it is justifiable that this facility was established. Cox's shipping agency of Charing Cross, London were engaged by the army to ensure that all equipment and personal effects were returned to officers' next of kin. It is not surprising that given the importance of the task, it was dealt with

with great care and precision. The officers field kit itself was quite comprehensive, as this War Office directive illustrates:

> *Every officer must provide himself in England before departure with the following articles:-*
>
> *Compass, Haversack, Cup, Mess tin, Electric torch and refills, Water bottle, Binoculars or telescope, Pistol, Blankets, Map case, Whistle*
>
> *These may be obtained on payment from the Army Ordnance Department, if they are available, by application through the unit to which the officer belongs or is attached. He must in addition purchase privately:-*
>
> *Great-coat or coat (warm British), Waterproof, Canvas bucket or enamel basin, Grease or vaseline, Soap, Holdall containing knife, fork, and spoon, Housewife, Hairbrush and comb, Valise, Tooth brush, Towel, Shaving brush, Spare pair of boots, Razor, Khaki clothing, Clasp knife, Shirts and Underclothing, Luminous watch (preferably of railway guard pattern)*
>
> *Eiderdowns or a sleeping bag may be taken instead of blankets, and an Army Correspondence Book and Field Service note-book should be in every officer's possession.*
>
> *The only camp kit that is absolutely necessary for all theatres of war is a rubber or canvas bath, and for all theatres except France, a bed. A few articles of additional kit are laid down for those proceeding to Salonika, Mesopotamia, and Egypt.*[34]

The articles which the officer was not using immediately in the attack would be packed into a valise – a large folding suitcase and would have been collected by the battalion for storage. In addition to this equipment, personal items were also conscientiously itemised for return to the next of kin. In the case of D company's Second Lieutenant John Morgan, commissioned from the ranks of the 1st Battalion Royal Irish Rifles in November 1914 and killed on 16 May 1915, the effects consisted of the following:

Prayer book -1, Tobacco Box-1, Cigarette Cases – 2, Compass-1, Nail clippers-1,

Badges,Collar-2, Stud-1, Pocket Case-1, Whistle-1, Scissors, folding-1, Fountain pen-1, Pipe-1, Rosary-1, Wrist watch-1, Clasp knife-1, Notebook-1 containing 2 1/2d stamps, photo-1, religious charms. Two pence English, One Franc 65 Cents French. Handkerchiefs – 2, Links, silver-1[35]

Telegram notifying death of 2nd Lieutenant John Morgan
(Image courtesy of National Archives, WO 339/18920)

The greatest contrast between officers and men, however, related to efforts to elicit information of those who were missing. The efforts carried out by and on behalf of those of high social standing, bear little resemblance to those of the working class. Not that there was anything wrong with this. Everyone, no matter what class, who had lost a family member did everything in their power to discover what had happened, it was just that those with more resources – both financial and through social contacts, were able to make more comprehensive efforts. The local newspapers of June and July 1915 contained many appeals such as that relating to Private Robert Beattie highlighted at the beginning of the chapter, in every edition:

- Every effort to trace Private Hugh John Cairns, 4354, 2nd Inniskillings, who has been missing since the engagement at Festubert on 16th May, has failed. His sister, Miss Minnie Cairns, Sandy Row, Coalisland, is very anxious for news of him.
- Unofficial news is to hand that Pte Alfred Campbell, 2nd Inniskillings was killed in action on May 16th at Richebourg. No confirmation is obtainable from the War Office and the man's mother who resides at 4 Connswater St, Belfast, would be glad to hear from anyone who could give her any information.
- News is urgently required as to the fate of Pte John Archer, 2nd Inniskillings of whom nothing has been heard since 13th May. His whereabouts is unknown to the War Office, and his father, Mr T Archer of 56 Turin St, Belfast would be grateful for any information concerning him.
- News is urgently awaited as to the fate of Pte Joseph Henry, 2354, 2nd Inniskillings, who was reported missing after the engagement at Festubert on 16th May. His parents, who reside at 5 Spinner Sq. Belfast, would be glad to hear from anyone who could give information about their son.
- Mrs McNulty, 16 Fulton Place, Derry, will be grateful for any information regarding her husband, Pte Robert McNulty, 2nd Inniskillings, who has been posted as missing since May.
- Mrs Porter, 111 Sugarfield Street, Belfast anxiously awaits news of her husband, Pte Thomas Porter 6567, 2nd Inniskillings who was reported missing on 16th May and has not been heard of since. Porter was a reservist, employed at Milford Weaving Company, and a member of West Belfast UVF.[36]

In reality, for these working class relatives of missing soldiers, the first intimation they would have had that anything was amiss would be the lack of letters from the front, perhaps accompanied by coverage in the local press of the involvement of the battalion in a battle. If their loved one's name did not appear in the casualty lists and no letters were received from comrades, the next option was to contact the War Office by telegram as is indicated in some of the instances highlighted. The last option was to publish an appeal such as those above, in the hope that some fellow soldier may have some information as to their fate. The agony of waiting and not knowing must have been unbearable, but for those of limited resources and means, there was nothing else to do but wait, in the hope that some information would be forthcoming.

Even for those with a ready source of information within the battalion, there were difficulties in obtaining tangible evidence. One such case was that of 19-year-old Corporal Henry Sidney Victor Donaldson, attached to D company. The son of Nixon Donaldson, the Royal Irish Constabulary Sergeant in Dungannon, he was a young man with a promising career ahead having achieved two promotions in the year since he had enlisted. He had been in France just over a month before the battle, but he had family connections in the battalion, his uncle, Serjeant Robert Le Gear, being attached to B company. Following the battle and in the absence of any official confirmation, the responsibility to find information fell on Serjeant Le Gear. This must have been an onerous task for him due to the post battle confusion and the physical state of the battlefield, weighed against the expectation of the family for him to produce answers. In a moving letter to his sister, he tried to prepare the family for the inevitable:

I have put off writing to you for the last few days hoping against hope for good news, but you must be prepared for the worst. You no doubt have heard of the great charge of the Inniskillings, and the taking of several lines of trenches which has crowned the Regiment with glory. The taking of these well-fortified positions by us entailed a number of killed and wounded, but amongst the lists at HQ I can find no account of Sidney. Now don't grieve, for if he has fallen in the glorious charge he has died a noble death in defence of the Empire and the glorious cause we are fighting for. I may be able to let you know fuller particulars in a few days, but up to the present he is down as missing. He may have gone up with the first batch of wounded, or he may be mixed up with other battalions, which would account for him not being able to join his own for several days. I am still hoping for the best. I am sorry I was not near him to see him through. The battle is still raging all along the line and the Germans are beginning to learn the kind of men who make up General French's contemptible little army.[37]

All the efforts of his uncle, at the front and with intimate knowledge of military systems came to nothing and seven weeks after the battle the following notice appeared in the *Belfast News Letter*:

Corporal HVS Donaldson, 2nd Battalion Inniskillings, son of Sgt Donaldson, RIC Mark Street, Dungannon, is stated in the latest casualty list to be missing. He could not be traced after the severe fighting at Festubert, where the Inniskillings gained so much credit, although his uncle, Sgt Le Gear, of the same Battalion, made every enquiry about him on the spot.[38]

No trace of Corporal Donaldson was found and he is commemorated on Le Touret Memorial to the Missing and on both Dungannon War Memorial and at St Anne's Church of Ireland, Dungannon. If the family of Corporal Donaldson with their connections to the battalion were unable to find closure, how much more difficult was it for those with no such access?

For those at the other end of the social scale – those with influence and access – although their anxiety was no greater, there were further steps that could be taken. In the immediate aftermath of the battle, there were conflicting accounts of the fate of Lieutenant John Houghton Stewart.[39] As early as 21 May his father Major George Powell Stewart, the commandant of the Inniskillings depot in Omagh, County Tyrone, received a pro forma telegram from the War Office stating, 'Regret to inform you that 2 Lt JH Stewart, Inniskilling Fusiliers was wounded 17 May. Further news when received will be wired.'[40] At that time that was also the view of his friend and colleague Lieutenant Alexander, who in a letter to his mother dated 19 May commenting on the battle stated, 'John S was wounded, but I know no more about him, but hope to tell you more when I hear.'[41] Four days later and with no further news, Lieutenant Alexander, obviously feeling some responsibility, revisited the issue when again writing to his mother. 'I cannot write to Col George Stewart as I have no news of his son but everything is being done to find out. I fear he is missing, it is very awkward not being able to write, but tomorrow I will have to write something.'[42] As time passed with still no concrete information, Lieutenant Alexander began to hint at other possibilities, 'No word of the missing officers. There is just a chance that Wingate and John Stewart might have been taken prisoner, but I'm sure the others must be killed.'[43]

Meanwhile, the family had not been idle. On 2 June 1915, Lieutenant Colonel Stewart wrote to the War Office as follows:

My son Lt JH Stewart 2nd Royal Inniskilling Fusiliers was reported as wounded and missing from the Battalion on May 16th 1915. The action I believe took place in the vicinity of Richebourg L'Avoue at which place the 2nd Royal Innis.

Fus. attacked and occupied the German trenches. As nothing has since been heard of 2nd Lt JH Stewart, I have the honour to request that enquiries may be made through the American Embassy in case he may be a prisoner of war.[44]

In order to emphasise the importance of the request, the details of the person making the enquiry were given on the official form as, Brigadier General Sir Hugh H Stewart, 77 Brigade, 26th Division, Sutton Veny, Wiltshire. This was Lieutenant Stewart's uncle, the 4th Baronet of Athenree, Co Tyrone. The reply from the Germans was returned on 16 August, indicating that they had no details of Lieutenant Stewart.

Whilst this request for information was taking its course, it appears that an enquiry was taking place within the battalion to establish who had last seen Lieutenant Stewart. Two statements exist from soldiers who claimed to have sighting information of the lieutenant during the attack. The first dated 16 July was from a Private Alec Birkett, who at the time was recovering from wounds at a hospital in Worcester. It stated, 'Informant saw this officer wounded on the 15th of May and he was left between the English and German lines.'[45] The second statement was taken on 19 July and the informant was a Private Greer attached to B company. He stated, 'He was wounded in the breast on May 16th and was carried in on a stretcher by Sgt Daley at midnight.'[46] Whilst it is certain the motivation of both soldiers was sound, neither statement added much to information already known.

Second Lieutenant John H Stewart and the photo of his sister Mary, recovered from the battlefield.
(Images courtesy of the National Archives, WO 339/22949)

On 19 July, the search for information concerning the fate of Lieutenant Stewart took a remarkable twist. *The Daily Sketch* – a nationwide tabloid daily newspaper, published photographs found in a pocket bible recovered from the Festubert battlefield by a Private Bell, 4th Seaforth Highlanders. The bible had Lieutenant Stewart's name inscribed and pictures were identified as that of Lieutenant Stewart's mother and his 15-year-old sister, Mary.

Contact was established between the family and the Seaforths, at that time still on active service in France and on 21 August, Private Bell replied to a letter from Lieutenant Colonel Stewart. In the letter he described in detail how on the night of 23 May, he had been detailed as part of a burial party bringing in the dead from the attack of 15/16 May. He described finding the body believed to be that of Lieutenant Stewart as follows:

The soldier was lying face downwards in a small shell hole where he had probably taken cover, and I think that while there he must have been hit by shrapnel, the head and one arm being badly wounded. I think the poor fellow must have been instantaneously killed.[47] He went on to state, *I am uncertain as to whether the body was that of an officer or not, he wore no equipment whereas the others I buried did, and he had no cap on. I buried him myself just where he had fallen.*[48]

At this stage Private Bell must have thought that this was the end of the matter, and he may at some stage have contemplated whether it might have been better to bury the bible with the body. For it was now that Lieutenant Colonel Stewart, in an effort to obtain closure, began to exercise his influence backed by his wealth. The final lines of Private Bell's statement created uncertainty and in a letter to the War Office in October 1915, Lieutenant Colonel Stewart outlined the action he had taken:

I have the honour to state:- In the Daily Sketch of July 19th 1915 appeared the enclosed copy of a photograph of my daughter. In a paragraph of the paper it was stated that the photo along with another of my wife was found in a bible on the battlefield with my son's name inside. The bible was found by a Private Lewis Bell, 4th Seaforth Highlanders and is now in my possession. I succeeded in getting into communication with Pte Bell and have since obtained leave from his CO at Fort George, paid for his journey over from Scotland and had him here to interrogate. He was unable to give me any further information other than what is contained in his letter. . . . . . The little pocket bible I identify as belonging to my son, Lt John Houghton Stewart, Royal Inniskilling Fusiliers.[49]

At that time, and perhaps influenced by the strong Stewart family regimental connections, the 2nd Inniskillings were still trying to confirm the exact fate of Lieutenant Stewart. On 24 October, the by then captain and adjutant of the battalion, Charles Alexander, took a statement on the subject from Acting Serjeant Lee, who on the night of the battle was a Lance Corporal in the platoon commanded by Lieutenant Stewart. His statement below, largely corroborates the details given by Private Bell and in itself is a valuable detailed account of D company's advance:

At Richebourg on the night of 15th/16th May, 1915, I was Lance Corporal in charge of No 6 Section, 14 Platoon, D Company. Lieutenant Stewart was commanding No 14 Platoon. At 11.30 pm, the charge started, my Company advanced in column of Platoons, No 13 Platoon leading, followed by No 14 Platoon about 30 yards behind. Bayonets were fixed, and each platoon extended to 3 paces. I was near Lt Stewart with the other NCO's just behind the platoon – No 13 Platoon occupied the first line of German breastworks and were immediately reinforced by No 14 Platoon – the distance we had advanced was about 350 yards – it was very dark, the only light being from flares. Lieut. Stewart was alright on arrival at this first German line – and was alright when I saw him about 12.10 am. At about 1230am I received a verbal message from Stewar? As follows, 'To OC D Company- think the enemy are enfilading our left flank.' I passed on the message and also sent back to find out was the message from Lt Stewart or from Captain and Adjutant GRV Steward. I ascertained this message was from Lt Stewart. About 1am, Lt Stewart was with the left section of the platoon and I myself was with the section on his right. I saw him fall. I was about eight yards away, about 5 bombs fell around the place where he fell. The Section eased off to the left and right at this spot. About this time the right half of the Company advanced under Captain Hewitt and took the enemy's second line. The enemy's breastworks were not a continuous line and the sections near where I was were unable to advance. Soon after this the Sections near me were ordered to move to their right. I had to go with my section, so was unable to go to the left to see about Lt Stewart whom I never saw again. I am the only NCO of No 14 Platoon who returned unwounded.[50]

With all this information and personal accounts to hand, it was still not until March 1916 that the War Office confirmed his death, stating, 'This officer was reported Wounded, no date, and Wounded and Missing, no date. On the strength of unofficial reports which have been received, it has been decided to accept for official purposes that his death occurred in action at Richebourg L'Avoue on 15th/16th May 1915.'[51]

The family appear to have accepted his fate earlier following the details provided by Private Bell and Acting Serjeant Lee. In memoriam services were held jointly in Lieutenant Stewart's memory on Monday 1 November 1915 at the family church, St Saviour's Grainville, Jersey, where the family pew was draped in black and at Carrickmore, Co. Tyrone, where the family attended.[52] The grave of Lieutenant John Houghton Stewart was never found and he is commemorated on Le Touret Memorial to the Missing and on the family memorial in St Saviour's Churchyard, Jersey. Such was the grief felt by Lieutenant Stewart's family, that no details of his fate were ever mentioned in the family circle whilst his parents were still alive.

Apart from the obvious priority of trying to establish the fate of a loved one, obtaining confirmation of a death also had important legal and financial considerations for the next of kin. Unbelievably, and further indication of the British nation's unpreparedness for war, there were no statutory pension provisions for soldiers' dependants until 1919. Prior to this pensions were discretionary. Before 1919 and as the war progressed, however, provision was made so that an individual's circumstances could be addressed. It was only from 1917 that parents and siblings who were dependants were eligible for a pension and again this was at the discretion of the War Office. Widows and dependent children may also have been eligible for a gratuity to meet expenses incurred following a soldier's death. This amounted to £5 for the widow of a soldier in the ranks and £1 for each child.

When a married man enlisted, he was given the opportunity to remit a proportion of his pay to his wife and family. This continued until it was replaced by a widow's allowance, unless he was reported missing. In that case, his pay was suspended pending clarification of his situation. If he was reported as a prisoner of war, his pay was reinstated from the day he went missing. Yet again, there were separate rules for officers and men, as officers who went missing who had dependants, could have their pay continued for up to three months. However, the onus to obtain continuing pay was somewhat unfairly placed on the wife or dependants. The procedure to be followed was outlined in the press on May 25

1915 as follows:

> *Steps to be taken by wives or dependants – To enable the War Office to decide the period for which pay is issuable under the above arrangements, it is necessary for wives or dependants of missing officers, on becoming aware that an officer is missing, to submit without delay applications on the appropriate forms which, when completed, should be sent to the Assistant Financial Secretary (F3) War Office.* [53]

Being reported as 'missing' then was the worst possible situation for the families of soldiers in the ranks and led to many cases of hardship for those with dependants.

Where a soldier had left a will, it eased the burden for relatives, as they had a legal document to enable them to sort out their financial affairs. However, where there was no will or it had been lost, there were additional difficulties for the next of kin to firstly prove eligibility before even considering applying for a pension. One such case was that of Private Robert Beattie, D company, highlighted at the beginning of this chapter. He was reported as 'missing in action' in the aftermath of the battle of Festubert. On 22 September 1916 – 16 months later, his mother was required to complete a form forwarded by the War Office to prove eligibility to his estate. The form presupposed that a statement had been made at some stage by the deceased regarding the disposal of his effects and addressed three questions to his mother:

1. *Exactly on what date and at what place the statement referred to was made by the deceased?*
2. *The exact words used by him in making the statement?*
3. *The full names and addresses of any persons other than yourself who were present at the time and heard the statement made.* [54]

The completed form then had to be signed by the applicant and the witness and the signatures verified by a professional person such as a doctor, or in the case of Robert Beattie, a Justice of the Peace. It is clear that the completion of this form was designed to assist and benefit families, but expecting a grieving relative to remember verbatim a conversation – in the case of Robert Beattie two-and-a-half years earlier, appears somewhat harsh.

It appeared to have been the case that the details of financial benefits were not widely understood and when the numbers of soldiers being killed every day throughout the war is taken into consideration, it was inevitable that cases of genuine hardship occurred.

One such case involved the next of kin of B company's Lieutenant Edward John White Abbott. Lieutenant Abbott had joined the Inniskillings 4th battalion in March 1908 and had been on secondment to the Royal Irish Fusiliers, returning to the Inniskillings 2nd battalion at the beginning of May. He was posted as missing following the battle leaving a wife Fanny and a son John aged one. By July 1915, nothing further had been heard and his wife who had already made contact with the financial secretary at the War Office regarding his pay as highlighted in the procedure above, felt obliged to put pen to paper again to highlight her predicament:

I hear from Cox' that they have not received my husband's pay since he was missing, May 15th. Would you see about this for me as I have only £1-0-0 left in the bank. I filled in the form you sent me over a week ago. If my husband has been killed do I get a grant from the government? Would you be good enough to answer this question?[55]

This enquiry proved successful as it was agreed to credit the bank account with pay for the period 18 May to 17 August 1915. In this period, enquiries took place within the battalion to ascertain Lieutenant Abbott's fate. Two separate reports from soldiers in the battalion taken in July indicated that he was killed by machine gun fire at the German wire. It was not until February 1916, however, that the War Office concluded in a document to assist in dealing with the estates of officers, 'that Lieutenant Abbott is dead, and his death occurred on or since the 17th May 1915.'[56]

Further assistance was to hand for Lieutenant Abbot's widow. In a display of solidarity which exemplifies the loyalty and close ties within the regiment, Lieutenant Abbott's original commanding officer, Lieutenant Colonel Kinsman of 4th Inniskillings made an ultimately successful application to the War Office, that Lieutenant Abbott's widow be awarded the enhanced pension due to a captain's widow, citing the fact that Lieutenant Abbott was the senior lieutenant in the battalion and that others junior to him had since been promoted to captain. In the case of Lieutenant Abbott's widow, the fact that he was posted as missing and his death not confirmed for seven months appeared to slow the process. This can be contrasted with the case of the dependents of 2nd Lieutenant John Morgan, whose death in hospital in Bethune was confirmed on 16 May. The pension for his widow Maude, was finalised as early as 21 June 1915, with the award of a yearly pension of £80 and a gratuity of £10.[57]

Whilst the vast majority of the Inniskillings who made the ultimate sacrifice were killed outright, or succumbed to their wounds before rescue on the battlefield, a total of eight soldiers entered the military medical chain, but subsequently died of their wounds in the week following the battle. Looking at the locations of their deaths gives some indication of the efficiency of the Royal Army Medical Corps effort to support the troops on the front line. On 17 May, 28-year-old Private David Finlay, from Seaview Street in Belfast, an iron worker in Belfast shipyard prior to enlisting, died of his wounds having been treated at the military hospital in Bethune, some six miles from the front line and was buried in Bethune Town Cemetery. On the same date, 20-year-old Private Michael Lawn, before the war a mill worker and talented footballer from Cookstown, County Tyrone, died of his wounds at Lillers, a small town 13 miles behind the front line which was used extensively by a number of casualty clearing stations throughout the war. He was buried in Lillers communal cemetery. On 25 May, some 70 miles behind the lines at Le Touquet on the French coast, 18-year-old Private John O'Farrell, prior to the war a farm labourer from Tullyniskane, Coalisland, County Tyrone, succumbed to his wounds. John O'Farrell died in one of the more unusual medical establishments. Officially called No 1 British Red Cross Hospital, it was known as the Duchess of Westminster's, as it had been established at the start of the war by the Duchess and some aristocratic lady friends who felt the need to do something to help. The hospital itself was housed in a former casino and the duchess and her friends having no medical expertise busied themselves by collecting details of the wounded. They utilised their talents to ensure that the morale of the men was kept up. This included greeting new arrivals in full evening dress, including tiaras and jewellery no matter what time of the day and with gramophones playing the latest tunes. The duchess also did rounds of the wards accompanied by her Irish wolfhound. To the soldiers just out of the hell of battle, it must have seemed like a different world. It can only be hoped that John O'Farrell was able to experience some comfort there in his last days. He is buried in the nearby Le Touquet Paris Plage communal cemetery.

For some of those wounded, a period in hospital was only a brief respite from the horrors of war. However, the tone of a letter sent by Private John Lynn, a neighbour of Private John O'Farrell in Coalisland to his parents some days after the battle, suggests a keenness to re-join the fray:

I am at present in a convalescent home, I got wounded in the head and back during the heavy fighting on Saturday and Sunday by a shell bursting on the edge of the trench, partly falling in on me. I had a narrow escape. They sent me to hospital, and they are all filled up, but I hope to be all right again and back with my Regiment... The fighting going on is very hot, and will be for some time until we get the enemy beaten back, and it will take beating to do it, and every man will be needed, but they will have to be beaten sooner or later, and the sooner the better.[58]

With so many men casualties and missing, the priority was to get the battalion up to active strength again as the period of rest and reorganisation was finite. On 21 May, the Inniskillings received replacements of one officer and 119 other ranks. In addition, Lieutenant Alexander received a temporary promotion to captain and was appointed adjutant. Lieutenant Cox became the new machine gun officer.

On the same date, Brigadier General Chichester, commander 5 Brigade, forwarded a report to 2nd Division Headquarters, which summarised the events of 15-17 May and highlighted issues of concern which were detrimental to further success. Chief among these was the performance by the artillery. In a scathing paragraph he stated:

Artillery fire was often inaccurate. This may have been due to indifferent climatic conditions and difficulty in observing effect of fire. But these conditions were not bad enough to cause losses to our own troops through shells falling in our original trenches and some as far back as the Rue du Bois. I received constant and daily reports of this bad shooting, and besides there were a considerable number of prematures. I consider there is nothing that so adversely affects the morale of troops as being shot at by their own artillery, and it is most urgent that more care is taken.[59]

According to Brigadier General Chichester, even though the attack had been delayed to allow for better weather conditions, the weather yet again played a part, and gives some idea of the conditions the Inniskillings had to contend with:

The wet weather made operations most difficult and progress along the trenches was very slow on account of the mud which in parts was 2 feet deep, and the rifles were clogged with it.' On the use of fixed bayonets at night, he commented, 'When fixed at night they glint in the light of flares. It would be better if they were blued or otherwise coloured.[60]

The full report of Brigadier General Chichester can be found at Appendix V.[61]

This view of the courage and initiative shown by the Inniskillings was shared by the recipient of the report, Major General Horne, officer commanding 2nd Division, who visited Burbure on the afternoon of 22 May and inspected the battalion, addressing them as follows:

Captain Crawford, officers, NCO's and men of the 2nd Battalion Royal Inniskilling Fusiliers – I have come here today just to say how proud I am of you and of the manner in which you charged across that bullet swept plain to the German trenches on the night of the 15th. From your name in the past it is only what I expected of the Inniskillings. I am indeed proud to have you in my Division. I came here to tell you so, and not only am I proud of you, but General French and your Corps commander are also, and your country has every reason to be.[62]

Over the next few days other complimentary messages were forwarded to the battalion and read to the men on parade by Captain Crawford. One was from Sir Douglas Haig to the Commander 5 Brigade:

General Sir Douglas Haig, KCB,KCIE,KCVO,ADC, General Commanding 1st Army has personally desired me to thank all ranks of the 5th Infantry Bde for their great gallantry and hard work during the recent operations, which although they did not result in any great gain of country, had other far reaching effects and achieved important results. The thanks of General Joffre have also been sent to the 1st Army for the way in which they have drawn the enemy's troops away from other parts, thus enabling the French to carry out plans which could not otherwise have been successful. Signed, AA Chichester Brig Gen, Commanding 5th Infantry Bde.[63]

Another message, which probably meant more to the men, was from the colonel of the regiment and recalled his rousing speech to them on Christmas Day 1914, which for those who had survived unscathed from that time, must have seemed like a long time ago:

Lt General Sir Archibald Murray, KCB, KCMG, CVO, DSO, Colonel of the Royal Inniskilling Fusiliers, has asked me to convey to the battalion his satisfaction at the manner in which they carried out the attack on the German trenches at Richebourg on 15th-16th May. He is convinced that the success was alone achieved by the gallantry and determination of all ranks to push forward at any cost. He is gratified to know that his address to them last Christmas day has borne fruit.[64]

On 24 May, Major General Sir Charles Munro, Officer Commanding I Corps visited Captain Crawford and passed on his congratulations on the battalion's performance on 15/16 May.

Quite what the men thought of these platitudes has not been recorded, but in the circumstances where well over half the battalion had become casualties, a few well-meaning words from remote generals would have done little to console.

The battalion, despite being the most successful of all the 5 Brigade battalions and suffering the most grievous losses, was not overly represented in the award of medals for gallantry. Whilst the awards of the Distinguished Conduct Medal – second only to the Victoria Cross for Warrant Officers and NCOs, was awarded to three – Serjeant McFarland, Acting Serjeant Hollinger and Corporal McNeill of the RAMC, there were no awards of the Military Cross for bravery carried out by officers, which is somewhat surprising given the high attrition rate and the obvious bravery of all the young officers who fell.[65] Captain Crawford, who commanded the battalion in the absence of Lieutenant Colonel Wilding, was promoted to major within the month. His stewardship of the battalion through the battle in all likelihood being a contributory factor.

As mentioned earlier, the first inkling many relatives would have had of the involvement of their loved ones in a battle would have been through the press. The leading national newspapers would have had military correspondents such as Lieutenant Colonel Repington, *The Times* correspondent whose reporting initiated the 1915 munitions crisis. Other national dailies had special correspondents, such as Percival Philips of the *Daily Express*, one of only five journalists accredited by the War Office. Percival Philips' work was then syndicated to other newspapers by agreement. One paper receiving Philips' work 'exclusively', was the *Belfast Evening Telegraph.*

There was great rivalry between the printed papers of the time, as that was the only way of getting information to a mass audience. The tone of reporting too had to be responsible, whilst portraying the actions of the British forces exclusively in a positive light. At this stage of the war the British public, having initially been under the misapprehension that the war would be over by Christmas 1914, were keen for good news stories, which the newspapers were only too glad to give them. This jingoistic reporting led to some problems, as frequently what was reported as an astounding success later turned out to be anything but. This accuracy was obviously influenced by the reticence of the War Office to have more than five accredited journalists and it would have been impressed upon these journalists that their continued access was dependent on supporting the War Office view. Any negative reporting was definitely not encouraged. The newspapers also published daily official casualty lists, with *The Times* being the premier source of information direct from the War Office. These lists were scoured on a daily basis by the regional daily newspapers, such as the *Belfast Evening Telegraph*, *Belfast Newsletter* and *Irish News and Belfast Morning News*, who then published details of local casualties.

In order to build up a comprehensive picture, the local press encouraged their readers to forward details of local casualties. Notices such as the following from the *Derry Journal* appeared in all the local papers:

> *If the relatives of soldiers in Derry and the North-West district who receive intimation of casualty to any members of their families in the fighting line send us the official notice we shall publish the facts. In this way only can accurate details of the name and regiment of the men concerned be ascertained.*[66]

The fact that the official notice was requested, aided the newspapers in providing accurate information to their readership. Private letters sent for publication which contained details of casualties not yet officially notified to the family, such as in the case of Private William Dickson, must have led to some difficult editorial decisions.

The provincial weekly papers by agreement, published some material taken from the regional dailies, but also included accounts from soldiers who were local to their readership area and on occasion publishing information not yet covered by the regional dailies. These papers also had the opportunity on reporting in greater depth on the activities of battalions recruiting locally and in the Inniskillings recruiting area there was no exception to this. In this context, it is of interest to see how the Battle of Festubert was reported to those anxiously waiting at home.[67]

The first intimation that any major engagement had taken place appeared in the newspapers of Monday, 17 May. *The Times*, noting that it was the 287th day of the war, commenced its war coverage on page eight with the headline, 'German Line Broken – Night Attack By Our Troops'. The article continued, 'In a night attack, between Saturday evening and Sunday morning, the British Army stormed and took the German position between Festubert and Richebourg L'Avoue. The hazards of such an enterprise are notorious but this was brilliantly successful, owing to the spirit and determination of the troops to which it was entrusted.'[68] On the same page under the headline, 'British Night Attacks – German Lines Stormed – A Mile of Ground Won – Our Brave Troops', were details of the official communique from Field Marshal French, dated May 16:

> *Our First Army has made a successful attack between Richebourg L'Avoue and Festubert, breaking the enemy's line over the greater part of a two mile front. The attack commenced at midnight south of Richebourg L'Avoue where we carried two successive lines of German breastworks on a front of 800 yards…fighting still continued in our favour and throughout the day our brave troops have fought splendidly.*[69]

Both articles emphasise the success of the venture but nowhere is any mention made of the cost involved in achieving the breakthrough. The communique from Sir John French was carried by both the *Belfast Evening Telegraph* and the *Belfast Newsletter* on 17 May, with the *Newsletter* headlining its report, 'Brilliant British Victory – Fierce Fighting Near La Bassée – Report From Commander in Chief – Enemy's Lines Carried – A Big Advance – Germans' Heavy Casualties.'[70] It is only when the report is read in its entirety is it made clear that the Germans' heavy casualties were actually inflicted by the French to the north of Arras and were not related to Festubert at all. At this early stage, there was no indication in any of the articles of the identity of any of the battalions involved.

The Times of May 18 carried a report from their military correspondent, Lieutenant Colonel Repington dated May 16. Under the headline, 'Great Night Attack.' This report begins in sensational style, 'Last night hell broke loose, and before the sun had risen this morning the British Army had stormed the German lines from Festubert and Richebourg L'Avoue.'[71]

The report goes on to allude that the night attack was carried out due to the shortage of high explosives, thereby maintaining and supporting his allegations published on May 14 concerning the failures at Aubers Ridge on May 9. This report was carried in its entirety by the three Belfast dailies, *Belfast Evening Telegraph*, *Newsletter* and *Irish News* along with other war news.

On May 19 Lord Kitchener, as Secretary of State for War addressed the House of Commons. His wide ranging speech on the state of the war on all fronts was reported in both daily and provincial weekly papers in the following days. He mentioned the night attack of 15 May commenting on its success and the fact that the action was continuing. He then stated:

> With regard to the Army at the front, in those recent operations our losses and those of the French have been heavy, but the task that our armies have accomplished necessitated great sacrifices, and the spirit and morale of our troops have never been higher than at the present moment.[72]

There were no further details of how extensive the casualties were, but the manner and location in which the news was delivered, was clearly intended to prepare the British public for bad news.

Over the next few days the efficiency of the excellent army postal service began to overtake any self-imposed silence undertaken by the newspapers in conjunction with the War Office to enable next of kin to be officially informed. On Saturday 22 May in its 'Derry Casualties' column, the *Londonderry Sentinel* published the details of a number of soldiers wounded in action at Festubert:

- In a field postcard to his father, Mr William Wray, Wapping Lane, Londonderry, Private Samuel Wray, Royal Inniskilling Fusiliers, states that he was wounded on the 16th May, but is doing well.
- Mrs Catherine Carson, 138 Bluebellhill Terrace has received intimation that her son Private Daniel Carson, D Company of the 2nd Royal Inniskilling Fusiliers was wounded in one of the recent engagements in France, and has been sent to the base. It is understood that he is going on well.
- Messrs Devine and Sons, Strand Road, have received a card stating that Private Toye, of the 2nd Battalion Royal Inniskilling

Fusiliers, who previous to the war was employed by that firm, has been wounded and is at present in hospital in France.[73]

Given the close knit relationships between families in the north of Ireland in general and particularly the close ties engendered by the regiment, it is prudent to state that it was at this time, around one week after the battle that the Inniskillings' 'family' at home were aware that their loved ones had been involved in a major engagement.

On Monday, 24 May the first official casualty lists appeared, although at that stage it was confined to officers, with the deaths of Second Lieutenant Morgan and Lieutenant Hinds being reported in *The Times* roll of honour of that date. This reporting was picked up by both the *Belfast Evening Telegraph* and the *Belfast Newsletter* who provided a paragraph of biographical material on both:

The death is announced from wounds of Second Lieutenant J.J.L Morgan, 2nd Batt. Royal Inniskilling Fusiliers. Deceased was a son of Colour Sergeant Musketry Instructor John Morgan, who was for 23 years connected with the 4th Battalion Royal Irish Rifles at Newtownards. He was born in that town and entered the army at an early age. He had seen considerable service in India, and on his return from the East seven months ago was raised to commissioned rank and sent to the front to join the 2nd Battalion Inniskillings, whose perils he has shared ever since. He was married last November to Miss Sainty, who will be remembered by many as schoolmistress in Victoria Barracks, and whose present address is York Road, Aldershot. Members of the old YMCA Tennis Club will recollect Mr Morgan as captain. He was well known in the city, and news of his death has caused sorrow to a large circle of friends. Lieutenant SV Morgan, adjutant of the 3rd Battalion Royal Irish Rifles, Dublin, is a brother of the deceased, who was a first rate soldier, as his promotion to commissioned rank proved.[74]

A telegram has been received announcing that Lieutenant Ralph William Gore Hinds, 2nd Battalion Royal Inniskilling Fusiliers, was killed in action last Sunday. He was a son of Lieutenant Colonel W.R. Gore Hinds, a retired officer of the Royal Army Medical Corps, who now resides at 16 Royal Terrace East, Kingstown. His promotion to the rank of Lieutenant came in January 1914, after nearly three years' service.[75]

By May 26 details of rank and file casualties – mostly those wounded and who were able to get a message home and accounts contained in private letters sent to relatives from survivors of the battle, began to appear in both the regional daily and provincial weekly papers, with evidence of sharing of the detail in order to reach a wider audience. An example of this was the letters from Lance Corporal McIntyre, which appeared in his local papers, the *Mid Ulster Mail* and the *Tyrone Courier* but also in the regional *Belfast Evening Telegraph*.

It was not until 29 May that there was any official recognition of the Inniskillings' involvement in the battle. The *Belfast Evening Telegraph* of this date carried a full page article by Percival Phillips under the headline, 'Battle of Festubert–Stirring Narrative-Inniskillings' Feat – Stories of British Heroism – Bayonet and Bomb Charges.' Hinting at restrictions that had been placed on reporting, he continued, 'I am permitted to give details of the part played in the first three days' operations around Festubert by many famous British regiments.' The article covers the exploits of a number of the battalions involved and in relation to the Inniskillings stated:

> The Inniskillings had a trying ordeal. The Battalion took part in the first attack of Saturday night (the 15th), half advancing on either side of a thoroughfare known as 'The Cinder Track' in order to make an assault on the German trenches which were at an angle. The regiment which was to have supported the attack was delayed, and the Germans turned their concentrated machine gun fire on the left of the Inniskillings' line, holding it back. The two right companies made a successful dash across 350 yards of broken ground into the trench. The battalion lost very heavily and was shelled all day on Sunday as it held the captured position.[76]

For those families who had heard nothing from the front, this was ominous news.

Throughout the first weeks of June, the regional dailies continued to report on casualties from Festubert as details came to light, but the war had moved on, and events in other areas of the Western Front and Gallipoli dominated the daily news. The provincial papers,, however, in areas where Inniskillings traditionally recruited, concentrated their focus on the battle and continued to publish accounts from letters sent from the front. In addition, on June 4 the *Tyrone Constitution* editorial was entitled, 'The Gallant Inniskillings'. The editorial eulogised both the first and second battalions, commencing, 'The lengthy lists of casualties in the Royal Inniskilling Fusiliers, both from France and the Dardanelles, which have been coming to hand daily for the past fortnight, is sufficient evidence that this famous old regiment so closely identified with the north-west counties of Tyrone, Fermanagh, Derry and Donegal, has been once more in the thickest part of the fight and has nobly upheld its ancient traditions for valour and gallantry won on many a foreign field.'[77]

Also in June, both the *Fermanagh Herald* and the *Ulster Herald* carried a full page article concerning the battle, entitled 'Dash of the Inniskillings – First in the Enemy's Trenches'.[78] In both these weekly provincial papers, this was a compilation of reports which had already appeared in daily papers and accounts from letters, some of which had previously appeared in other newspapers. However, these articles had the effect of constructing a picture of the Inniskillings' experience, whilst ensuring that, especially for the families of those still missing, a high public profile was maintained.

Towards the end of June 1915, nearly six weeks after the battle, it is significant to note that only around 50 Inniskillings had been reported in the press as having been killed as a result of the battle. However, an article in the *Belfast Evening Telegraph* of Tuesday, 29 June 1915 was to change that perception. The *Belfast Evening Telegraph* ran a daily feature entitled *Ulster Military News*, which contained details of decorations and details of those killed or wounded. On this date under the sub headline, 'Rank and File-Royal Inniskilling Fusiliers' was the following:

> *The following non-commissioned officers and men of the 2nd Battalion Royal Inniskilling Fusiliers have been missing since the engagement at Festubert on 16th ult., in which the Inniskillings played so valiant a part:-*[79]

There then follows an article of 203 names by rank and number. The list is reproduced as Appendix VI.[80]

Any optimism that families who had heard nothing from their loved ones had held, would have disappeared at that point when the enormity of the losses were revealed, although some families still held out faint hope as the appeals in the newspapers throughout July highlighted previously indicate. In reality, the men named were all dead and it remains the case that none of the 203 named as missing have a known grave and all are commemorated on Le Touret Memorial to the Missing. The fact that the list of missing was published some 46 days after the battalion went into action had the effect of lessening the impact in the general public consciousness. In all likelihood it was the case that the War Office in conjunction with the battalion wished to exhaust every avenue, including checking wounded and PoW details before publishing the list. However, the war had moved on and for all but the families of those missing and the battalion, Festubert was but a distant memory.

1   This column appeared daily in the *Belfast Newsletter* throughout the war with details of promotions, appointments, instances of gallantry, notification of deaths and appeals for those missing. Private Robert Beattie was 21 when he was killed, most likely in the initial advance on 15/16 May. He was attached to D company and has no known grave. He is commemorated on the Le Touret Memorial to the Missing.

2   Alexander, CAM. *With the 2nd Battalion Royal Inniskilling Fusiliers in France 1914-16.* p.35

3   National Archives. WO 95/1350 2nd Battalion Royal Inniskilling Fusiliers war diary

4   National Archives. WO 95/1343/2. 5 Infantry Brigade war diary

5   National Archives. WO 95/1285/2. 2nd Division war diary

6   5 Infantry Brigade war diary. op.cit.

7   Fox, Sir Frank, *The Royal Inniskilling Fusiliers in the World War.* p.53

8   Edmonds, BG Sir J. *Military Operations France and Belgium, 1915.* P.58

9   Fox, op.cit., p.72

10 Grayson,R.S. *Belfast Boys. How Unionists and Nationalists fought and died together in the First World War.* p.34.

11 War Office. *Soldiers Died in the Great War. 1914-1919. Part 32 The Royal Inniskilling Fusiliers*

12 www.cwgc.org Only 8 of this total were reported as having died of wounds in the period stated.

13 Mitchell TJ & Smyth GM, *History of the Great War, Medical Services, Casualties and Medical Statistics of the Great War.* p.13 Table 2

14 Both forms of message had a similar style. The telegram started '*Deeply regret to inform you that...*' Whilst the letter began, '*It is my painful duty to inform you that a report has been received from the War Office notifying the death of...*"

15 Corrigan, G *Sepoys in the Trenches, The Indian Corps on the Western Front 1914-15.* p.208

16 National Archives. WO 95/1285/2 App 491. 2nd Division war diary. It is unlikely that these burials took place with any ceremony. It was more a practical step to clear access areas for health reasons.

17 Referred to as Magee in some official military documents.

18 Presybyterian Historical Society of Ireland. *The Presbyterian Church in Ireland Roll of Honour 1914-1919.* p76. Private Robert Nugent 9836, 1st Battalion Royal Inniskilling Fusiliers, died of wounds on 15 February 1917 and is buried at St Sever Cemetery, Rouen, France. Having five sons serving seems a lot, but with the larger families of the time, this was by no means unique. The parents of Alexander McIlree from Cookstown, attached to D company and also killed at Festubert, had eight sons serving.

19 *The Times* roll of honour, 29 May 1915 p.9

20 *Belfast Newsletter*, Ulster and the War column, 15 June 1915. Private Joseph McCart, had been with the battalion at the front since August 1914. He has no known grave.

21 *Tyrone Constitution*, 4 June 1915 p.3. The letter was addressed to a Mr Joseph Doonan, Dungannon, County Tyrone.

22 *Mid Ulster Mail*, 29 May 1915 p.7.

23 Ibid

24 *Tyrone Constitution*, 4 June 1915 p.3

25 *Royal Aero Club Newsletter* available online at www.ancestry.co.uk. To enhance the rate at which pilots could be produced, the Army enlisted the help of the British Royal Aero Club, who trained the pilots for a fee of £75. This fee was paid for by the army to suitable candidates.

26 Clutterbuck, Colonel L A.(undated) *The Bond of Sacrifice, A Biographical Record of British Officers who Fell in the Great War, Vol 2, January to June 1915*, p224

27 PRONI. D/4121/F/4/B/2/6/6A. CAM Alexander papers 19 May 1915

28 National Archives. WO 339/7836 Lieutenant RWG Hinds service record

29 Ibid. Orchard farm was a strongpoint in the Givenchy sector, some five miles from the battlefield where Lieutenant Hinds was killed. In all likelihood the mention of Orchard farm was an administrative error.

30 Ibid

31 The other three identified Inniskillings are, 3908 Private Robert McNulty, 3764 Private WD Watson, and 4553 Private William Williamson.

32 www.cwgc.org

33 www.soldierswills@nationalarchives.ie

34 www.timesarchiveonline.co.uk 29 December 1917.Accessed 21 January 2014

35 National Archives. WO 339/18920 2nd Lieutenant JJL Morgan service record.

36 A representative sample. All taken from Ulster and the War Column, *Belfast Newsletter* between 21 June and 10 July 1915.

37 *Mid Ulster Mail*, 5 June 1915 p.9

38 *Belfast Newsletter*, Ulster and the War column, 8 July 1915

39 Many documents refer to him as 2nd Lieutenant. He had in fact been promoted Lieutenant with effect from 1 May 1915.

40 National Archives WO 339/22949 Lieutenant JH Stewart service record.

41 PRONI D/4121/F/4/B/2/6/6A 19 May 1915. CAM Alexander papers

42 PRONI D/4121/F/4/B/2/6/7 23 May 1915. Ibid

43 PRONI D/4121/F/4/B/2/6/9 28 May 1915. Ibid

44 Lieutenant JH Stewart service record. op.cit., The American embassy referred to is in Berlin and acted as a go-between for such requests.

45 Ibid

46 Ibid

47 Ibid. From the tone of the letter and the vocabulary used it is very likely that Private Bell had assistance from some of his officers in compiling the reply.

48 Ibid. Private Bell was discharged from the Army on 31 May 1916.

49 Ibid

50   Ibid. Statement of acting Serjeant Edward Lee 26 October 1915. Serjeant Lee later transferred to the Royal Scots Regiment, survived the war and continued to serve in the Army

51   Ibid. The unofficial reports are believed to be those of Private Lewis Bell and acting Serjeant Edward Lee.

52   www.greatwar.ci.net

53   *Londonderry Sentinel* 25 May 1915, p.8

54   www.soldierswills.ie. Will of Private Robert Beattie. Military document, Effects-Form 150

55   National Archives. WO 339/8980. Lieutenant Edward John White Abbott service record.

56   Ibid. Research indicates that he was actually killed on 16 May. He has no known grave and in another anomaly, his name appears as attached to the Royal Irish Fusiliers on the Menin Gate Memorial at Ypres, whereas it should appear on the Le Touret Memorial to the Missing, with his fellow Inniskillings. Information forwarded to CWGC who have acknowledged the anomaly and have included an amendment on their website.

57   National Archives. WO339/18920 2nd Lieutenant JJL Morgan service record. Mrs Maude Morgan had a double tragedy to contend with. Pregnant with their first child when her husband was killed, their son only survived for four months.

58   *Tyrone Constitution* 4 June 1915, p.2. Private Lynn recovered and rejoined the Regiment's 1st Battalion. He was killed just over a year later and is buried at Lijssenthoek military cemetery, Belgium. He was one of four brothers to fall in the war.

59   National Archives. WO 95/1343/2. 5 Infantry Brigade war diary.

60   Ibid. This was obviously a consideration that was overlooked at the planning stage.

61   National Archives. WO 95/1343/2 5 Infantry Brigade War Diary, Appendix LII

62   Alexander, op.cit., p.49

63   Ibid

64   Ibid

65   Captain Hewitt, OC D company was awarded the Military Cross which was gazetted in January 1916. It has not been possible to ascertain if this was for the action at Festubert.

66   *Derry Journal* 28 May 1915, p.8

67   *The Belfast Evening Telegraph* contained comprehensive and informative coverage of the war on all fronts. Included in each issue throughout the war was a column entitled Ulster Military News. It included official despatches and communications but focused on areas of conflict where local men from throughout the Province were serving. There were accounts from local soldiers by way of letters to family and friends, appeals for information from family and coverage of the exploits and fate of local men who were serving in other British, Canadian, Australian and New Zealand Regiments The *Belfast News Letter* (which maintained a London office) provided comprehensive coverage of the war, including the political situation pertaining in the government at that time, the munitions scandal being an example. There are reports from all the fronts in the conflict, giving it an international perspective. The focus, however is on local men from across the community and the experiences of the local units. Whilst not publishing as many first-hand accounts as the *Telegraph*, there are detailed entries regarding those killed and injured, mostly contained in its 'Ulster and the War' column, which appeared daily.

The *Irish News and Belfast Morning News* also provided informative and wide ranging coverage of the war, but with a slightly different accent to the other dailies. Unsurprisingly, as a pro 'home rule' newspaper, emphasis is more on an all Ireland view with considerable coverage of the exploits and experiences of units from other parts of the island, eg, *Irish News* 25 May p.6 headline – How Dublins and Munsters faced the Turks – Irish Bravery-Detailed account follows including, 'Dublin mans' story'. Interestingly, for a Belfast based newspaper, this coverage surpasses that given to units recruiting locally, and there are few accounts of the experiences of local men from either side of the community, compared to that evidenced in both the *Telegraph* and *News Letter.*

68   *The Times*, Monday 17 May 1915, p.8

69   Ibid

70   *Belfast Newsletter* 17 May 1915 p.5

71   *The Times,* 18 May 1915 p.8

72   *Tyrone Constitution*, 21 May 1915, p.5

73   *Londonderry Sentinel*, Saturday, 22 May 1915, p.5

74   *Belfast Evening Telegraph*, 24 May 1915, p.3. 2nd Lieutenant Morgan was married at St Patricks Church, Donegall Street, Belfast on 22 November 1914

75   *Belfast Newsletter*, 24 May 1915, p.12

76   *Belfast Evening Telegraph*, 29 May 1915, p.6

77   *Tyrone Constitution*, Friday 4 June 1915

78   *Fermanagh Herald* Saturday, 5 June 1915, p.5, *Ulster Herald*, Saturday, June 5, p.7

79   *Belfast Evening Telegraph*, Tuesday, 29 June 1915, p.6. The same list was published in the *Tyrone Constitution* of Friday, 2 July 1915

80   *Belfast Evening Telegraph*, 29 June 1915.

··· CHAPTER 9 ···
RETROSPECTIVE

If only high explosive arrived in the requisite quantities we could 'break thro' this tremendous crust of defence which has been forming and consolidating throughout the winter: once we have done it I think we may get the Devils on the run. How I should love to have a real good 'go' at them in the open with lots of cavalry and horse artillery and run them to earth. Well! It may come.[1] (Sir John French in a letter sent to his long term mistress, Winifred Bennett on 24 May 1915, showing that he had still not grasped the realities of trench warfare.)

The Battle of Festubert lasted from 15 to 27 May 1915. It will be remembered that the purpose of carrying out this offensive action was a continuance of the policy of utilising the British Expeditionary Force to draw German reinforcements away from attacks by the French, in this case to attempt to capture Vimy Ridge to the south. Following on from the disaster that was Aubers Ridge, did Festubert achieve its stated objectives and what impact did the course that the battle followed have on the Inniskillings?

It will be recalled that the objectives of the attack were to advance to the road named La Quinque Rue, by means of a two-pronged attack carried out by the 2nd Division (assisted by a brigade of the Meerut Division), and the 7th Division. The advance was to comprise a two-pronged attack by each of these divisions advancing around 1,000 yards, with the 2nd Division advancing at night, followed by the 7th Division at dawn the next day. The strategic aim of this battle was that the Germans would be forced to send reinforcements from the Vimy area to assist in containing the British advance.

From this strategic standpoint, it could be argued that the battle was a partial success. Whilst initially German reinforcements were brought south from the Armentieres area, on 19 May the German 2nd Guards Reserve Infantry Division was brought from Vimy and relieved the beleaguered 55th and 57th Infantry regiments, which had borne the brunt of the British assault. The Guards division had initially been brought from Alsace in the east of the country to Doaui as reinforcements against the French offensive, but very quickly slotted into position in the German front line where they were to remain for nine months.

In his authoritative, 'The German Army on the Western Front, 1915', Jack Sheldon contends that Festubert was dealt with by the Germans much in the same way that Neuve Chapelle had been and that it caused the Germans no great difficulty. The official history, Military Operations France and Belgium, 1915 compiled by Sir James Edmonds and published in 1928, in comparing the battle with Aubers Ridge stated, 'Thus, though no German reserves had been called on to deal with the attack in the battle of Aubers Ridge on the 9th May, the operations at Festubert had brought to the battle every German who could be spared.'[2] Whilst it was definitely not the case that every German who could be spared was brought to the battle, Sheldon argues that there is an element of post-war gloss on this statement and highlights that the reinforcements sent south from Armentieres (from the 139th and 179th Regiments), were not complete battalions and each comprised less than a thousand men. He further argues that the redeployment of the 2nd Guards Reserve Infantry Division was a minor inconvenience to the Germans.

Notwithstanding the argument that the battalions sent from Armentieres were local reinforcements, there is no doubt whatsoever that the 2nd Guards Reserve Infantry Division had to be redeployed from its initial assignment solely due to the successes achieved by the British attack. That this redeployment did not substantially affect the German effort at Vimy is immaterial, the plain facts were that the British attack at Festubert caused the Germans to think hard about their defensive line and therefore in doing so, achieved a partial strategic success.

As seen already, the British 2nd and 7th Divisions did meet at La Quinque Rue, albeit it took 36 hours before the 1st Kings (Liverpool Regiment) and the 2nd Royal Scots Fusiliers met as described previously. But the success was not the complete pincer movement as envisaged in the initial plan. Following the initial night attack, no advance was made to the left of the Inniskillings initial position at the cinder track. The successes after the initial advance were all to the right of the cinder track towards Festubert which left the German front line assuming a sharp bend at this point. It could be argued that the low lying ground seized in the subsequent attacks between 16 and 27 May was of little tactical value and that the real prize of gaining a foothold which would have enabled a renewed attack on Aubers Ridge eluded the British. An indicator of this is the fact that the Germans voluntarily ceded ground on 17 May unbeknownst to the British to establish a better defensive line, thereby protecting their elevated positions on Aubers Ridge. As it turned out the British were unable to seize the ridge until October 1918.

As regards the human costs, in keeping with the assaults at Neuve Chapelle and Aubers Ridge, the British lost heavily. Total British casualties for the duration of the battle were 710 officers and 15,938[3] other ranks dead, wounded or missing. Of these, the 2nd Division containing the Inniskillings lost 178 officers and 5,267[4] other ranks in their five day involvement. By contrast, and in keeping with the maxim that it was much easier to defend a position than to attack it, total German casualties numbered 5,000, including 800 taken prisoner.[5]

The Officer Commanding 2nd Division, Major General Henry Horne was realistic if somewhat cold about the losses. In a letter home to his wife on 18 May he stated, 'Casualties very heavy. One must not allow oneself to think of them, but must accept that it is for God and country.'[6] The somewhat unemotional comments of General Horne in accepting such losses can be put into context when one considers the casualties sustained by the French. Interestingly, having pressured Sir John French to commit to battle when the British were unprepared, the French took a more laissez faire attitude to their attempt, supposedly simultaneous, to capture Vimy Ridge. Their offensive commenced on 15 May, the same as the British, with their Tenth army making little progress. The attack was abandoned on 18 May, not resuming again until 7 June when some ground was made. This advance was made possible only after they had been reinforced by the redeployment of the British 2nd Division, already badly mauled at Festubert. This phase finished on 10 June and resumed again on 16 June until 18 June when efforts were ended. Vimy Ridge remained in German hands until 9 April 1917 when the Canadians captured it. The French efforts in May and June 1915 to capture the ridge resulted in 2,260 officers and 100,273 other ranks killed, wounded and missing.[7]

From the position of the French high command the efforts of the British in utilising scarce resources whilst pounding away at the German lines continually for 12 days, resulting in the redeployment of German reserves did not appear to provide much assistance, or for that matter, mollify. The French Army performance was far from exceptional, but in the spiteful climate which existed between the Allies at that time, General Foch sought again to blame the British for French military deficiencies. The following quote from the *French Official History* emphasised his disdain:

> *The attack of the Tenth Army was supposed to benefit from an attack to the north*
> *by the British First Army, but this operation, which was preceded by a completely*
> *inadequate artillery bombardment, stalled almost completely on the 9th, then*

petered out and was not resumed again until the 16th. This failure, followed by
inaction from the period 10th-15th, allowed the Germans to concentrate against
the 10th Army all the forces newly arrived in the area.[8]

The British performance at Festubert whilst sustaining heavy casualties was
certainly an improvement on the previous battles at Neuve Chapelle and Aubers
Ridge. Partial objectives had been achieved in the face of determined defence and
the learning process of trench warfare was cumulative. Unfortunately the process
of learning had a high human cost.

How then had the course of the battle developed? How also did this impact
on the Inniskillings?

Following the battle of Aubers Ridge, there was always going to be a further
British offensive. As the junior partner in the alliance, the British had two options.
Firstly, do nothing and wait until they had sufficient men and munitions or
secondly, assist the French with whatever resources they had available. The first
option would have resulted in a split in the alliance and in reality was no option
at all. The British then were caught between a rock and a hard place – and they
had to cut their cloth accordingly.

Planning for the battle was left to General Haig and his divisional generals.
Haig had long been acutely aware of the deficiencies in British preparedness for
war and knew that the British forces would struggle for a considerable period
before achieving their maximum potential. As early as 4 August 1914, the day
war broke out, Haig addressed a war council at Downing Street. In addition to
endorsing the creation of a new army, he addressed the issue of the type of conflict
that he foresaw:

> *Great Britain and Germany would be fighting for their existence. Therefore the*
> *war would be a long war and neither would accept defeat after a short struggle.*
> *I knew that German writers had stated in their books that a modern war in*
> *Europe would not last more than a few months. In my opinion, that was what*
> *they hoped for and what they were planning to make it. I held that we must*
> *organise our resources for a **war of several years**.*[9]

As a firm believer in the principle of a 'long war', Haig was cognisant that he
had to utilise his scarce resources as best that he could. In this context, it was no
surprise that from the outbreak of war he became a sponsor of the man who was

to command the 2nd Division at Festubert – Major General Henry Sinclair Horne. Horne had first come to not only the then Lieutenant Colonel Haig's attention, but also that of the then Temporary Major General John French and the then Lieutenant General Kitchener for his competent handling of his artillery battery during the South African War. By 1912, Horne had been appointed Inspector of the Royal Horse and Royal Field Artillery, a role which brought him into close contact with Haig, who was the commander in chief at Aldershot. The outbreak of war found Horne in France where Haig entrusted him with the command of a rearguard, comprising infantry, cavalry and artillery, on the retreat from Mons. His adept handling of this force further enhanced his reputation as someone who could be trusted and on Haig's recommendation he was appointed as the commander 2nd Division on 31 December 1914, a rarity for an artilleryman to command a Division of 20,000 infantry.[10]

This appointment negates the view of Haig by some revisionist historians as a bungling butcher who threw away thousands of lives. Put simply, Horne had proved himself competent in his numerous dealings with Haig, who regarded him as the best man for the job. The fact that he was a fellow ascetic Scot added to the attraction. Horne shared Haig's 'long war' view and realised that methods of warfare had to change to accommodate the new realities of trench warfare. Prior to his most recent promotion he had worked on Haig's behalf to develop and enhance coordination between the Royal Flying Corps and the Royal Artillery, both realising that the RFC were invaluable in accurately pinpointing enemy batteries for the artillery.

By the time planning for Festubert came around, both realised that following the experiences of Neuve Chapelle and Aubers Ridge, the short bombardment had to be discarded as ineffective. The policy of attrition instigated prior to Festubert was an innovative step and the idea of a 36 hour bombardment to destroy the German defences was certainly a good idea, but whilst the policy was sound, to attempt to implement it without the necessary resources was a serious mistake, which it could be contended was bound to lead to failure.

Haig had to carry through the plan for the offensive, but the state of the artillery pieces and both the shortage of and quality of ammunition at this stage of the war determined the outcome of the battle before a single soldier stepped out into no-man's-land.[11] General Sir Martin Farndale in his commanding, 'History of the Royal Regiment of Artillery, Western Front 1914-18' remarks on the shortages of ammunition at the end of the battle, 'Slowly operations came to an end, primarily due to the almost total lack of ammunition.'[12] The lack of coordination between the divisional artillery continued to cause a considerable number of deaths on the British side from 'friendly fire' and this was no different at Festubert. The unpalatable truth was that this had been identified as a problem at Neuve Chapelle and Aubers Ridge, yet nothing had been done to remedy the situation. Quite simply, the British artillery was not up to the task of destroying the German defensive positions and in particular the embedded and fortified machine gun positions. In common with the other arms of the British Army, the artillery was evolving its tactics to cope with a new type of warfare and the rapid expansion in both artillery pieces and ammunition would take some time to bear fruits.

It was a similar case with the nascent skill of aerial reconnaissance, with which General Horne had had such a prominent role in developing. Great strides had been made, targets could be identified for counter battery work and more or less accurate trench maps could be created from aerial photographs. However, due to the creativity of the German defenders in embedding their machine gun posts in the parapet construction, they were all but invisible from the air. Failure to pinpoint these for subsequent direct targeting by the artillery had devastating consequences for the attacking infantry.

It appears that the decision to conduct a night attack was one taken by General Horne. He had seen the carnage inflicted on the allied forces as the result of the daylight assault against fortified positions the week previously at Aubers Ridge, and in an attempt to protect as many soldiers as possible decided on a night time assault with all its inherent risks identified in the *Field Service Regulations*. Whilst supportive of his subordinate's decision, General Haig was aware of the risks and took the prudent step of ensuring that a back-up plan was available for implementation. As his diary entry of 15 May records:

> *After lunch I motored to Lestrem and saw Willcocks, and arranged that if night attack failed, a general offensive would start at 3.15am tomorrow at the same time as the 7th Division attack. If that failed, a bombardment of at least 6 hours would take place, and fresh troops organised for a third attack. The time at which this latter would be made would be ordered by me.* [13]

In a further attempt to give those undertaking the night assault the best chance possible, the tactic of deploying into no-man's-land prior to zero hour was implemented. As it turned out, this tactic ensured the initial complete success of the assault by 6 Brigade on the Inniskillings right and in all probability greatly assisted the advance of the Inniskillings D company. These were tactics which to a large extent were successful. The innovative tactic of intermittent firing prior to zero hour to confuse the Germans, as employed by the Jullundur Brigade of the Lahore Division to the Inniskillings left, had the unfortunate effect of forewarning the Germans that an attack was due to take place.

However, these positive and negative outcomes indicate the 'trial and error' nature of trench warfare at that time. Haig was a cavalryman, Horne was an artilleryman, albeit with experience of managing infantry in combat as highlighted above in the retreat from Mons. But that experience was totally different from the trench warfare which was now developing. It should be remembered that this type of warfare was still in its infancy and all armies were adapting to the new challenges. As mentioned above, it was much easier to defend than to attack and the situation dictated that the British had to attack. The official history, complied by Sir James Edmonds describes the results of the battle as 'tantalising'.[14] It could be argued that that is an accurate reflection. Gains to an average depth of 600 yards on a width of four miles of front were made and were certainly deemed a success at that time. But had a number of other factors, such as the performance of the artillery and the failure to recognise the German withdrawal been addressed, then the sacrifices of the 'poor bloody infantry' may have been more palatable. To castigate the British generals over losses incurred whilst implementing innovative ideas, however, is patently unfair. Quite simply, they had no realistic option.

Piecing together the Inniskillings experience of the battle has been difficult, primarily due to the paucity of information contained within the battalion war diary. The Inniskillings diary contains little more than the disposition of companies prior to the attack, the fact that D company was successful and a list of officer rank casualties. In contrast, the diary entry of the 1st Battalion King's Royal Rifle Corps to the Inniskillings right comprises a detailed account extending to five pages. The responsibility for keeping the diary was that of the adjutant, in the case of the Inniskillings, Captain GRV Steward, DSO. He was amongst the officers wounded in the battle, so it may have fallen to someone else with no intimate knowledge of what took place to complete the diary. Along with the KRRC diary, the diaries of the other battalions in the brigade and personal accounts, have assisted in the understanding of how events unfolded for the Inniskillings.

The 5 Brigade special instructions outlining how the advance was to proceed, stated that the objective for the Inniskillings and the Worcesters was:

The 1st and 2nd line of German parapets from R7 (Inclusive) to a point NW of V5 and to get in touch with the Meerut Division at that point.[15]

As previously mentioned this entailed for the Inniskillings, an advance of 400 yards across a frontage of 250 yards. Successful completion of this manoeuvre depended heavily on the element of surprise being maintained and successful coordination between the Inniskillings and the Worcesters to mutually support each other. Unfortunately, neither of these came to pass. The intermittent rifle fire from the Jullundur Brigade ensured that the Germans opposite 5 Infantry Brigade sector were alert, awaiting an attack and able to respond instantly. The 2nd Leicesters who were to the left of the Worcesters – two to the left of the Inniskillings reported that during the evening of 15 May, the Germans shouted across, 'Come on over, we are ready for you.'[16] Whether this was an act of bravado by some German soldier is debatable, but the fact was that in concert with the Inniskillings both the Leicesters and the Worcesters had all their attacking companies out unhindered in front of the British breastworks prior to zero hour at 11.30 pm. There is a consensus amongst the above British participants that the Germans illuminated the battlefield and opened concentrated fire before the zero hour of 11.30 pm, with the Worcesters timing this at 11.28 pm. In his after action report, the commander of 5 Brigade suggested that the Germans were aware that British attacks generally took place on the hour or half hour and that the firing was a precautionary measure. There is nothing in the German account to back this up, however, Major Schulz of 2nd Battalion 55th Infantry Regiment confirmed that they had been alerted by the intermittent rifle fire:

After the arrival of darkness a sudden barrage of fire from the enemy infantry that lasted only a couple of minutes started up. After an hour the barrage of fire picked up again. Now we were warned. In the trenches, observation posts, batteries, everything was ready for conflict.[17]

The heavy fire of the defenders appears to have been confined to those attached to the 55th Infantry Regiment, which was primarily opposite the British 5 Brigade. To their left was the 57th Infantry Regiment which was facing the British 6 Brigade and appears to have been taken by surprise by the attack. The intensity of the fire put down by the German defenders of the 55th ensured that neither the Leicesters nor the Worcesters were able to breach their defences. The Leicesters' attack was called off at midnight and the surviving Worcesters were unable to advance or retreat and as a result were unable to regroup for a further attack. This situation meant that the Inniskillings had no protection to their left for a distance of over 400 yards. The lack of protection enabled the German defenders in the machine gun positions to the left of the Inniskillings to direct enfilading fire at them, as well as the direct fire coming from the defenders in front. It should be recalled that this was exactly the same fate that befell the Munsters in exactly the same position the week previously. Obviously lessons were not learnt from the Munsters' experience and any artillery fire directed at these machine gun emplacements during the bombardment failed utterly – even after the concerns repeatedly raised by the Worcesters and the Inniskillings on the eve of the battle. The Inniskillings' A company bore the brunt of this murderous fire – a fact borne out by the exceptionally heavy casualties. That D company managed to breach and secure not only the first but also the second German line is nothing short of miraculous. In securing the captured lines, they were ably assisted by the leading companies of the Ox and Bucks LI and tribute should be paid to the initiative shown by them.

After the initial assault, the same problem that had bedevilled the attacks at Neuve Chapelle and Aubers Ridge – effective communications, came to the fore. As highlighted in the account of the battle, brigade headquarters had no idea for a number of hours as to how the battle was progressing and were reliant on individual battalion commanders for updates. If effective battlefield communications had been available, more progress and less casualties would have ensued. This an issue which features heavily in the after action report of Brigadier General Chichester, Commanding 5 Brigade. In the initial paragraph he identified as an issue:

> The time it takes to convey orders to troops. Telephonic communication nearly always broke down and cannot be relied on.[18]

The only option was to rely on runners carrying messages back and forward across no-man's-land, which in the circumstances was a death sentence, as proved in the case of Second Lieutenant Morgan and no doubt many unnamed others.

Accepted practice at the time was to retrieve the wounded from the battlefield back to the British front line for onward transportation to the rear, a process which was well honed and worked in most circumstances. On this occasion this was to prove disastrous. The failure of the artillery to neutralise the German batteries behind their front line ensured that the British front lines were under constant bombardment all day on 16 May. The result was twofold. Firstly, the stretcher bearers could not get forward to retrieve those wounded and secondly, that those retrieved were often killed on reaching the supposed safety of the British lines. General Chichester also pointed out that the method of recovering the wounded was haphazard. The issue of eight stretchers per battalion was wholly inadequate and led to those bearers being totally fatigued and unable to carry on in the exceptionally physically demanding conditions and he recommended that a reserve of stretchers and bearers be retained to take the wounded from the front line to the first aid posts, leaving the battalion stretcher bearers to concentrate in locating and retrieving casualties.

The practice of each man wearing a distinguishing white square of cloth on his chest and back did not appear to have been thought through properly. White squares worn on the back would have enabled those monitoring the battle to see how the advance progressed, but those on the chest merely identified the troops to the German defenders and served as an attractive target, especially when flares were used to illuminate the battlefield. The use of flares had another previously unforeseen disadvantage to the attackers. The light glinted off the fixed bayonets of the troops, providing further indicators to the defenders of the progress of the attack.

In essence then, factors beyond the Inniskillings control mitigated against them achieving their objective. Most serious among these was the failure of the artillery to adequately destroy the German defences. The failure of the battalions to their left to breach the German positions left them horribly exposed and the confusion engendered by inadequate communications compounded the confusion of the battlefield. No battalion of the Meerut division to the Inniskillings left breached the German lines. The battalions of 6 Brigade to the right had better success, as they were able to exploit the element of surprise. The Inniskillings were the only battalion in the initial attack to breach and capture the German lines from an alert, experienced and battle hardened enemy, a fact acknowledged by Brigadier General Chichester in the final paragraph of his report of 21 May:

> *The battalions of the Brigade did all that could be done and the successful charge of the 2nd ROYAL INNISKILLING FUSILIERS under a murderous fire, notwithstanding a loss of 18 Officers and 650 other ranks, showed great gallantry and dash.*[19]

The period of rest, recuperation and reorganisation for the Inniskillings at Burbure was by necessity short. However, whilst there, and as an effort to lift morale, a concert was organised by Serjeant Davies, the RSM Serjeant Major Maguire and the battalion's Roman Catholic chaplain, Reverend Father MacCabe. The concert was deemed a great success. In the regimental journal, 'The Sprig' the efforts of Father MacCabe at this exceptionally trying time were acknowledged:

> The Battalion is very fortunate to have the services of Rev Father MacCabe, who is indefatigable in his efforts for the spiritual welfare of the men, very often under the most trying and dangerous of circumstances.[20]

The efforts to raise spirits seem to have been successful. In a letter to his mother dated 29 May, Lieutenant Alexander (who had been appointed adjutant, replacing the wounded Captain Steward), commented:

> We want officers, there is no one to spare to look after the Transport in billets so I keep an eye on them. We are all well rested now and the men very cheerful. There are a great number missing but the majority of them we believe are dead.[21]

On 25 May as the Inniskillings rested at Burbure, General Foch made a request to General Sir John French for further assistance. As a result, the British were obliged to accede to a request from the French to take over a little more of the front line, to release the French 58th Division to resume the assault on Vimy Ridge. The 2nd Division were identified as the replacements and on 29 May the Inniskillings with the rest of their 5 Brigade colleagues marched the twenty miles to Vermelles. This position was seven miles south east of the Festubert battlefield towards Loos and in effect this manoeuvre meant an expansion of the British sector. On arrival, the Inniskillings were detailed as Brigade reserve and to their delight had relatively luxurious quarters, compared to their previous experiences. The Battalion headquarters even had electric lighting which was run from a coal mine behind the lines. The Inniskillings remained in this area until the end of July when, as part of a major reorganisation, they were withdrawn from 2nd Division and appointed as part of the headquarters troop of the new Third Army. From this time the Inniskillings were in preparation for the next major offensive – the Battle of the Somme.

The Battle of Festubert therefore can be seen as something of a watershed for the 2nd Inniskillings. After this engagement the original battalion had basically ceased to exist. The May edition of *The Sprig* had highlighted that only 120 of those who had gone to France on 23 August, 1914 were still with the battalion, and that was before Festubert. Prior to the battle, replacements came from Reservists and Special Reservists, but this resource was now exhausted. There had always been competing demands on this resource with the 1st Inniskillings, who were undergoing a similar torrid time at Gallipoli but with the raising of Kitchener's New Army, potential reinforcements were directed to the Inniskillings' service battalions, particularly the 5th and 6th Battalions, who also went to Gallipoli, as reinforcements in August 1915. The paucity of indigenous recruits, coupled with the fact that conscription was never introduced for political reasons in Ireland, meant that replacements came from wherever they could be found. This led to the diminution of the Irish content of the battalion and it could be argued a dilution of the regiments' family ethos.

Research by the author bears out the changes in the structure of the battalion. Up to and including Festubert, 14.6 per cent of the fatal casualties incurred were born or enlisted outside Ireland. From Festubert until the end of the war, this percentage had risen to 76.8 per cent.[23] Prior to Festubert, replacements who were subsequently killed tended to be from other Irish regiments. After Festubert, these came from units as geographically diverse as the Duke of Cornwall's Light Infantry and the Royal Scots – and nearly every regiment in between.

The fate of the 2nd Inniskillings was something over which they had no control. In common with many of the regular army battalions they were fought to destruction from their entry into the conflict on 23 August 1914, until their ultimate test on 15/16 May 1915, a period of 266 days continuous active service. In common with other battalions, they were used to 'try and test' the new concept of trench warfare – and they were not found wanting. The heavy casualties that they suffered were regrettably the norm for the time. The fact that the Inniskillings had a small geographical recruiting area exacerbated the scale and impact of the losses. Unfortunately, similar heavy casualties were to be incurred by the Inniskillings as a regiment the following July at the Somme.

The Inniskillings carried out their duties at Festubert with great bravery against overwhelming odds and the fact that they had some success is testament to the professionalism and integrity of all those involved. They were a credit to their battalion, to their regiment and to their country. We owe them a huge debt of gratitude. Hopefully this account will go some way to bring their experience to the wider audience it deserves.

Postscript

The author had the opportunity to visit the battlefield in March 2014. In keeping with the fact that Festubert is a somewhat forgotten battle, the battlefield is not marked in any way, there are no signposts and no memorials. Utilising maps from the time and with the excellent navigation skills of the author's wife, the cinder track was found, still in existence off the Rue Du Bois on the D171 road from Neuve Chapelle to Bethune around three quarters of a mile from the Port Arthur roundabout and fittingly, just under two miles from Le Touret Memorial to the Missing.[24]

The visit was planned intentionally for spring, as although the fields had been sown, the crops were no more than a few inches high. Leaving the Rue du Bois and walking up the cinder track the battlefield opened to the left and right and comprised open farmland. The British front line position, again calculated from available maps, is easily identifiable as the dyke which had to be bridged prior to the attack is still in existence, although it has been dredged, reinforced and culverted in places.

Although the ground has been farmed constantly since it was reclaimed after the First World War, it is liberally strewn with battlefield debris. On the author's visit, ammunition clips, bone fragments, remains of boots and pottery were clearly visible lying on the surface. The ground is completely flat as the cinder track leads to the German line and beyond to the long demolished Ferme Du Bois. Standing at the British front line it was a sobering and emotional experience to realise that thousands of young men, including the author's great uncle are buried in the fields to the left and right.

The time spent at the battlefield coincided with beautiful sun-kissed early spring days with the ground firm and dry underfoot, a far cry from the conditions of a century ago. As the author walked the cinder track, a drove of hares were spotted playing on the ground that A company Inniskillings advanced across. In the dyke, an otter was spotted calmly going about its business. Although the battlefield is not marked, it is fitting that it is a peaceful place, reclaimed by nature.

View along cinder track from Rue de Bois, March 2014
(Author's collection)

*View from British Front line. German front line was just in front of the copse of trees
in the distance. A Company, 2nd Inniskillings advanced in the field on the left of the
cinder track, D company advanced in the field on the right.*
(Author's collection)

1   Holmes,R. *The Little Field Marshal, A Life of Sir John French*, London, Cassell, p294

2   Edmonds, BG Sir J. *Military Operations France and Belgium, 1915.* p.82

3   Ibid p.76

4   Ibid.

5   Ibid.

6   Farr, D. *The Silent General. Horne of the First Army*, p.58

7   Edmonds. op.cit., p.80

8   Sheldon, J. *The German Army on the Western Front, 1915*, p.160

9   Sheffield, G & Bourne,J (Eds) *Douglas Haig, War Diaries and Letters. 1914-1918*, p.54

10 Farr. op.cit., p.47

11 National Archives. CAB 44/20. In a handwritten note written in 1927 on the draft for the official history compiled by Sir James Edmonds, Field Marshal Haig stated, *'Much of the Artillery ammunition was very faulty until 1917.'*

12 Farndale, Gen Sir M, *History of the Royal Regiment of Artillery, Western Front 1914-18.* P.109. No artillery piece on the British side had more than 40 rounds left at the close of the battle, with some in single figures.

13 Sheffield, G & Bourne, J. op.cit., p.124. Lieutenant General Sir J Willcocks was the commander of the Indian Corps.

14 Edmonds. op.cit., p78

15 National Archives. WO 95/1343/2. 5 Infantry Brigade war diary Appendix XLIV- Special Instructions

16 National Archives. WO 95/3945/2 2nd Battalion Leicestershire Regiment war diary

17 Schulz, Major D. *Infanterie Regiment Graf Bulow von Dennewitz, Nr 55 im Weltkriege.* p.92

18 National Archives. WO 95/1343/2 5 Infantry Brigade war diary, Appendix LII. Report of Brigadier General Chichester to HQ 2nd Division, 21 May 1915.

19 Ibid.

20 *The Sprig of Shillelagh*, July 1915, p.162

21 PRONI D4121/F/4/B/2/6/8. 29 May 1915. CAM Alexander papers. Lt Alexander was wounded on 22 July 1915, when German artillery shelled the battalion's billets in Bethune.

22 *The Sprig*, op.cit., May 1915, p124

23 Research carried out by analysing all deaths for the 2nd Inniskillings recorded in *Soldiers Died in the Great War, 1914-1919*, part 32 Royal Inniskilling Fusiliers, pps 17-28

24 In Edward Hancock's 2005 book in the Battleground Europe series, *Aubers Ridge*, the cinder track is described as now being the 'Rue du Quesgniot'. This may have been another cinder track at one time, but it is situated half a mile further along the D171 towards Port Arthur and from research of available maps of the time is definitely not the cinder track from which 2nd Royal Munster Fusiliers advanced on 9 May and the 2nd Royal Inniskilling Fusiliers advanced on the night of the 15 May.

APPENDIX I

'Need for Shells'. Article by Lt Col Repington, *The Times* Military correspondent
Friday 14 May 1915

THE TIMES, FRIDAY, MAY 14, 1915.

BIG FRENCH VICTORY.

CAPTURE OF CARENCY.

A BATTLESHIP LOST.

CRISIS IN ITALY.

BOTHA'S GREAT SUCCESS.

[294th Day of War.]

CARENCY TAKEN BY ASSAULT.

BRILLIANT SUCCESS OF THE FRENCH.

HOUSE TO HOUSE FIGHTING.

PARIS, MAY 12.

ANOTHER VILLAGE CAPTURED.

THE BOIS LE PRETRE IN FRENCH HANDS.

THE BERLIN VERSION.

AMSTERDAM, MAY 12.

TRENCHES DESTROYED NEAR YPRES.

BRITISH LINE UNCHANGED.

NEED FOR SHELLS.

BRITISH ATTACKS CHECKED.

LIMITED SUPPLY THE CAUSE.

A LESSON FROM FRANCE.

From Our Military Correspondent.

NORTHERN FRANCE, MAY 12.

FORMIDABLE DEFENCES.

LACK OF HIGH EXPLOSIVE.

OUR URGENT NEEDS.

ITALIAN CABINET RESIGNS.

A GRAVE SITUATION.

LATE WAR NEWS.

EXCITEMENT IN ROME.

GIOLITTIAN EX-MINISTERS ROUGHLY HANDLED.

[FROM OUR CORRESPONDENT.]

ROME, MAY 13.

SIGNOR GIOLITTI'S POSITION.

Lucca.

THE BATTLE IN GALLIPOLI.

D'ANNUNZIO'S PROPAGANDA.

ROME, MAY 13.

GERMAN LOSSES, 30,000.

MAY 13.

GOLIATH LOST IN THE STRAITS.

TORPEDOED BY TURKS AT NIGHT.

BRITISH SUBMARINE RAID.

TURKISH REPORT.

AMSTERDAM, MAY 13.

GERMAN SUBMARINES IN THE MEDITERRANEAN.

ATHENS, MAY 13.

EARLIER CLOSING OF BANKS.

THEATRES.

VARIETIES, &c.

APPENDIX 10.

I. CORPS OPERATION ORDER No. 83

14th May, 1915.

1. The First Army will resume its offensive tonight.

2. Its object is to press forward to Violaines and Beau Puits, **Map 5.** establishing a defensive flank on the La Bassée—Estaires road on **Sketch** the left and maintaining the right at Givenchy.

3. The main attack will be carried out by the I. and Indian Corps.

4. The first objective is the general line of the road Festubert— La Quinque Rue—La Tourelle—Port Arthur. This position is to be consolidated when won.

5. The task of the I. Corps (2nd and 7th Divisions) is to secure the line of the road Festubert—La Tourelle from Points M.3 to R.13.

6. The Indian Corps is to assault the German front system of trenches between the ditches running S.S.E. to N.N.W. through Points V.5 and V.6, secure the German second line breastwork and Point V.6, and establish a flank at this point connecting with our present line.

This assault is to be delivered at 11.30 P.M. tonight simultaneously with that of 2nd Division.

As opportunity offers the Indian Corps will subsequently attack outwards towards the line Points V.5.E—V.6.E—59, and having secured that, will push on and secure the road from Port Arthur to La Tourelle, as the attack of the 2nd Division progresses.

7. To carry out the task of the I. Corps :—

(a) The 2nd Division will assault the German front system of trenches between Point R.1 and the right of the Indian Corps and secure the line R.1—R.3—R.5—R.7—V.4 under cover of darkness.

This assault will be delivered at 11.30 P.M. tonight in close touch with the assault of the Indian Corps.

At 3.15 A.M. tomorrow the 2nd Division will continue to press its attack simultaneously with that of the 7th Division and secure the Ferme Cour d'Avoué and the line of the Festubert—La Tourelle road from Points P.14 to R.13 both inclusive.

(b) The 7th Division will assault the German position on the front Points N.1—P.5 at 3.15 A.M. tomorrow.

First objective :—the enemy's front system of trenches.

Second objective :—the line of the road from Points M.3 to P.14 at which point close touch is to be established with 2nd Division.

8. Under the direction of the Divisional Commanders concerned, a deliberate bombardment of the enemy's positions will be maintained throughout today and tonight up to the hours fixed respectively for the assaults of 2nd and 7th Divisions, in accordance with instructions already issued. Fire will then be lifted clear of the actual portions of the hostile line to be assaulted.

440   APPENDICES 10 AND 11

The 1st Group, H.A.R., will also take part in this bombardment in accordance with a programme arranged under the supervision of the M.G.R.A., 1st Army, which has been communicated to divisions.

9. (a) The 4th (Guards) Brigade will form the Corps Reserve in readiness to move at short notice from 11.30 P.M. tonight.

(b) The 1st Bn. Queen's Regt. will be under the direct orders of the Corps Commander in its billets and in readiness to move at one hour's notice from 3 A.M. tomorrow. Horses of the baggage and supply wagons of this battalion need not be harnessed.

R. WHIGHAM, Brig. General,
Issued at 1 P.M.   General Staff, 1st Corps.

APPENDIX 11.

2ND DIVISION INSTRUCTIONS

Map 5. 1. [This paragraph deals with Artillery Instructions.]

2. Infantry Attack.

The infantry attacks will be delivered by the 6th and 5th Infantry Brigades.

Frontage.

6th Infantry Brigade—From R.1 to the bend in the German line between R.6 and V.1 (inclusive).

5th Infantry Brigade—From that point (exclusive) to the northwest corner of the salient between V.3 and V.6.

1st Objective.

6th Infantry Brigade—The first and second line of German parapets between R.1 and R.7 (exclusive). R.1 to Q.2 to be blocked.

5th Infantry Brigade—The first and second line of German parapets from R.7 (inclusive) to a point N.W. of V.5 and to get into touch with the Meerut Division at that point.

Arrangements for assembling the attacking and supporting columns must be carefully thought out and arranged.

Every endeavour will be made to render the attack a surprise.

The attacking line should be deployed in good time in front of the breastwork and in front of any obstacle which exists close to the breastwork.

The maintenance of the correct direction of the attack is very important. Portions of the German trenches in front of which it is known that the wire is adequately destroyed should be selected, and every precaution taken by aid of compass bearings, landmarks, etc. to lead directly towards them.

The advance should be made in absolute silence and at a walk till close to the German line where a rush will be made and the enemy cleared out with bombs and the bayonet.

APPENDIX 11   441

The supporting line should follow close on the attacking line in order to reinforce it and give it impetus to carry it on to the second line of breastworks. The 3rd and 4th lines will bring the necessary tools and will be accompanied by R.E. to convert both the German 1st and 2nd line breastworks for our use, and to consolidate the position gained as rapidly as possible.

It is very important that the leading lines when successful, are adequately supported without delay and reinforcements sent out as required, by driblets if necessary.

Parties will be detailed at once to commence digging and preparing communicating trenches.

The distribution of the R.E. will be as usual, three men accompanying the leading troops to search for mines.

A further advance will not be made till 3.15 A.M.

Flanks will be secured by demolishing a few traverses and utilizing the material to form a barrier. This will leave a space which can be denied to the Germans by bombing. Care must be taken to avoid bombing the men of the Meerut Division attacking on our left.

As soon as the position is established, machine guns and trench mortars will be brought up.

Rations will be carried as usual and it is important that water bottles should be full.

Communications by wire, and visual signalling will be established.

Bangalore torpedoes have been issued for the destruction of any unexpected wire.

Cutting tools such as axes, billhooks, etc. should be carried, as hedges may require to be dealt with.

3. At 3.15 A.M. the advance will be commenced on the objectives detailed, in ordinary battle formation, scouts being thrown well forward and patrols being pushed to the flanks to obtain touch with the 7th Division, and with the Meerut Division if this has not already been gained.

4. It is stated that on 9th May the infantry attacks were incorrectly timed because officers did not trust their watches and imagined that they could tell when the moment of attack had come by the lifting of the artillery fire.

It must be strongly impressed on all ranks that no change in the fire of our artillery will be apparent either to the ear or to the eye when the moment comes for the assault. The attack to be simultaneous must start absolutely punctually at the hour named, and although the infantry cannot perceive it, the artillery range will also be lengthened at that hour.

A staff officer will visit R.A. and Brigade H.Q. during the afternoon to give the exact time.

LOUIS VAUGHAN, Lieut.-Colonel,
S.G.S.O., 2nd Division.

Issued at 9.30 P.M.
13th May, 1915.

APPENDIX III

5 Infantry Brigade Special Instructions, 14 May 1915

S E C R E T.

5TH INFANTRY BRIGADE.

··*·*·*·*·*·*·*·*·*·*·*·*·*·*·*·*·*·*

SPECIAL INSTRUCTIONS.

1.   The 5th Brigade will attack the German trenches on their front from the bend in the German line (exclusive) between R.6 and V.1 to the N.W. corner of the salient between V.3 and V.6.

    1st Objective. The 1st and 2nd line of German parapets from R.7 (inclusive) to a point N.W. of V.5 and to get in touch with MEERUT Division at that point.
    A further advance will not be made till after daylight.

2.   The detail of the attack will be as follows:-
    (a) Frontage - 570 yards - two battalions front.
        INNISKILLING FUSILIERS from communication trench W.of CINDER TRACK (exclusive) to ditch 150 yards East of CINDER TRACK. Frontage 250 yards.
        WORCESTERS from this point to ditch just E. of communication trench running through COPSE. Frontage 320 yards.
    (b) The attack is to be carried out by successive lines at intervals of about 100 yards. Especial care must be taken to ensure adequate support being given.
    (c) Working parties will be supplied by supporting battalions OXFORDS and GLASGOWS. The working parties for the 1st line will go as a third line. They will each consist of a platoon made up to 50 men with 1 N.C.O. and 4 men R.E.
    (d) When the first line has been taken, the second line will be assaulted, the INNISKILLINGS assaulting from the line - their right to V.1, the WORCESTERS from the line - V.3 Northwards to the N.W.corner of the salient.
        Between V.1 and V.3 no further advance will be made until the 2nd line trenches facing West and running South from R.7 and from about V.4 have been captured. The attack on these will be supported by machine gun fire from the captured German front line just W.of V.3 and by a bombing attack up the communication trench running South from near V.2. Four machine guns will accompany the WORCESTERS 2nd line for this purpose.
    (e) The successful capture of R.7 and V.4 will be shewn by lighting torches at these points.
        The two flank attacks will then drive the enemy from the trench between them by bombing attacks up the trench. This bombing attack will then be supported by a frontal attack from the line V.1 - V.3.
        Bridges must be carried to bridge the stream between the two lines and these must be placed in position as soon as the torches denote the arrival at R.7 and about V.4. Special parties to carry bridges must be detailed for this purpose.

Forming up.
3.   The two battalions allotted to the attack will form their men up on the front line and in the two cover trenches 50 and 100 yards in rear of the front line.
    The OXFORDS and GLASGOWS will form up on B, C, and D lines.
    The H.L.I. will be formed up H.Q. and 2 Coys in dug-outs at house S.9.a.91 and remainder in dug-outs and breastworks about house S.9.a.58.
    The two first lines should be deployed in front of our parapets in the old trench before the time for the assault, their places in the breastworks being taken by succeeding lines. As one line goes forward the succeeding one should take its place.

Timing of Attack.
    It is essential that the start of the attack be simultaneous. Watches will be accurately set.
    The attack will be carried out in absolute silence and at a walk until the enemy's trench is approached when it will be rushed.
    It must be strongly impressed on all ranks that no change in the fire of our artillery will be apparent either to the eye or the ear when the moment comes for assault. The attack to be simultaneous must start absolutely punctually at the hour named.
    Although the Infantry cannot perceive it, the artillery range will also be lengthened at that hour.

(2)

Direction.
5.   The maintenance of the correct direction of attack is very important. During the day the position of gaps in the wire must be accurately marked, so thatvleaders can guide straight to them.

Bombs and S.A.A.
6.   Battalions will complete with bombs today.

Bomb reserve depots (each containing 500 bombs) are in front breastwork at exit of communication trench 150 yards East of CINDER TRACK and 250 yards East of CINDER TRACK.

Special parties must be told off from battalions doing the attack to carry up bombs, care being taken to show them beforehand where they are to take them to.

S.A.A.Stores. (each containing 100 boxes) exist at the same places.

A further reserve of bombs and S.A.A. is at house S.9.a.91 and about house S.9.a.58.

These reserve stores will be under guards furnished by H.L.I.

R.E.Stores.
7.   Depots of R.E.Stores are near the bomb stores in the front line. Reserve Depot is in house on RUE DU BOIS next the FACTORY.

Medical.
8.   Advanced Dressing Station will be established at X roads. Stretcher parties will only use the two new communication trenches. Sentries will be posted by H.L.I. on the exit of each of the communication trenches in the front breastworks.

Working Parties.
9.   The OXFORDS and GLASGOWS will provide the following working parties:-

(a)   One platoon OXFORDS to report to O.C.INN:FUS: at S.9.a.91 at 6 p.m. (For work on German 1st line).

(b)   One platoon GLASGOWS (to be made up to 50 men) to report to O.C.WORCESTERS at S.3.c.55 at 5 p.m. (For work on German 1st line).

(c)   One platoon OXFORDS to report to O.C.INN: FUS: at S.9.a.91 at 6 p.m. (For work on German 2nd line).

(d)   One platoon GLASGOWS (made up to 50 men) to report to O.C. WORCESTERS at S.3.c.55 at 5 p.m. (For work on German 2nd Line).

(e),(f),(g) & (h) - 100 men each of H.L.I. to make 4 communication trenches up to German front line. To be detailed by O.C.,H.L.I., but to remain at S.9.a.91 till called for.

9.   1 N.C.O. and 9 men H.L.I. to report to Trench Mortar Officer at house S.9.a.91 at 4 p.m.

R.E.
10.   O.C.5th Field Coy.R.E.,will detail one N.C.O. and 4 men for each of the above parties.

He will also tell off 1 N.C.O. and 3 men to accompany the front line of the INNISKILLINGS and WORCESTERS to look for mines or telephone communication in German trenches.

The above to report to O.C.WORCESTERS at S.3.c.55 at 5 p.m. and to O.C.INN: FUS: at house S.9.a.91 at 6 p.m.

11.   Masks must be dipped in solution during the day and be carried by all men.

12.   Communications. Battalion Head Quarters have been wired up in dug-outs in the front line. Brigade Head Quarters will be on the RUE DU BOIS. Buried lines connect there.

Captain,

14th May,1915.   Brigade Major 5th Infantry Brigade.

S E C R E T.

5TH INFANTRY BRIGADE.
SPECIAL   INSTRUCTIONS.

(Continued).

13. Distinguishing Marks.

Distinguishing marks (white patches back and front) are being issued approximately 1000 to WORCESTERS and INNISKILLINGS each.

14. Working Parties.

All working parties will carry one shovel and 25 sandbags per man. Sandbags will be drawn at 9 p.m. at R.E. Store in RUE DU BOIS (house next FACTORY).

15. Reports.

Officers Commanding Battalions will furnish reports as soon as the tactical situation changes at all. If there is no change they will be furnished every half hour.

If reinforcements are asked for the message must state clearly where they are required e.g., INNISKILLINGS right when OXFORDS will reinforce.

16. Bayonets.   Bayonets will be fixed before leaving our trench.

17. Colours.
Distinguishing marks of Divisions are as follows:-
2nd Division = YELLOW flags and screens.
7th Division - RED flags with white bars.
MEERUT Division - White diagonal cross, corners of flag
red and black.

14th May,1915.   Brigade Major 5th Infantry Brigade.

Captain,

214

APPENDIX IV

5 Infantry Brigade Operation Order No 29, 15 May 1915

S E C R E T.

Copy NO...... 30

O P E R A T I O N   O R D E R   NO: 29

BY

BRIGADIER GENERAL A.A.CHICHESTER., D.S.O., COMMANDING 5TH INFANTRY BDE.

Reference (1/10,000 Trench Map.
(1/40,000 Squared Map.
(Sketch shewing Trenches.

In the Field,
15th May,1915.

1.   (a)   The 1ST ARMY is resuming its offensive tonight with the object of pressing forward to VIOLAINES and BEAU PUITS.
     (b)   The INDIAN CORPS will assault simultaneously with 2ND DIVISION, being on their immediate left,and establish a flank through V.8 to our present line.
     (c)   The 7TH DIVISION is to assault at 3-15 a.m. tomorrow morning on the front N.1 - P.5.
     (d)   The 1ST CORPS have orders to secure the line of the road FESTUBERT - LA TOURELLE from points M.3 to R.13.

2.   (a)   The 2ND DIVISION is to assault the German front trenches between R.1 and the right of the INDIAN CORPS at 11-30 p.m., tonight and secure the line R.1 - R.3 - R.5 - R.7 - V.4 under cover of darkness; at 3-15 a.m. tomorrow it is to press its attack simultaneously with 7TH DIVISION to secure the FERME COUR D'AVOUE and the line of the FESTUBERT - LA TOURELLE road from points P.14 to R.13 both inclusive.
     (b)   The 6TH BRIGADE are attacking on the front R.1 to the bend in the German line between R.6 and V.1 (inclusive).

3.   The 5TH BRIGADE will assault:-
     (a)   The German first line of trenches from the bend in the German line between R.6 and V.1 (exclusive) to the N.W.corner of the salient between V.3 and V.6.
     (b)   The German second line from R.7 (inclusive) to a point N.W. of V.5 and get into touch with the MEERUT Division at that point.
     (c)   At 3-15 a.m. the advance will be continued with the object of capturing FERME DU BOIS, establishing itself on the line Q.12 (exclusive) to R.13 (inclusive) maintaining touch with the INDIAN CORPS.
     The communication trench running S.E. to N.W. through Q.15 will be included in the 6TH BRIGADE Front.

4.   (a)   The 2ND ROYAL INNISKILLING FUSILIERS and the 2ND WORCESTER REGIMENT will carry out the assault.
     (b)   Frontages. As laid down in Special Instructions already sent out. The 2ND OXF.& BUCKS L.I. and the GLASGOW HIGHLANDERS will support the INNISKILLING FUSILIERS and the 2ND WORCESTERSHIRE REGIMENT respectively.
     (c)   The 2ND HIGHLAND LIGHT INFANTRY will be in Reserve at XXX S.9.a.58.
     (d)   The 5TH FIELD COY: R.E., will be in Reserve at S.9.a.91.
     (e)   No.3 TRENCH MORTAR BATTERY will advance to V.1 in support as soon as the German front line has been captured.
     (f)   CENTRE SECTION,NO:7 MOUNTAIN BATTERY will remain in RICHEBOURG ready to move.

5.   The position when gained must be immediately consolidated. The work of consolidation except as regards communication trenches will be continued after daylight. The special working parties detailed for this will therefore not be withdrawn by their battalions.

6.   In the event of a partial success, Officers Commanding attacking battalions must hold on to and support any portion of the German line gained, organising further attacks towards the flanks before daylight.

7.   The 2ND R.INN:FUS: and the 2ND WORC: R., will be closed up on the front line breastworks and the two new cover trenches behind by 9 p.m.
     The GLASGOW HIGHLANDERS will pass house S.9.a.91 at 9 p.m. and move to their places of assembly.
     The 2ND OXF.& BUCKS L.I.will pass house S.9.a.91 at 9-45 p.m.
     The 5TH FIELD COY: R.E.,will arrive S.9.a.91 at 10-15 p.m.

31

(2)

The 2ND HIGHLAND LIGHT INFANTRY will arrive at S.9.a.59 at 10-30 p.m.

9.   Advance Dressing Station at X roads S.3.c.

9.   BRIGADE AMMUNITION RESERVE and 1ST LINE TRANSPORT will remain in their present position.

10.   Units will each send a representative with at least 2 watches to get the correct time at Brigade Head Quarters about 7 p.m.

11.   BRIGADE HEAD QUARTERS will be at house 8.9.a.91 from 10-30 p.m.

                                        Captain,
                        Brigade Major 5th Infantry Brigade.

Issued at 4-30 p.m.
      Copy No.1 to INN:FUS.
        "   " 2 " WORC.R.
        "   " 3 " OXF.
        "   " 4 " H.L.I.
        "   " 5 " GLASGOWS.
        "   " 6 " 5TH FIELD CO: R.E.
        "   " 7 " 5TH FIELD AMBCE.
        "   " 8 " No.3 TRENCH MORTAR BTY.
        "   " 9 " No.7 MOUNTAIN BATTERY.
        "   " 10 " ½ Troop S.IRISH HORSE.
        "   " 11   WAR DIARY.
        "   " 12)
        n   13) BRIGADE STAFF.
               14)
               15)
        ****

APPENDIX V

Summary of events 15-17 May 1915 by Brigadier General Chichester,
commanding 5 Infantry Brigade

Appendix LII

41

Head Quarters,

2nd Division.

Report herewith on the operations of the 15th, 16th and 17th May,1915. I attach a Summary of Events (as in War Diary).

The points I wish to draw attention to are as follows:-

SIGNALS. (1) The long time it takes to convey orders to troops. Telephonic communication nearly always breaks down and cannot be relied on.

ORDERS. (2). The experience of the last few days shows that when it is necessary to issue orders for a new attack,e.g.,against a tactical point which is holding up a further advance, a Brigade Commander should give at least 5 hour's notice to Battalion Commanders in this present state of trench warfare. No doubt if and when movement becomes freer this limit of time might be modified.This period should allow of time for messengers to reach a Battalion Commanding Officer and enable him to organise the new attack. To do which he has to explain the situation and issue orders to his Company Commanders who are not easy to get at in narrow trenches u under heavy fire. Whilst this is going on the artillery bombardment can be developed.

OVERCROWDING.(3). If an attack fails and supports have closed up to take the places of those lines gone forward when the latter recoil the trenches are overcrowded. Supports can be pushed forward too soon. Battalion Commanding Officers must maintain the closest touch with units in front to know when to push forward in support.

HOUR OF ATTACK. (4). Enemy's fire broke out two minutes before our night attack was delivered at 11-30. They may possibly do this before every hour or ½ hour on chance as our attacks are generally delivered at these times. Suggest some other time for future assaults.

42

COMMUNICATING TRENCHES. (5). After a successful attack at least two communicating trenches per Battalion should be made linking our original front line with the enemy trenches. These should be constructed by troops from the rear and not by those of the Brigade intended for the further advance next day.

PREVIOUS PREPARATION OF COMMUNICATION AND COVER. (6). The communicating and cover trenches in and from the RUE DU BOIS were indifferently constructed and were without traverses. Undue casualties occurred in consequence. Considering the time at disposal for making these, better cover should have been provided.

ARTILLERY. (7). Artillery fire was often inaccurate. This may have been due to indifferent climatic conditions and difficulty in observing effect of fire. But these conditions were not bad enough to cause losses to our own troops through shells falling in our original trenches and some as far back as the RUE DU BOIS. I received constant and daily reports of this bad shooting, and there were besides a considerable number of prematures. I consider there is nothing that so adversely affects the morale of troops as being shot by their own artillery, and it is most urgent that more care be taken.

TELEPHONE WIRES. (8). Wires from Advanced Brigade Report centre to the stations in the first line trenches should have been deeply buried.

WEATHER. (9). The wet weather made operations most difficult and progress along the trenches was very slow on account of the mud which in parts was 5 feet deep, and the rifles were clogged with it.

WOUNDED. (10). The collection of wounded was very difficult partly due to congestion in communication trenches and paucity of stretchers. Eight stretchers per Battalion is inadequate. Previous to warfare of this description a reserve of

PAGE 3.

WOUNDED. (continued)	a reserve of stretchers should be established in the 1st line of trenches and special bearer parties should be attached to Battalions to deal with the wounded between the front line and the 1st Aid Posts. It was here where the difficulty was greatest. Stretchers too are of necessity used as beds and taken off in ambulances. Arrangements should be made for ambulances to bring back other stretchers to maintain the supply of them at the front. Stretcher bearers very often do not know where to go for the wounded, so Battalion arrangements should be made for guides to direct them.
HOLES IN PARAPETS.	(11). Generally too small for men with packs. Should be at least 3' square.
BRIDGES.	(12). The ones placed in advance near our front lines were too weak. They broke up.
DISTINGUISHING MARKS AT NIGHT.	(13). It is thought that with flares they may show men up when placed in front. Suggested they be put only on the pack.
BAYONETS.	(14). When fixed at night they glint in the light of flares. It would be better if they were blued or otherwise coloured.
FLAGS.	(15). These were most useful, but there were not enough of them. There should be at least 20 per battalion. All those we had are gone.
GENERAL CONDUCT.	(16). The Battalions of the Brigade did all that could be done and the successful charge of the 2ND ROYAL INNISKILLING FUSILIERS under a murderous fire, notwithstanding a loss of 10 Officers and 660 Other Ranks, showed great gallantry and dash.

Maps will be brought forward later.

A.H. Chichester

BRIG.-GENERAL,

21st May, 1915.   Commanding 5th Infantry Brigade.

APPENDIX VI

List of Missing, *Belfast Evening Telegraph*, 29 June 1915

ULSTER MILITARY NEWS.

REGIMENTAL LOSSES.

TWO BROTHERS KILLED.

ANOTHER D.C.M. FOR BELFAST.

700 MISSING INNISKILLINGS.

WOUNDED TERRITORIAL OFFICER.

RANK AND FILE.

ROYAL INNISKILLING FUSILIERS.

ROYAL IRISH RIFLES.

IRISH GUARDS AND FUSILIERS.

APPENDIX VII
List of fatalities compiled by author

BATTLE OF FESTUBERT FATALITIES
A COMPANY

Number	Rank	Name	KIA/MIA/DOW	Origin
	Lt	Oliver George Norman Stacke	KIA	London
	2nd Lt	Lionel St George Mordaunt-Smith	KIA	Rugby, Warwickshire
4582	CSM	Joseph Crilly	KIA	Dublin
2214	Sjt	George Donaghy	MIA/KIA	Londonderry
7879	Sjt	Sidney Hopkirk	MIA/KIA	London
19750	Cpl	Thomas Connor	MIA/KIA	Dublin
9091	Cpl	William Gleghorn	MIA/KIA	Antrim
10286	Cpl	John Joseph Hanly	MIA/KIA	Burma
8684	Cpl	George Riley	MIA/KIA	Middlesex
9831	Cpl	Archibald Scott	MIA/KIA	Londonderry
8309	Cpl	Charles Wilks	MIA/KIA	Middlesex
4062	L/Cpl	John Doherty	MIA/KIA	Londonderry
2304	L/Cpl	Patrick Doherty	MIA/KIA	Enniskillen
2904	Pte	Dominic Adams	MIA/KIA	Belfast
8172	Pte	John Arbuthnot	MIA/KIA	Stewartstown, Co. Tyrone
4536	Pte	George Baxter	MIA/KIA	Belfast
17936	Pte	Henry Birrell	MIA/KIA	Perth, Scotland
17179	Pte	Walter Body	MIA/KIA	Durham
3932	Pte	Robert James Boyd	MIA/KIA	Ballyclare, Co. Antrim
4436	Pte	Charles Cassidy	MIA/KIA	Londonderry
8155	Pte	Edward Caves	MIA/KIA	Belfast
7701	Pte	David Collins	MIA/KIA	Belfast
17008	Pte	George Connor	MIA/KIA	Liverpool
15141	Pte	Horace Percival Cooper	MIA/KIA	Hertfordshire
11757	Pte	Michael Crampsey	MIA/KIA	Londonderry
17939	Pte	Thomas Cullen	MIA/KIA	Dublin
3437	Pte	Robert Cunningham	MIA/KIA	Strabane, Co. Tyrone
8272	Pte	Emmett Davenport	MIA/KIA	Newry, Co. Down
8532	Pte	Hugh Dempsey	KIA	Belfast
4186	Pte	Charles Doherty	MIA/KIA	Garvagh, Co. Londonderry
6064	Pte	Patrick Doyle	MIA/KIA	Omagh
2693	Pte	Samuel Evans	MIA/KIA	Enniskillen
2527	Pte	James Fleming	MIA/KIA	Banagher, Co. Londonderry
8061	Pte	Thomas Francey	KIA	Ballymena
4028	Pte	Patrick Gallagher	MIA/KIA	Falcarragh, Co. Donegal
9910	Pte	Hugh Gilmore	MIA/KIA	Belfast
8436	Pte	Henry Gray	MIA/KIA	Ballynahinch, Co. Down
18285	Pte	James Greener	MIA/KIA	Durham
3699	Pte	James Hamilton	MIA/KIA	Gortin, Co. Tyrone
7642	Pte	Mark Harrigan	MIA/KIA	Londonderry

Number	Rank	Name	KIA/MIA/DOW	Origin
3814	Pte	John Heaney	MIA/KIA	Londonderry
10726	Pte	James Ingram	MIA/KIA	Belfast
10569	Pte	William Johnston	MIA/KIA	Moneymore, Co. Londonderry
4348	Pte	George Kayes	MIA/KIA	Belfast
6256	Pte	Thomas Kealey	MIA/KIA	Belfast
6902	Pte	Charles Lavery	MIA/KIA	Lisburn
10739	Pte	Edward Lavery	KIA	Lisburn
7581	Pte	James Mahoney	MIA/KIA	Limerick
12107	Pte	Daniel Marrs	MIA/KIA	Kilkeel, Co. Down
4306	Pte	Bernard Molloy	MIA/KIA	Londonderry
4446	Pte	George Mullan	MIA/KIA	Omagh
10474	Pte	John Mullan	MIA/KIA	Belfast
7534	Pte	Joseph McCart	MIA/KIA	Gilford, Co. Down
10495	Pte	Alexander McConnell	MIA/KIA	Belfast
3580	Pte	James McConnell	MIA/KIA	Strabane, Co. Tyrone
8033	Pte	Bernard Francis McDermott	MIA/KIA	Monaghan
11161	Pte	William McDowell	MIA/KIA	Belfast
3449	Pte	John McFadden	MIA/KIA	Lanarkshire
18769	Pte	John McGee	MIA/KIA	Belleek, Co. Fermanagh
3829	Pte	Patrick McGinley	MIA/KIA	Sion Mills, Co. Tyrone
10448	Pte	William McGinty	MIA/KIA	Enniskillen
2255	Pte	Joseph McGowan	MIA/KIA	Londonderry
2444	Pte	Joseph McLaughlin	MIA/KIA	Strabane, Co. Tyrone
7802	Pte	John McKnight	MIA/KIA	Fivemiletown, Co. Tyrone
10887	Pte	Robert T McMullan	MIA/KIA	Killyleagh, Co. Down
8431	Pte	Frederick McNabb	MIA/KIA	Trillick, Co. Tyrone
2536	Pte	Samuel McNally	MIA/KIA	Magherafelt, Co. Londonderry
9246	Pte	James Newell	MIA/KIA	Saintfield, Co. Down
11162	Pte	James Nugent	MIA/KIA	Belfast
7315	Pte	Thomas O'Kane	MIA/KIA	Garvagh, Co. Londonderry
6762	Pte	Robert James O'Rorke	MIA/KIA	Monkstown, Co. Antrim
8556	Pte	Alexander Peoples	MIA/KIA	Strabane, Co. Tyrone
8725	Pte	Harry Raymond	MIA/KIA	Croydon
3820	Pte	Andrew Rush	MIA/KIA	Lifford, Co. Donegal
3585	Pte	James Speers	MIA/KIA	Aughnacloy, Co. Tyrone
14383	Pte	Patrick Joseph Stafford	MIA/KIA	Dublin
4490	Pte	William Steele	MIA/KIA	Renfrewshire
10379	Pte	James White	MIA/KIA	Belfast
4292	Pte	James Walsh	MIA/KIA	Strabane, Co. Tyrone
11763	Pte	John Whearty	MIA/KIA	Belfast
11009	Pte	David Young	MIA/KIA	Belfast

B COMPANY

Number	Rank	Name	KIA/MIA/DOW	Origin
	Lt	Edward J W Abbott	KIA	Plymouth
4488	CSM	Alfred Ernest Jackson	KIA	London
7873	Sjt	Thomas Waugh	KIA	Belfast
10291	Cpl	Frank Henry Bushell	MIA/KIA	London
9019	Cpl	Henry Thomas Hunt	MIA/KIA	Middlesex
17782	Cpl	Thomas John Quinn	MIA/KIA	Portrush, Co. Antrim
8721	Cpl	William Riley	MIA/KIA	Ballynahinch, Co. Down
4354	L/Cpl	Hugh John Cairns	MIA/KIA	Coalisland, Co. Tyrone
3872	L/Cpl	Joseph Deane	MIA/KIA	Londonderry
3430	Pte	Richard Anderson	MIA/KIA	Belfast
10665	Pte	John Armstrong	MIA/KIA	Lisburn
3630	Pte	James Baird	MIA/KIA	Londonderry
4581	Pte	Samuel Bingham	MIA/KIA	Belfast
17781	Pte	George Brent	MIA/KIA	Liverpool
7542	Pte	Thomas Brown	MIA/KIA	Lanarkshire
3514	Pte	John Currie	MIA/KIA	Ballymena
3835	Pte	Patrick Cuthbert	KIA	Londonderry
19968	Pte	Archibald Devine	MIA/KIA	Liverpool
4077	Pte	William Richard Dickson	KIA	Dungannon
2318	Pte	James Duffy	MIA/KIA	Enniskillen
4300	Pte	William Joseph Ewings	MIA/KIA	Sixmilecross, Co. Tyrone
7852	Pte	George Foster	KIA	Strabane, Co. Tyrone
4019	Pte	Henry Fullerton	MIA/KIA	Belfast
2942	Pte	Joseph Garry	MIA/KIA	Drogheda, Co. Meath
4487	Pte	William Glasgow	MIA/KIA	Lanarkshire
3192	Pte	Thomas Gordon	MIA/KIA	Ballymena
3919	Pte	Michael Herron	MIA/KIA	Stranorlar, Co. Donegal
10479	Pte	James Dominick Lawlor	MIA/KIA	Belfast
2604	Pte	William James Maze	MIA/KIA	Belfast
3523	Pte	Alexander Moorhead	MIA/KIA	Ardstraw, Co. Tyrone
10581	Pte	William Morrison	MIA/KIA	Milford, Co. Donegal
9702	Pte	Joseph McGrath	MIA/KIA	Belfast
17759	Pte	Patrick McGuinness	MIA/KIA	Lisburn
3857	Pte	John McLaughlin	MIA/KIA	Londonderry
7601	Pte	John McManus	MIA/KIA	Enniskillen
3908	Pte	Robert McNulty	MIA/KIA	Londonderry
8238	Pte	John Shevlin	MIA/KIA	Belfast
9055	Pte	George Wright	KIA	Aughnacloy, Co. Tyrone
9319	Pte	William Smyth Wylie	MIA/KIA	Belfast

C COMPANY

Number	Rank	Name	KIA/MIA/DOW	Origin
8788	Sjt	John Carty	MIA/KIA	Roscommon
8707	Sjt	Maurice Edward Wigg	KIA	Southampton
5730	Cpl	Thomas Adams	MIA/KIA	Middlesex
4480	L/Cpl	Andrew Murray	MIA/KIA	Lanarkshire
9003	L/Cpl	William Sharkey	MIA/KIA	Omagh
18188	Pte	Thomas Burke	MIA/KIA	Sligo
19905	Pte	Charles Conaghan	MIA/KIA	Donegal
3232	Pte	Hugh Gribbon	MIA/KIA	Belfast
16438	Pte	Patrick Henry	MIA/KIA	Belfast
11098	Pte	James Kyles	MIA/KIA	Belfast
4286	Pte	James Lowry	MIA/KIA	Belfast
3324	Pte	Joseph Murray	MIA/KIA	Strabane, Co. Tyrone
10055	Pte	Patrick McGowan	MIA/KIA	Kinlough, Co. Leitrim
3422	Pte	Samuel Patton	MIA/KIA	Belfast
6567	Pte	Thomas Porter	MIA/KIA	Belfast
18196	Pte	Charles Robertson	MIA/KIA	Cushendun, Co. Antrim
10684	Pte	William Shaw	KIA	Carrickfergus, Co. Antrim
4153	Pte	Michael Smyth	MIA/KIA	Donagheady, Co. Tyrone
10647	Pte	Alfred Stewart	MIA/KIA	Belfast
3543	Pte	Patrick Taylor	MIA/KIA	Cookstown, Co. Tyrone
4687	Pte	Patrick Wray	MIA/KIA	Londonderry

D COMPANY

Number	Rank	Name	KIA/MIA/DOW	Origin
	Lt	John H Stewart	KIA	Jersey
	2nd Lt	John James Leo Morgan	KIA	Newtownards, Co. Down
6854	CSM	Mervyn James Williams	KIA	Blackrock, Co. Dublin
7990	Sjt	Harwood Eldred Ansell	KIA	Surrey
9565	Sjt	John Johnston McGonigle	KIA	Donemana, Co. Tyrone
7679	Cpl	William John Brolly	KIA	Ballymoney, Co. Antrim
10699	Cpl	Henry Victor Sidney Donaldson	MIA/KIA	Moville, Co. Donegal
3685	Cpl	Hugh Maguire	MIA/KIA	Londonderry
6311	Cpl	Thomas Sproule	MIA/KIA	Newtowncunningham, Co. Donegal
7285	L/Cpl	Thomas Armstrong	MIA/KIA	Derrylin, Co. Fermanagh
17181	L/Cpl	Patrick Campbell	MIA/KIA	Renfrewshire
7470	L/Cpl	William John Pedlow	MIA/KIA	Portadown, Co. Armagh
9171	L/Cpl	George Watson	MIA/KIA	Belfast
4597	Pte	John Archer	MIA/KIA	Belfast
3350	Pte	Robert Beattie	MIA/KIA	Belfast
2591	Pte	James Cavanagh	MIA/KIA	Sligo

Number	Rank	Name	KIA/MIA/DOW	Origin
4088	Pte	Francis Collins	KIA	Ardstraw, Co. Tyrone
2903	Pte	Arthur Jos. Connolly	MIA/KIA	Belfast
17044	Pte	Thomas Ellison	MIA/KIA	Liverpool
3966	Pte	Bernard Gallagher	MIA/KIA	Donemana, Co. Tyrone
2638	Pte	Hugh Gavin	MIA/KIA	Belfast
2308	Pte	Daniel Gilmore	MIA/KIA	Enniskillen
3139	Pte	Patrick Goodfellow	MIA/KIA	Enniskillen
4698	Pte	William Hegarty	MIA/KIA	Faughanvale, Co. Londonderry
18980	Pte	Francis Hudson	MIA/KIA	Castledawson, Co. Londonderry
3626	Pte	Samuel Kane	MIA/KIA	Stranorlar, Co. Donegal
9389	Pte	James Kelly	MIA/KIA	Buncrana, Co. Donegal
4218	Pte	Michael Kelly	MIA/KIA	Ballyshannon, Co. Donegal
8016	Pte	Robert Lawless	MIA/KIA	Cookstown, Co. Tyrone
2864	Pte	John Thomas Logan	MIA/KIA	Maguiresbridge, Co. Fermanagh
4284	Pte	Peter Logue	MIA/KIA	Ramelton, Co Donegal
7454	Pte	Thomas Marshal	MIA/KIA	Newry, Co. Down
4264	Pte	James McAlinden	MIA/KIA	Belfast
10121	Pte	Hugh McCarney	MIA/KIA	Omagh
2889	Pte	Francis McCarroll	MIA/KIA	Lisnaskea, Co. Fermanagh
12125	Pte	Mark McDermott	MIA/KIA	Newtownbutler, Co. Fermanagh
10555	Pte	Frederick McDonald	MIA/KIA	Birr, King's County (Co.Offaly)
6998	Pte	William McHugh	MIA/KIA	Londonderry
4304	Pte	Alexander McIlree	MIA/KIA	Cookstown, Co. Tyrone
2189	Pte	Daniel McLeod	MIA/KIA	Londonderry
2726	Pte	John McLoughlin	MIA/KIA	Blacklion, Co. Cavan
10741	Pte	John McMorran	MIA/KIA	Belfast
8097	Pte	John McPartland	MIA/KIA	Belturbet, Co. Cavan
4557	Pte	John McVeigh	MIA/KIA	Londonderry
3108	Pte	Joseph Nelson	KIA	Belfast
3620	Pte	James Owens	MIA/KIA	Moneymore, Co. Londonderry
17365	Pte	James Owen	MIA/KIA	Liverpool
3411	Pte	William John Patton	MIA/KIA	Belfast
2592	Pte	Thomas Quinn	MIA/KIA	Maguiresbridge, Co. Fermanagh
11610	Pte	William Quinn	MIA/KIA	Belfast
7452	Pte	William Reid	MIA/KIA	Newtownstewart, Co. Tyrone

Number	Rank	Name	KIA/MIA/DOW	Origin
4311	Pte	Patrick Sheehan	MIA/KIA	Londonderry
2294	Pte	John Smith	MIA/KIA	Enniskillen
7181	Pte	William Speers	MIA/KIA	Londonderry
3785	Pte	Samuel Stewart	MIA/KIA	Strabane, Co. Tyrone
10860	Pte	Samuel Stewart	MIA/KIA	Barrow-in-Furness, Lancashire
4456	Pte	William McCreadie Stewart	MIA/KIA	Coleraine, Co. Londonderry
6315	Pte	John Strain	MIA/KIA	Belfast
3959	Pte	Charles Teague	MIA/KIA	Omagh
2444	Pte	Thomas Thompson	MIA/KIA	Belfast
3764	Pte	William David Watson	MIA/KIA	Fintona, Co. Tyrone
13226	Pte	Thomas Whelan	MIA/KIA	Rathrush, Co. Carlow
7650	Pte	John White	MIA/KIA	Newry, Co. Down
3677	Pte	William Williamson	MIA/KIA	Londonderry
11601	Pte	Robert John Wills	MIA/KIA	Dublin

MACHINE GUN SECTION/GRENADIERS/UNABLE TO IDENTIFY COMPANY

Number	Rank	Name	KIA/MIA/DOW	Origin
	Lt	Ralph William Gore Hinds (MG)	KIA	Dublin
	2nd Lt	Herbert William Hyde	KIA	Rugby, Warwickshire
	2nd Lt	Alfred Douglas Wingate (Grenadiers)	KIA	Bombay, India
	2nd Lt	William James Whittington	KIA	Petersfield, Hampshire
4662	Sjt	Thomas Mowbray	KIA	Londonderry
8179	L/Cpl	James Cairey	KIA	Castledermot, Co. Kildare
7622	L/Cpl	Arthur William Roedear	KIA	Essex
8739	L/Cpl	William Roullier	KIA	London
8089	L/Cpl	Henry Small	KIA	London
2901	Pte	James Blackwood	KIA	Belfast
10478	Pte	Alfred John Campbell	KIA	Belfast
3729	Pte	James Campbell	KIA	Strabane, Co. Tyrone
9047	Pte	Bernard Casey	KIA	Lanarkshire
9216	Pte	Edward Coleman	KIA	Co. Londonderry
7473	Pte	David Dobbin	KIA	Drumbo, Co. Down
4454	Pte	Neil Doherty	KIA	Londonderry
4425	Pte	Hugh Duncan (Doherty)	KIA	Donaghmore, Co. Donegal
10701	Pte	Sidney Ellis	KIA	Hampshire
4309	Pte	William Feeney	KIA	Londonderry
7755	Pte	David Finlay	DOW 17 May	Portrush, Co. Antrim
10483	Pte	Alfred Frame	KIA	Bessbrook, Co. Down
7706	Pte	William Francis	KIA	Newtownards, Co. Down
7706	Pte	William Frances	DOW 19 May	Belfast
13743	Pte	John Gallagher	KIA	Londonderry
2638	Pte	Hugh Gavin	KIA	Belfast

Number	Rank	Name	KIA/MIA/DOW	Origin
3479	Pte	Joseph Gilmore	KIA	Belfast
7005	Pte	James Graham	KIA	St Mary's, Co. Westmeath
4278	Pte	Robert Hamilton	KIA	Ramelton, Co. Donegal
2354	Pte	Joseph Henry	KIA	Dungannon
7861	Pte	Ernest Fred. Hone	KIA	London
4685	Pte	Hugh Kelly	KIA	Donemana, Co. Tyrone
4340	Pte	Patrick Kelly	KIA	Cappagh, Co. Tyrone
4064	Pte	Michael Lawn	DOW 17 May	Strabane, Co. Tyrone
18551	Pte	Thomas Letherbarrow	KIA	Liverpool
10436	Pte	James Logan	KIA	Belfast
4168	Pte	Thomas Long	KIA	Londonderry
10861	Pte	William Montgomery	KIA	Belfast
10513	Pte	John Leo Mooney	KIA	Belfast
2320	Pte	David Mowbray	DOW 19 May	Londonderry
3413	Pte	Edward Mulholland	KIA	Plumbridge, Co. Tyrone
1781	Pte	Hugh Mulligan	DOW 18 May	Derrygonnelly, Co. Fermanagh
11600	Pte	James McCaw	KIA	Belfast
3566	Pte	Thomas McClurg	KIA	Belfast
7239	Pte	Henry McConnellogue	KIA	Londonderry
18153	Pte	William McCully	KIA	Lanarkshire
10887	Pte	Robert Thomas McMullan	KIA	Killyleagh, Co. Down
3740	Pte	Henry McNamee	KIA	Drumkeen, Co. Donegal
3488	Pte	James Nesbitt	DOW 26 May	Belfast
4149	Pte	David Norris (MG)	KIA	Londonderry
4418	Pte	John O'Farrell	DOW 25 May	Coalisland, Co. Tyrone
3015	Pte	Ernest Patterson	KIA	Belfast
4364	Pte	George Pepper	KIA	Ennis, Co. Clare
8409	Pte	Robert Stewart	DOW 17 May	Donaghadee, Co. Down
19249	Pte	Robert Tinnion	KIA	Cockermouth, Cumbria
2497	Pte	Patrick Towell	KIA	Dublin
10509	Pte	William Walsh	KIA	Halifax, Yorkshire
4553	Pte	William Williamson	KIA	Belfast
4165	Pte	S Wright	KIA	Belfast

Details verified through Soldiers Died in the Great War, Commonwealth War Graves Commission, Ireland's Memorial Records and 1901 and 1911 Census of Ireland.

APPENDIX VIII

The strange case of 2nd Lt Stanley Holland Morter

Whilst researching the battle of Festubert and its aftermath, I came across the following in the Ulster and the War column of the *Belfast News Letter* dated 11 June 1915:

> **Second Lieutenant Morter** – News is to hand of the death of another officer of the 2nd Battalion Royal Inniskilling Fusiliers in the person of Second Lieutenant Stanley Holland Morter, who was killed in action on 5th Inst. In France. Deceased was the only child of the late Captain Percy Morter of the Gordon Highlanders (who was killed in action in December) and of Mrs Grace Morter, 18 Morningside Gardens, Edinburgh. He was educated at Birkenhead Institute, joined the army at the outbreak of war and had only been three weeks at the front when he lost his life, in his 19th year.[1]

My interest was aroused as at first glance this appeared to possibly be a young officer sent out as a replacement for those killed at Festubert and himself being tragically killed three weeks after arriving with the battalion. It looked like a promising lead for further research and possible inclusion in the narrative.

In carrying out initial research, I found that this notice had been picked up by other papers, including the *Fermanagh Herald* and the *Irish Independent*. A similar notice appeared in the July edition of the *Sprig of Shillelagh*, the regimental journal of the Royal Inniskilling Fusiliers, amongst obituaries for other 2nd Battalion officers who were killed at Festubert including Lt Ralph Hinds, 2nd Lieutenants John Morgan, Lionel Mordaunt-Smith, and William Whittington.[2]

Research was then carried out with the Commonwealth War Graves Commission and on the Officers died in the Great War database, but there was no mention of either Stanley Holland Morter or his father, Percy. Further checks were carried out on various genealogical databases for both military records, details of births, marriages and deaths and census details in England, Scotland and Ireland, but no positive matches were found. A check with the Inniskillings Museum failed to uncover any further details, as did checks on records at the National Archives where officers' records are held, at the Royal Military College Sandhurst, and with the *London Gazette*, which holds details of commissions and appointments.

Thinking of the possibility of the surname being misspelt, I carried out the same checks on alternative spellings, such as Mortar, Marter, Morton, and Morten, but still with no joy. Thinking that the middle name of 'Holland' may have been the mother's birth name, I again carried out research of births, marriages and deaths, but with negative results.

A check of the 2nd battalion Royal Inniskilling Fusiliers War Diary for June 1915 reveals the following:

> June 2-7, Relieved Oxfords in trenches x 1 near Fosse No 7 de Bethune on Lens road. Casualties.[3]

There being no casualties listed, a check was made on the Commonwealth War Graves Commission and Soldiers Died in the Great War databases. Four soldiers were killed in that period in the trenches, all of them holding the rank of private. Another private died of wounds in the same period in a base hospital. None have a name which remotely resembles Morter.

Further research revealed that there is no Stanley Holland Morter listed on the Birkenhead Institute Roll of Honour, although Captain PH Morter of the Gordon Highlanders is commemorated on the Southport Civic War Memorial on Merseyside.

Having reached a dead end whatever path I took, I posted a query on the Great War Forum and to my surprise found that this individual had already been the subject of much attention there. Of particular interest was the fact that in addition to the Irish press, there was coverage in the *Liverpool Echo*.[4]

On 2 January 1915, the following notice appeared under the heading, 'Killed in Action':

> MORTER – December 19, killed in action in France, aged 47 years. Captain Percy Holland Morter, Gordon Highlanders, the devoted and beloved husband of Grace Morter, Morningside Gardens, Edinburgh, (late of Cheshire and Birkdale)[5]

On 9 June 1915, the following notice appeared under the heading, 'Killed in Action':

> MORTER – June 5, killed in action aged 19 years, Second Lieutenant Stanley Holland Morter serving with the Inniskilling Fusiliers, only

child of the late Captain Percy Morter, Gordon Highlanders, (also killed in action) and of Grace Morter of 18 Morningside Gardens, Edinburgh.

BIRKENHEAD INSTITUTE OLD BOY

SECOND-LIEUTENANT S. H. MORTER.

Our photograph is that of Second-Lieutenant Stanley Holland Morter, of the Inniskilling Fusiliers, only son of the late Captain Stanley Morter, whose death in action we announced last night. He joined at the beginning of the war, and was drafted to the front about three weeks ago. He was educated at Birkenhead Institute, and formerly resided at Edinburgh.

Of greater interest was the edition of the same paper of 10 July 1915 which contained a photograph and obituary.

In all there were over 100 posts as those with knowledge and interest tried to solve the mystery. No-one however has come up with any positive identification of the persons named as Stanley Holland Morter and Percy Morter.

Many theories as to what the truth is have been put forward, including enlisting under a false name, creating a false identity to support some financial scam, or in a perverse plan to elicit sympathy, but none can be conclusively proven. In the absence of any information to the contrary it would appear that neither Stanley Holland Morter, or Percy Morter ever existed.

As mentioned above, the name PH Morter appears on the Southport Civic War Memorial however, details of this may have been taken from local newspapers such as the *Liverpool Echo*, without any further research being carried out. Pressures on newspapers at the time as the sole form of popular media, may have resulted in the notices being circulated throughout England and Ireland without further checks being carried out, but the inclusion of Stanley Holland Morter as an obituary in the regimental journal intrigues me. Surely someone within the regiment would have asked the question, who is he?

It is the case that someone for whatever reason, went to an awful lot of time and trouble to create these identities and forward details to newspapers. Why, remains a mystery.

---

1   *Belfast News Letter*, 11 June 1915

2   *The Sprig of Shillelagh*, July 1915, p173

3   The National Archives, WO 95/1350/1 2nd Battalion Royal Inniskilling Fusiliers War Diary

4   *Liverpool Echo*, 9 June 1915 and 10 July 1915, accessed on www.1914-18invisionzone.com. Accessed 29 Nov 2013

5   Ibid, 2 January 1915

BIBLIOGRAPHY

THE NATIONAL ARCHIVES, KEW

CAB 44/20 Draft of History of the Great War based on official documents

WO 95/1249/2 39 Brigade Royal Field Artillery War Diary

WO 95/1279 2nd Battalion Royal Munster Fusiliers War Diary

WO 95/1285/2 2nd Division: Headquarters War Diary

WO 95/1330/2 5 Field Company Royal Engineers War Diary

WO 95/1337/1 5 Field Ambulance War Diary

WO 95/1343/2 5 Infantry Brigade: Headquarters War Diary

WO 95/1347 2nd Battalion Highland Light Infantry War Diary

WO 95/1347 9th Battalion Highland Light Infantry War Diary

WO 95/1348 2nd Battalion Oxfordshire and Buckinghamshire Light Infantry
War Diary

WO 95/1350 2nd Battalion Royal Inniskilling Fusiliers War Diary

WO 95/1351 2nd Battalion Worcestershire Regiment War Diary

WO 95/1358 1st Battalion Kings Royal Rifle Corps War Diary

WO 95/1730 1st Battalion Royal Irish Rifles War Diary

WO 95/3945/2 2nd Battalion Leicestershire Regiment War Diary

WO 95/3938/4 Meerut Division, 107th Pioneers War Diary

WO 76/356 pps 98-103, Service record of Captain Charles Caulfield Hewitt

WO 339/7836 Service Record Lt Ralph William Gore Hinds

WO 339/8980 Service Record Lt Edward John White Abbott

WO 339/15799 Service Record, 2nd Lt Lionel St George Mordaunt-Smith

WO 339/18920 Service Record 2nd Lt John Joseph Leo Morgan

WO 339/22949 Service Record Lt John Houghton Stewart

PUBLIC RECORDS OFFICE NORTHERN IRELAND

Letters from Lt Charles Alexander to his mother.

D/4121/F/4/B/2/5/7 – 13 February 1915

D/4121/F/4/B/2/5/8A – 25 February 1915

D/4121/F/4/B/2/5/10A – 6 March 1915

D/4121/F/4/B/2/5/11A – 9 March 1915

D/4121/F/4/B/2/5/15 – 23 March 1915

D/4121/F/4/B/2/6/1 – 1 May 1915

D/4121/F/4/B/2/6/2A – 3 May 1915

D/4121/F/4/B/2/6/5A – 13 May 1915
D/4121/F/4/B/2/6/6A – 19 May 1915
D/4121/F/4/B/2/6/7 – 23 May 1915
D/4121/F/4/B/2/6/9 – 28 May 1915
Handwritten note describing the duties of a Transport Officer
D/4121/F/4/D/1/17

NEWSPAPERS AND JOURNALS

Belfast Evening Telegraph
24 May 1915
27 May 1915
29 May 1915
29 June 1915
22 May 1916
Belfast News Letter
26 March 1915
14 May 1915
18 May 1915
27 May 1915
11 June 1915
9 June 1915
15 June 1915
23 June 1915
24 June 1915
8 July 1915
Irish News and Belfast Morning News
27 May 1915
29 May 1915
Fermanagh Herald
5 June 1915
Mid Ulster Mail
15 May 1915
29 May 1915
5 June 1915
Tyrone Constitution
21 May 1915

4 June 1915
2 July 1915
Tyrone Courier
22 April 1915
The Derry Journal
17 May 1915
24 May 1915
28 May 1915
The Londonderry Sentinel
22 May 1915
25 May 1915
The Times
18 March 1915
14 May 1915
17 May 1915
29 May 1915
The Dover Express and East Kent Times
 3 October 1913
2 January 1914
18 March 1914
The Liverpool Echo
2 January 1915
9 June 1915
10 July 1915
The Sprig of Shillelagh, Regimental journal of the Royal Inniskilling Fusiliers
May 1915, p124
July 1915, p162
July 1915, p173
September 1915, p211
January 1916, p274
Quarterly Journal of the Royal Meteorological Society, Vol 41 Issue 176, pps 338 &
341, July 1915
The London Gazette
30 June 1915
11 March 1916

BOOKS

Alexander CAM, (Undated), *With the 2nd Battalion the Royal Inniskilling Fusiliers in France, 1914-1916,* Omagh, Tyrone Constitution.

Anon. (1918), *Historical Notes on German Divisions. Part 1, Active Divisions Engaged on the British Front in France Up To January 1918.* France, Army Printing and Stationary Services.

Ballard R with Dunmore S, (1995), *Exploring the Lusitania.* London, Weidenfeld and Nicolson.

Batchelor P and Matson C, (2011) *VC's of the First World War: The Western Front 1915.* Stroud,The History Press.

Black W R (2012) *Dispatches from the World: The Life of Percival Phillips, War Correspondent,* Bloomington Indiana, Author House (Kindle E Book).

Bowman, T (2003) *The Irish Regiments in the Great War, Discipline and Morale.* Manchester, Manchester University Press

Bridger G, (2009), *Battleground Europe, The Battle Of Neuve Chapelle*, (Kindle Ebook), Barnsley, Pen & Sword.

Bristow A, (1995), *A Serious Disappointment: The Battle of Aubers Ridge 1915 and the Munitions Scandal*, London, Leo Cooper.

Brown M, (1991)*The Imperial War Museum Book of the First World War,* London, Guild Publishing.

Bull S Dr, (2002), *World War 1 Trench Warfare (1) 1914-1916,* Oxford, Osprey Publishing.

Chapin, H (Undated) *One Man's War: Letters from a Soldier Killed at the Battle of Loos.* (Kindle E Book).

Clarke A, (1991), *The Donkeys*, London, Pimlico.

Clutterbuck, Colonel LA, with Dooner, Colonel WT and Denison, Commander CA (Undated). *The Bond of Sacrifice, A Biographical Record of British Officers who Fell in the Great War, Vol 2, January to June 1915.* Uckfield, Naval & Military Press.

Conan Doyle A, (1915), *The British Campaign in France and Flanders 1915,* London, Hodder and Stoughton.

Corrigan G, (2006), *Sepoys in the Trenches. The Indian Corps on the Western Front 1914-1915,* Stroud, Spellmount.

Edmonds, Sir J.E (1928) *Military Operations France and Belgium 1915,* London, MacMillan and Co.

Farndale, General Sir Martin, (1986) *History of the Royal Regiment of Artillery. Western Front 1914-1918*, London, Royal Artillery Institution

Farr, D (2009), *The Silent General. Horne of the First Army*, Solihull, Helion & Co.

Fox, Sir F, OBE, *The Royal Inniskilling Fusiliers in the World War*, Uckfield, Naval and Military Press.

General Staff, War Office, (1911) *Manual of Field Engineering*. London, HMSO.

General Staff War Office (1912), *Field Service Regulations, Part I, Operations*. HMSO, London

General Staff, War Office, (1914) *Infantry Training (4-Company Organisation)*. London, HMSO.

Gilbert M, (1994), *First World War*, London, Harper and Collins.

Graves, R (1957) *Goodbye To All That*, London, Penguin (Kindle E book).

Grayson RS, (2009), *Belfast Boys, How Unionists and Nationalists Fought and Died Together in the First World War*. London, Continuum Books.

Griffith P, (1994), *Battle Tactics of the Western Front, The British Army's Art of Attack 1916-1918*. New Haven and London, Yale University Press.

Hammerton Sir JA, (Undated), *A Popular History of the Great War, Volume 2, Extension of the Struggle:1915*. London, The Fleetway House.

Hancock E, (2005), *Aubers Ridge*, Barnsley, Pen and Sword Books Ltd.

Hart P, (2013)*The Great War*, London, Profile Books (Kindle E Book).

Holmes R, (2005), *The Little Field Marshal, A Life of Sir John French*. London, Cassell Military Paperbacks.

Holmes R, (2008) *Fatal Avenue: A Travellers History of the Battlefields of Northern France and Flanders, 1346-1945*, London, Vintage.

Holt T &V, (2007), *Concise Illustrated Battlefield Guide, The Western Front – North*. Barnsley, Pen and Sword Military.

Hughes G, (2012), *The Hounds of Ulster: A History of the Northern Irish Regiments in the Great War,* Bern, Peter Lang.

Johnstone T, (1992), *Orange Green and Khaki, The Story of the Irish Regiments in the Great War, 1914-1918*. Dublin, Gill and McMillan.

Jones N, (1983), *The War Walk, A Journey along the Western Front*. London, Robert Hale.

Jones HA, (1969) *The War in the Air, being the story of the part played in the Great War by the Royal Air Force*. Volume 2, London, Hamish Hamilton.

Kearsey A, (Undated), *1915 Campaign in France: The Battles of Aubers Ridge, Festubert and Loos,* 2nd Ed, Uckfield, Naval and Military Press.

Laffin J, (1973), *Letters from the Front, 1914-1918.* London, JM Dent.

Laurie GB, (Laurie, F V-L, Ed) (1921), *Letters of Lieut.-Colonel George Brenton Laurie, (commanding 1st Battalion Royal Irish Rifles),* Aldershot, Gale&Polden, (Kindle Ebook).

Lewis-Stempel J, (2010) *Six Weeks: The Short and Gallant Life of the British Officer in the First World War,* London, Orion Books (Kindle E Book).

Macdonald L, (1997), *1915: The Death of Innocence,* London, Penguin.

Mitchell, Major TJ & Smith GM (1931), *Medical Services. Casualties and Medical Statistics of the Great War.* London, Imperial War Museum and Nashville Tennessee, Battery Press Incorporated.

Neillands R, (2004), *The Great War Generals on the Western Front 1914-1918,* London, Magpie Books.

Neillands R, (2013), *The Death of Glory: The Western Front, 1915,* London, Endeavour Press Ltd.

Pound, R. (1964), *The Lost Generation,* London, Constable.

Richards, F, (1933), *Old Soldiers Never Die,* London, Faber and Faber.

Rickard JLM, (1918) *The Story of the Munsters at Etreux, Festubert, Rue Du Bois and Hulloch.* London, Hodder and Stoughton.

Schulz D, (1928), *Infanterie Regiment Graf Bulow von Dennewitz, Nr 55 im Weltkriege.* Max Staerde, Detmold.

Sheffield G and Bourne J, (Eds) (2005). *Douglas Haig. War Diaries and Letters 1914-1918,* London, Weidenfeld and Nicholson.

Sheldon J, (1995), *The German Army on the Western Front 1915.* Barnsley, Pen and Sword Military.

Simkins P, Jukes, G & Hickey M, (2003) *The First World War: The War To End All Wars.* Oxford, Osprey Publishing Ltd.

Stacke, H FitzM (1928), *The Worcestershire Regiment in the Great War, Volume 1.* Uckfield, Naval and Military Press.

Swinton ED and Percy AIP, (1916). *A Year Ago. Eye-Witness Narrative of the war from March 30th to July 18th, 1915,* London, Edward Arnold.

Taylor AJP, (1966),*The First World War, An Illustrated History,* London, Penguin.

The Presbyterian Historical Society of Ireland, (Undated), *The Presbyterian Church in Ireland Roll of Honour, 1914-1919,* Uckfield, Naval & Military Press

& The Imperial War Museum.

Van Emden R, (2010), *The Soldiers' War. The Great War through veteran's eyes*, London, Bloomsbury, (Kindle E Book).

Van Emden R, (2011), *The Quick and the Dead, Fallen Soldiers and their Families in the Great War*, London, Bloomsbury, (Kindle E Book).

War Office (1920) *Soldiers Died In The Great War 1914-19, Part 32 The Royal Inniskilling Fusiliers*, Suffolk, Hayward & Son.

Westlake R, (2001) *British Battalions on the Western Front, January to June 1915*, Barnsley, Leo Cooper.

Wyrall E, (1921), *The History of the Second Division, Volume 1, 1914-1916.* London, Thomas Nelson and Sons.

WEBSITES

www.ancestry.co.uk
www.britishnewspaperarchive.co.uk
www.cookstownwardead.co.uk
www.dungannonwardead.co.uk
www.cwgc.org
www.greatwarbelfastclippings.com
www.greatwar.ci.net
www.laugharnememorial.co.uk
www.lennonwylie.co.uk
www.lightbobs.com
www.linfieldfc.com
www.londongazette.co.uk
www.measuringworth.com
www.minerva.mic.ul.ie
www.nationalarchives.gov.uk

www.nationalarchives.ie
www.norwayheritage.com
www.oldmagazinearticles.com
www.ourheroesinmemoriam.co.uk
www.soldierswills.ie
www.timesarchiveonline.co.uk
www.trove.gov.au
www.westernfrontassociation.com
www.wikepedia.org
www.1914-1918.net

INDEX

238